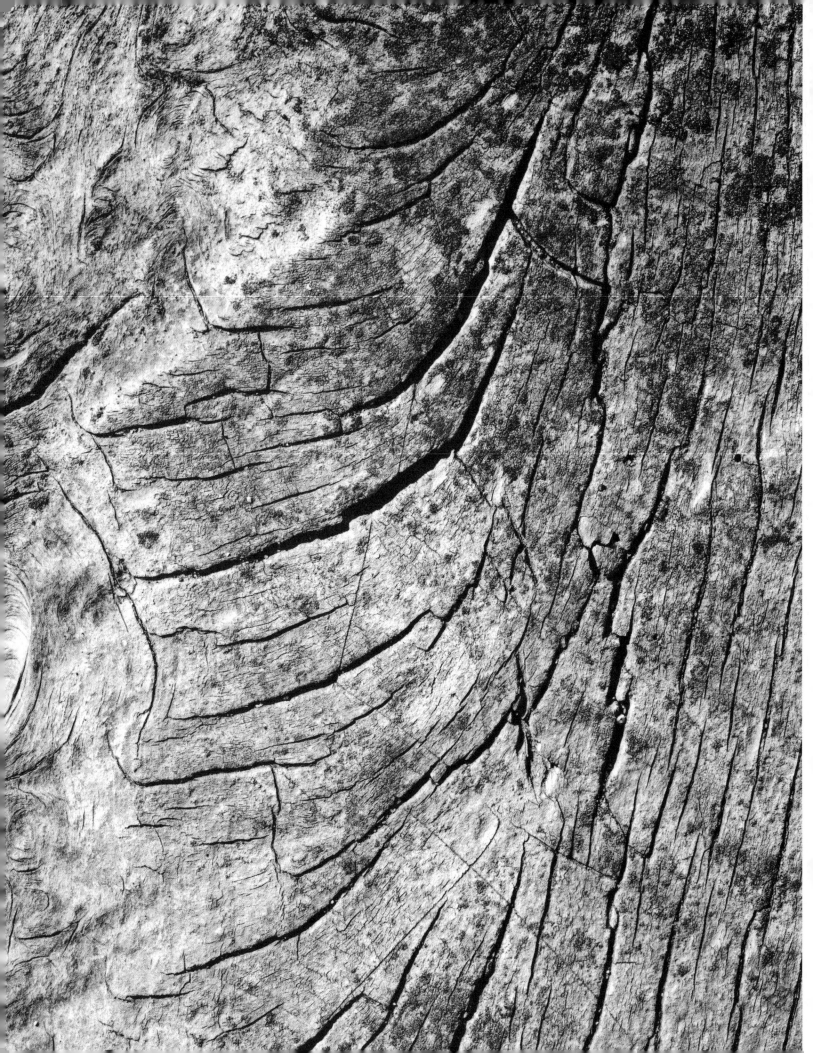

Atelier Crenn

Metamorphosis of Taste

Dominique Crenn

with Karen Leibowitz

Atelier Crenn
Metamorphosis of Taste

Photographs by Ed Anderson

HOUGHTON MIFFLIN HARCOURT
BOSTON NEW YORK 2015

For information about permission to reproduce selections
from this book, write to trade.permissions@hmhco.com or to Permissions,
Houghton Mifflin Harcourt Publishing Company,
3 Park Avenue, 19th Floor,
New York, New York 10016.

www.hmhco.com

Library of Congress Cataloging-in-Publication Data
Crenn, Dominique.
Atelier Crenn : metamorphosis of taste / Dominique Crenn with
    Karen Leibowitz ; Photography by Ed Anderson.
pages cm
ISBN 978-0-544-44467-6 (hardback)
ISBN 978-0-544-44468-3 (ebook)
1. Cooking, French. 2. Seasonal cooking. 3. Atelier Crenn
(Restaurant) I. Title.
TX719.C74 2015
641.5944 --dc23
2015017438

Design by Level, Calistoga, CA
Printed in the United States of America
DOW 10 9 8 7 6 5 4
4500608150

FOR PAPA CRENN

Contents

ACKNOWLEDGMENTS

THIS BOOK WOULD NOT EXIST without the contributions of many, many people.

I want to thank everyone who has ever stepped inside Atelier Crenn, from stagiaires to chefs de cuisine, from bussers to managers, from visiting guests to regular customers, and from my business partner, Michelle Astorian, to the investors who have helped transform my dream and my vision into reality. Together, we have made Atelier Crenn what it is.

In the course of writing this book, I have drawn enormous support and inspiration from my coauthor, Karen Leibowitz, who translated the amorphous spirit of Atelier Crenn into words. I would also like to thank Juan Contreras, who spent many hours explaining his meticulous work as pastry chef; Mehdi Boudiab, who generously contributed to the bread recipes; and all the staff, who helped harness the details of our kitchen into written form. I am grateful that Ed Anderson, our photographer, captured the aesthetic of Atelier Crenn for these pages, and that Ty Lettau did the same for us online. My agent, Michael Psaltis, has believed in me for years, and my editor, Justin Schwartz, allowed us the freedom to create a book that truly reflects Atelier Crenn. Heartfelt thanks are due to Nancy Silverton, for her lovely foreword, to Wendy MacNaughton, for her participation in the creative process during my earliest book discussions with Karen, and to Karen's husband, Anthony Myint, for his ongoing engagement with the book at every stage of its development.

Thanks, also, to all of the chefs and other artists who have inspired and continue to inspire me, including Dan Barber, Jean-Michel Basquiat, Baudelaire, Simone de Beauvoir, Michel Bras, Pascal-Adolphe-Jean Dagnan-Bouveret, Frédéric Chopin, Salvador Dalí, Jimi Hendrix, David Kinch, Joan Miró, Wolfgang Amadeus Mozart, Nathan Myhrvold, Daniel Patterson, Olivier Roellinger, and Jeremiah Tower.

This book is dedicated to everyone I love—

especially Louise, Allain, and Jean-Christophe Crenn

DOMINIQUE CRENN is like a Marvel superhero.

If you are familiar with Marvel superheroes, you know they lead two lives. They have their superhero lives where they leap or fly or cling to buildings all over town fighting evil people and saving the world from doom.

And then they have their regular life where they look like normal folk, and you wouldn't even know they are anything special. The Incredible Hulk, for example, is Dr. Bruce Banner, a physicist. The Amazing Spiderman is Peter Parker, a student and photographer in his everyday life. Thor, the Norse god of thunder and lightning, is Dr. Donald Blake, a respected surgeon.

And Dominque Crenn, the acclaimed superhero chef is, in her regular life, a cook.

I think in her heart, in that very artistic heart of hers, she might have fun being the superhero chef—who wouldn't?—but she is most in her element, most in her purest state of bliss, when she is being a cook.

Still, like all superheroes, it is fun to see the transformation. It's exciting to see her magically transform from cook to superhero chef.

I have seen superhero Dominique single-handedly take a celebrity chef–studded food event that was heading toward doldrums and transform it into a joyous, free-spirited party with her super powers of unrestrained spontaneity, mischievousness, merrymaking, and beauty.

And I have seen regular Dominque inconspicuously walk into my restaurant in Los Angeles, dressed casually, and quietly take a seat at the Mozzarella Bar. I've seen her ask the server about the dishes like she didn't know foie gras from chopped liver. I've seen her quietly study the plate when it arrived, sniff, and slowly taste. A cook still learning. Or at least hoping to learn.

And, to me, that is the mark of the great ones. The chefs, the cooks, who after all the acclaim, all the stars and rave reviews, are still leaning, still searching for flavor. That's Dominque Crenn.

I first met Dominique Crenn two years ago at a food event in downtown Los Angeles. She was sitting at a table with a mutual friend, quietly sipping a glass of white wine. We quickly hit it off, talking about our worlds in the kitchen.

I learned she was, like me, deeply influenced by her father, who you will read about in this book's opening pages. He was an artist, and I think Dominque is an artist. A poet, too.

When you go through this book, I think you will agree. Go to one of the opening chapters, Metamorphosis, and read perhaps the loveliest, most poetic menu ever called "Chef's Grand Tasting Menu." Poetic Culinary. Read and you will understand.

But her food isn't about words. It isn't about looks, though it is certainly fun to behold. Her food is about soul. It is about childhood. It is about passions. But, and this is a giant "but," it is about deliciousness. Front and center, it is about how damn good her food tastes.

Hey, what did I say? Dominique Crenn might be a superhero chef. But, really, Dominique Crenn is a cook.

Nancy Silverton

Atelier

ATELIER CRENN is named after a little studio behind my childhood home in north-western France, where my father used to paint pictures inspired by the natural world around us in Brittany, from seascapes to landscapes to still-lives of the food grown on our family's farms. We called his studio "Atelier Papa Crenn," and it was a haven to me as a child who often felt out of step with the mainstream culture. While my father painted, he shared with me a love of art that continues to this day, more than fifteen years after we lost him, and he inspired me to become an artist myself. My father always encouraged my painting, writing, and cooking as equally valid artistic endeavors, so when I opened my first restaurant in 2011, I wanted it to be a testament to the values he instilled in me. I hung his paintings on the wall, wrote my menus as poems, and drew my inspiration from nature.

In French, the word *atelier* can be used to refer to an artist's studio or an artisan's workshop, and I like the way it embodies the intersection between art and artisanship in the culinary world. When I first started cooking, it might have been laughable for a chef to claim to make art, but these days, I have noticed a dawning awareness that food can be a medium for artistic expression. I recently read about a study in which salads plated as exact replicas of paintings by Bauhaus painter Wassily Kandinsky were found to be more delicious than the same ingredients presented as a random hodge-podge, and this confirmed my intuition that the visual aspect of food affects our perception of taste.[1] But it's deeper than a simple matter of making the food look pretty—after all, Kandinsky's compositions are challengingly modern, abstract, and even discordant in design—it's about creating and communicating an intention, a feeling, a memory, or an idea. It may sound sentimental to talk about cooking with love, but the truth is, food can touch us in the same way as a poem, a painting, or a song, if we open ourselves to receiving its meaning.

In many ways, however, the culinary arts have been lagging behind other art forms and are only now beginning to catch up. During the first half of the twentieth century, modernism revolutionized literature, music, dance, theater, and the visual arts, but cooking was not swept up in the movement. Explorations of subjectivity, perspective, memory, technology, improvisation, and abstraction blossomed among the other arts, but there was little if any corresponding experimentation in the culinary world. When cooking finally began to evolve

---

1. Amy Fleming, "Why does artistically presented food taste better?" The Guardian (UK), June 20, 2014. www.theguardian.com/lifeandstyle/wordofmouth/2014/jun/20/why-does-artistically-presented-food -taste-better.

in these directions in the twenty-first century, many people struggled to understand what was happening by calling the movement "molecular gastronomy," but eventually a more apt description took hold: "modernist cuisine."

In the same way that modernist techniques like stream of consciousness opened the door to an entirely new kind of literature, modernist culinary techniques offer a chance to push cooking into unexplored territory. Personally, I am very inspired by artists like Salvador Dalí and Virginia Woolf, whose work centers on memory, dreams, sensations, and time. When taste memories from childhood develop into the refined pleasures of adulthood at Atelier Crenn, the experience reminds us that our sensations are never static, which is a central lesson of modernist art. In this book, I focus on my own aesthetic interests and preoccupations, but these are not the only themes chefs can explore. I believe that once we begin to imagine the aesthetic possibilities of cuisine, the potential for meaning is infinite. With this book, I invite every cook in the world, from professional chefs to home cooks, to regard the kitchen as an atelier, and to get to work. Food is Art.

Memory

LOOKING BACK on my childhood, I can see the makings of a chef, but at the time, it wasn't obvious. First of all, I was a girl. In France at the time, female chefs were very rare. Back then, there was quite a wide gulf between the familial, nurturing, daily practice of cooking that I saw women doing at home, and the cooking that happened behind closed doors at restaurants. But I always loved food. I was raised on my mother's excellent home cooking, which tends toward classic French and specifically Breton regional specialties incorporating wonderfully fresh seafood and produce. That alone might have been enough to inspire me to cook, but I was also lucky enough to be exposed to some of the greatest restaurants in the world at a very young age. My father's best friend was the food critic for *Le Télégramme*, a major newspaper in Brittany, and my father often accompanied him on his tasting trips. As my passion for food became increasingly evident, they started inviting me along, and I enjoyed my first grand tasting menu when I was eight or nine years old. We were at Jean-Pierre Crouzil, a three-star restaurant located just ten kilometers from the coast in Brittany, and my memory of that day feels like a revelation, a spiritual vision. Before that meal, I had no idea it was possible to make food taste that way, and from then on, I just wanted to know more. Around that time, I told my mother I wanted to be a chef (and a policeman).

As I grew into a teenager, my temperament seemed ill-suited to the kitchen because I was so physically restless that I had little patience for slow-and-steady kitchen work. I loved being outdoors, and it was only much later that I realized that nature would be a touchstone for me as a chef. I still loved food, but I also loved soccer, judo, handball, and running. In retrospect, I wonder if judo helped me streamline my movements during service, or if running helped me push through to the end of every night. I'm not sure, but I do know my competitive streak would propel me to work harder, faster, and longer, just to prove that I could—even though I was a girl.

Throughout my youth, my father, Alain Crenn, was a politician representing Brittany in the National Assembly, so we spent much of the year living in Versailles, near Paris. But our family was and still is deeply rooted in Brittany. That was our home, with Breton ancestors stretching back countless generations on both my mother's and father's sides of the family. Every summer, I helped out on my grandmother's potato farm and spent a lot of time at my uncle's cattle and pig ranch. I probably spent more days of the year in Versailles than in Brittany, but when people ask where I grew up, I instinctively feel that I am from Brittany. That is where I absorbed the culture and agriculture that shaped me as a chef and as a person.

After I finished school, I traveled around Europe and ate at some awe-inspiring restaurants, and then returned to Paris to study economics and business. In those years, it finally dawned on me that my childhood ambition to be a chef was my true calling after all, but the French culinary establishment was very rigid in those days. As a woman, the only positions available to me were in the front of the house. (Even now, the culture of haute cuisine in France is not very welcoming to women, though we have seen some improvement. A record sixteen Frenchwomen earned Michelin stars in 2014, including the incredible chef Anne-Sophie Pic, who heads two Michelin-starred restaurants. Pic is about my age, but her father and grandfather were both chefs, and even she was consigned to the front of the house at her family's restaurant for a few years after her father's death, before she took the reins and recovered Maison Pic's third Michelin star.)

At that point, becoming a chef seemed impossible, but I kept dreaming, and I kept eating, and I kept reading about food. I devoured everything from Jean-Anthelme Brillat-Savarin's brilliant Enlightenment-era philosophy of gastronomy, *The Physiology of Taste*, to the latest international culinary magazines. (This was the early nineties, and France was a bit late in adopting the Internet, so news traveled slowly.) I read with interest about California cuisine and its adaptation of rustic French cooking in a new light and a different landscape. I read about Chef Jeremiah Tower leaving Chez Panisse to start his own restaurant, called Stars, where each cook developed the dishes for their station from scratch every day. It sounded like the opposite of the brigade system in French restaurants, where an aspiring cook starts as a kitchen apprentice at age fifteen and scarcely has a chance to voice an opinion until he (or very rarely, she) is middle-aged. *If only France were like California*, I said to myself, *then I could find out if I've got what it takes to be a chef.* If only, if only, if only, I said, while I spun my wheels in Paris, cooking at home while dreaming of restaurants.

Then one day, I boarded a plane, like a child running off to join the circus . . .

"Damn everything but the circus! …

The average 'painter' 'sculptor' 'poet'

'composer' 'playwright'

is a person who cannot leap

through a hoop from the back of a

galloping horse, make people laugh

with a clown's mouth,

orchestrate twenty lions."

—e.e. cummings, *Him: A Play*

It was 1992. I had walked in confidently the day before, no circus school on my résumé. No résumé, in fact. I approached the ringmaster, looked him in the eye, and said in my (at the time, even more pronounced) French accent that I loved *le cirque*, that I thought that he had the best circus in town, and that I wanted to work for him. Jeremiah Tower told me to come back the next day.

My first day at the circus I thought I would be downstairs with the other apprentices, far away from the crowd, the flames, the spectacle. Dressed crisply in my whites, I had prepped that afternoon with the other artists, trying to do what anyone asked of me quickly, cleanly, and well; answering requests with a soft and perhaps all-too-earnest "*Oui, Chef.*" I tried not to betray that my mind was abuzz with uncertainty. I hoped I could blend in, not foul anything up, and perhaps no one would notice that I didn't belong there yet. As showtime approached, I began to slink off downstairs, but the ringmaster caught me in his spotlight and addressed me:

"Dominique, you'll be on the line with Sean tonight."

Was my sharp in-breath audible to anyone other than me? Perhaps I was heard confidently replying, "*Oui, Chef.*"

As the big top began to fill, I could feel the pulse and the expectation of the crowd. The performers assumed their posts and reviewed their preparations one last time. The knife-thrower, standing behind high piles of ice and four or five different kinds of oysters, would soon be moving at top speed, lightning fast but moving decisively, steel shining: in, slide, pop. In slide pop. Inslidepop. Inslidepop!

The juggler at *garde manger* eyed his immaculately cleaned lettuces and *mise en place*. The striking colors befitted a circus: vibrant green mâche, shining vinaigrettes, milky white artisanal goat cheese, deep red beets, bright ruby citrus, bloodred house-dried tomato, and pale frisée—this was the early '90s, after all! Soon all these ingredients would be in the air, the juggler tossing one or two hundred salads before the night was over.

The tightrope walkers in pastry knew they had very little room for error, especially with the soufflé and the bonbon. They had some routines that involved less risk ("French" cream with berries, ice cream with hot fudge and caramel), but these were still executed perfectly, and the crowd adored them.

The circus began.

Gorgeous in their suits, the gymnasts moved gracefully across the floor, occasionally performing bizarre contortions in response to the crowd's demands. They moved deftly back and forth, in and out, a tumbling act performed according to a hidden logic known only to the initiated.

Soon, the flamethrower to my left was expertly searing scallops, grilling ahi, and roasting king salmon. Every time I looked up, the ringmaster caught my eye. I smiled a smile meant to instill confidence. I was cooking the parsnip puree, potato, and couscous. I wondered what my role would be in this *cirque*. "Am I the clown? Was I sent to the grill my first day to provide amusement for everyone else?" I also remembered the showgirls of the old circuses. "Am I here to be a pretty face?" I didn't have too much time to think about it between stirring my pots and plating four, five, six, seven dishes at a time. To my right is Sean, the strongman. In addition to roasting his pork loin in the wood oven, he is grilling rib eye and duck breast. He is doing the heavy lifting.

I realized that whatever our official roles, we were all trapeze artists, catching and releasing in turn, watching one another to coordinate our timing, our flights through the air. I made the couscous and passed it to Sean. Release. Sean plated his pork loin and spooned his demiglace. Release. Another artist picked it up and added wilted greens. Release. The gymnast came and carried it out into the din.

I began to see that the ringmaster had an act of his own. Every so often, he slipped out of the kitchen and floated onto the dining room floor. Faces and arms opened for him. Jokes, reminiscences, and flirtations wafted his way. He was not merely a ringmaster but a magician. The spell emanated from him. He conjured the whole spectacle and I wanted him to show me how to do it.

When I started at Stars, in San Francisco, I was primed for restaurant life, but I was certainly not prepared. I had studied, traveled, and dabbled in cooking at home, but I hadn't forgotten the thrill of fine dining, and that memory brought me to Tower's kitchen with my bold request to join in. Over time, I learned how much sweat, focus, presence, and humility go into a great restaurant, but I still feel the magic when it all appears to be an effortless performance. At Stars, I met so many incredible cooks, including Mark Franz and Emily Luchetti, who are now chef and pastry chef at Farallon, and Loretta Keller, who opened Coco500. In San Francisco, I finally felt accepted within a community of cooks. Over the next few years, I worked at Campton Place and other restaurants, where I acquired some new skills and friends, particularly French émigrés, like Roland Passot (La Folie), Hubert Keller (Fleur de Lys), and Jean-Pierre Dubray (The Dining Room at the Ritz-Carlton). When friends of theirs were opening a big restaurant in the InterContinental Hotel in Jakarta, they offered me the job of executive chef.

To be perfectly honest, I was not enthusiastic at first. I had fallen in love with the Bay Area, and I had never been to Indonesia, so why would I move there? But when I learned more about the concept, I was intrigued: I would be the first female executive chef in Indonesia, leading an all-female staff of cooks at the first Californian-French restaurant in the country. Up to this point, my career trajectory was a bit strange, having been shut out of the kitchen until my late twenties, then suddenly zooming from my first job to executive chef of a huge operation in less than five years. Yet my experience motivated me, because I had an opportunity to open doors that had been closed to me. So, I went to Jakarta in 1997, and it was like nothing I'd ever experienced before. The sights, the sounds, the smells, the tastes . . . and the heat! It was a humbling, challenging experience, but so satisfying to help expand opportunities for women in the restaurant industry. Unfortunately, my sojourn in Indonesia coincided with a period of tremendous political strife following the 1997 Asian financial crisis. President Suharto's thirty-three-year rule was crumbling under the pressures of violence around the country, especially in Jakarta. It was not safe for me to stay. So in 1998, I returned to the United States. After Indonesia, I spent a few years in southern California, first as executive chef of the Manhattan Country Club in Manhattan Beach and later at Abode in Santa Monica, where I was called a "chef to watch" by *Esquire* magazine. I also did some cooking at private events for some high-profile celebrities, and although it was exciting to be a part of that glamorous world and to cook for everyone from Juliette Binoche to then Vice President Al Gore, in the end, my heart was still in northern California. So when the InterContinental Hotel Group asked me to open the restaurant in their new San Francisco location, I jumped at the chance. After a period of traveling around Tuscany, eating and drinking very well, I returned to the Bay Area as executive chef of Luce, a Californian-Italian restaurant.

In some ways, working for a multinational hotel group is not ideal: dealing with room service, filling out corporate paperwork, and the relentlessness of serving breakfast, lunch, and dinner seven days a week. But in other ways, it's quite comfortable to have someone else take care of all the peripheral details like maintenance, insurance, bookkeeping, and so on. At Luce, I could really focus on cooking, and I started to find my own way as a chef. I experimented with ideas from around the world, and the menu started to edge away from the initial Californian-Italian concept to encompass my favorite flavors and techniques from France and Asia. Perhaps the best thing I did at Luce was hire Juan Contreras as my chef de cuisine; we worked together side by side at Luce, bouncing ideas off each other until we were both happy with the results. Ever since then, Juan has been my closest colleague and cooking partner, and he is now pastry chef at Atelier Crenn (see page 214). In this period, I also started to forge deeper relationships with local farmers and became more serious about the environmental ramifications of the restaurant industry. While at Luce, I founded a dinner series called "A Moveable Feast: 12 Chefs Celebrate 6 Farmers in a Series of Seasonal Suppers" as a benefit for the Center for Urban Education about Sustainable Agriculture, which promotes local, sustainable, organic food in the Bay Area. These dinners were really transformative for me, not only because I learned so much about produce and the environment, but also because I discovered the joy of engaging in substantive dialogue with other chefs.

The last ten years or so have seen a sea change in the culture of chefs, particularly within the world of fine dining. Whereas an earlier generation of chefs jealously guarded their secret recipes, the best chefs now meet for international conferences where they share their latest discoveries, discuss important ideas, and trade the phone numbers of their best suppliers. Of course, I never cared for the hierarchical model of kitchen management, but I absolutely love the way that dialogue has emerged as a culinary value, because it means that we are starting to operate more like an artistic community, which acknowledges influences and builds from one idea to the next. Whenever possible, I travel to new places to cook, host guest chefs in my own restaurant, and share what we are doing on the Internet. I find it exhilarating to participate in events like Le Grand Fooding in Paris or the Roots of American Food conference in Chicago, or even a one-night tribute to Jeremiah Tower with other Stars alumni. Working together with other chefs is not only fun and inspiring; it is also important as a shift in the culture of food. Finally, it seems, cooking is recognized as a form of communication, and chefs are coming together in dialogue.

Metamorphosis

ONCE I FOUND MY VOICE as a chef, things started to change pretty quickly. Luce earned a Michelin star in both its first and second years. *Esquire* named me Chef of the Year for 2008. I competed on *Iron Chef America* (and won!), and even vied to be *The Next Iron Chef*. As my profile rose, I started to field offers to go out on my own, but I was hesitant to leave. Finally, I took the plunge and decided to create a small restaurant where I would not only be chef, but also co-owner with my managing partner, Michele Astorian, who is also a Frenchwoman. My chef de cuisine, Juan Contreras, came along with me in a new role as pastry chef. In January 2011, we opened the doors at Atelier Crenn. By the end of the year, we had our first Michelin star. The next year, I became the first and only woman in America with two Michelin stars, and the next year, I was again the only female chef in the country with two stars, which is a source of both satisfaction and sadness for me. The 2015 guide awarded two stars to Emma Bengtsson and Suzette Gresham, and I would love to see Michelin honor more women chefs with two stars. (Especially if they can bump me up to three stars—after all, I still have a competitive streak!)

When opening Atelier Crenn, I put my heart and soul into every choice I made, from décor to pricing to kitchen design. The sign on the window spelling out "Atelier Crenn" was lettered by me, in my own proud-yet-nervous hand. The dining room is minimal, with plenty of wood and glass to create an atmosphere of timeless elegance. From the beginning, I wanted the food to be the focus of attention, but I imagined a luxuriant sort of minimalism, with invitingly soft furniture and attentive service. In the end, I think we struck a balance between meditative, quiet space with some light nods to Japanese Zen architecture on the one hand and the luxury of the French *grands restaurants* that captivated me as a child. (In other words, a reflection of the food at Atelier Crenn.) At first, we offered three tasting menus, but soon scaled down to a choice of two: the "Chef's Grand Tasting Menu," or a shorter progression of "Signature Courses."

Perhaps the most controversial decision I made in those early days was to subtitle the restaurant "Poetic Culinaria." What does that mean? It means that the experience of dining at Atelier Crenn should mirror the experience of an evening immersed in poetry, and that each dish should contribute to the meaning of the meal in the way that a line of poetry conveys a layer of significance to a poem. Not everyone reads poetry, but everyone eats, and everyone can be touched by an image, whether it is found in a book or on a plate. I want the food at Atelier Crenn to delight the palate the way a poem delights the ear, but beyond the pure pleasure principle, I want the restaurant to communicate on an emotional, spiritual, intellectual level. That is the meaning of poetic culinaria.

CHEF'S GRAND TASTING MENU

Summer has come and is full of sweet surprises

Under midnight glow, I can taste the sweetness of the sea,

hear mellow serenades of colors licorice and orange

I touch the earth and play

Where the broad ocean leans against the Spanish land,

I remember an oceanic feeling

Here, the earth proffers its juicy, vermilion gifts

and above the half moon floats, silky and smoky

In summer's green dappled light

the forest radiant with possibility

Nature rejoice! Chasing childhood memories

Feeling the black sand under my toes, I dreamed of

these creatures' languid movements

Walking deep in the woods, as the earth might have something to spare

bird song, see the water rippling from their visit

a token of summer

Summer has come, the sea beckons

Sweetness, bounty, thanks

The menu and the poem are constantly changing, in accordance with the seasons and our inspirations, but the first line of the poem always corresponds to our signature apéritif, a spherical Kir Breton (page 34). The poem progresses through small bites, like a trio of oyster, sea urchin, and salsify shaped like a cinnamon stick (pages 97, 107, and 59) to linger a bit with "vermilion" tomato (page 63) and "the half moon" of the veil on our onion soup (page 71). Toward the end, the poem leads us on a walk in the forest full of mushrooms and pine (page 79), and concludes with a salad and a progression of dessert courses from the pastry kitchen.

The poem sets the mood, gestures toward the colors and textures that the food will invoke, and invites the diner into an aesthetic mode of enjoyment, but it is not meant to be a strictly literal "translation" of each dish into a line of poetry. In fact, what I love about poetry is the way the meaning arrives at an oblique angle, defying the rules laid down in the dictionary; as Emily Dickinson wrote, "Tell all the truth but tell it slant." Similarly, the food at Atelier Crenn can be interpreted figuratively, as a poetic form of engagement with our ingredients and emotions. My tomato dish, for instance, refers on some level to the actual tomatoes that grew in my mother's garden, to a Platonic ideal of tomatoes in the cultural imagination, and to feelings of summery plenitude and warmth. To achieve this effect, we perform many culinary steps to alter the tomato—we juice some tomatoes, poach and shock other tomatoes in clarified tomato juice, reduce still more tomatoes into a compote—and yet we plate the dish to look a bit like a simple tomato, topped with a "vine" made of dehydrated basil. Why go to such great lengths to make a tomato look like a tomato? Well, it's not just a tomato, in the same way that it's not just a wheelbarrow when William Carlos Williams wrote:

so much depends

upon

a red wheel

barrow

glazed with rain

water

beside the white

chickens.

Let me be clear that I don't pretend to belong on the same level as William Carlos Williams, but I do feel inspired by his poem to stop, to consider, and to reflect on the world around us. At its best, cooking is an alchemical process that transforms ingredients beyond the simple chemical reactions sparked by heat and cold, oil and acid. The act of cooking is an engagement with tradition, community, time, and place. And for me, cooking is poetry.

A Day in the Life of Atelier Crenn

ATELIER CRENN embodies a unique combination of freedom and structure. We abide by a set of core principles that enable our creativity, and we believe that the rules we have set for ourselves actually spur us to be more creative. Take our produce, as an example: Everything we serve has to be picked within two days of coming to the restaurant. We expect deliveries every day, but we won't always know when that delivery will arrive or what size a particular product might be, and that presents a real challenge because it introduces variability at a restaurant that depends on consistency. Or take the fact that we've restricted ourselves to organic sugar, and we have to find a way to keep a dish white in spite of the trace amounts of molasses. It takes a few extra steps, but ultimately, that's how the restaurant thrives. We take pride in working harder to reach our goals within the guiding philosophy of the restaurant. On a day-to-day basis, the push and pull between creativity and constraint at Atelier Crenn means that we are free to try new things, but we adhere to a schedule and fulfill clearly defined responsibilities. As chef, it's my job to maintain the standards of Atelier Crenn, and I do it through a combination of help, commentary, criticism, and leading by example. I expect the staff to clean as carefully as they cook, because that's integral to our work in the kitchen. We spend long hours together every day, so it's important to create an environment that encourages camaraderie and discipline at the same time. Here's a day at Atelier Crenn, from morning until night.

9:00 A.M.

Three cooks arrive to start preparing all the recipes that have the longest lead time: stocks, soups, sauces, crackers, and breads. Almost no food carries over from one day to the next. We mostly start from scratch every morning, so we stay busy, and we don't have any designated prep cooks to carry on the early morning work. Each cook prepares the mise en place for his or her own station, methodically working through a long to-do list relating to three or four dishes, which will involve fifteen to twenty component recipes altogether.

11:00 A.M.

All of the machines get put away, all of the surfaces are scrubbed, all of the dishes are done, all of the sinks are washed and sanitized, and the floor is vacuumed.

12:00 P.M.

The remaining six cooks arrive, and the wheels of the kitchen really start turning. The interns start to arrive and the kitchen starts to get a little noisier with the sound of blenders and conversation, but the mood is generally focused. Preparations for our afternoon staff meal begins in this period. We are very serious about providing a healthy, delicious meal that covers all the food groups, and isn't just a collection of scraps and leftovers. We write a menu and all the cooks have a bit of staff meal on their prep lists. It is important that staff meal is made with the same care and quality of ingredients as the food we serve in the dining room.

2:00 P.M.

All of the machines get put away, all of the surfaces are scrubbed, all of the dishes are done, all of the sinks are washed and sanitized, and the floor is vacuumed.

2:15 P.M.

Back to our prep lists. The front-of-house staff starts to arrive, starting with the polisher at 3:00, though the kitchen team won't start to see most of them until lunch.

3:40 P.M.

We set up the staff meal while all of the machines get put away, all of the surfaces are scrubbed, all of the dishes are done, all of the sinks are washed and sanitized, and the floor is vacuumed.

3:55 P.M.

This is when the front- and back-of-house staff all stop what they're doing and eat lunch together. Some eat in the dining room, some eat in the private dining area in the back, and others take their food outside if the weather is nice. The only rule is that no one is allowed to work during lunch. Actually, there's another rule: When serving yourself, take only what you can eat, and eat only what you take. Our staff meals cover a wide range of cuisines, but I am particularly fond of our holiday staff meals, like Fourth of July barbecue or turkey in the days leading up to Thanksgiving. (The restaurant is closed for major family holidays, so the staff can go home, but we like celebrating together by cooking a meal based on the holiday theme.)

4:30 P.M.

During the final period of mise en place, the front of house cleans up the staff meal and packages any leftovers to take home at the end of the night. This is crunch time for the back of house, when we do all our last-minute tasks, ranging from herb kits to knife cuts. The only exception is on Friday and Saturday nights when we open half an hour earlier, and we lose our final mise en place period, so we just have to hustle harder during the day.

5:00 P.M.

I meet with the front of house regarding any changes or additions to the menu. In addition to the usual clean-up tasks, we also remove everything from the refrigerators in order to clean them thoroughly. We consolidate containers and organize our stations. We do all of our dishes in time for the dishwasher's arrival. (It's just common courtesy to bring the kitchen back to the spotless condition we found it in.)

5:00/5:30 P.M.

Service is when it all comes together. I float from station to station and help wherever the kitchen is being pressured the most, but I also make sure that any food leaving the kitchen is absolutely perfect. I love the energy of the kitchen. I work closely with the expediter, who controls the flow of traffic in and out of the kitchen, and I take a good look at every single plate. The restaurant only serves tasting menus, which means we can have more control and consistency than we would with an à la carte menu, but we try to be very accommodating to diners with restricted diets and allergies, and even in the best-run kitchens, there are always plenty of surprises.

It's also important to me to find time to visit the dining room during service, so that I can talk to diners and personally welcome them to Atelier Crenn. I feel that feeding people is a very beautiful, intimate connection, and so I want to connect in other ways as well: through eye contact, a handshake, conversation. I have met so many fascinating people this way. I know that many chefs would rather stay in the kitchen, but for me, visiting the dining room is one of the great pleasures of restaurant life.

1:00/2:00 A.M.

Stations that finish first head downstairs and clean the equipment in the basement. After the last dish goes out, everything in the kitchen gets broken down, scrubbed, and polished. We write our prep lists and have a quick kitchen meeting. And then, of course, a final kitchen cleaning period.

1:30 A.M. (SATURDAY ONLY)

This is the only time we listen to music in the kitchen, when all the guests have gone home, and we need some extra energy to power through our deep cleaning. We take apart the refrigerators, clean inside the stoves and behind the plates, scrub the ceiling and the drains. We clean every single sheet pan, pot, and piece of equipment. If it can be cleaned, we clean it on Saturday night. The entire back-of-house staff is there together, including the dishwasher, and the whole process takes three to four hours. We have Sunday and Monday off to recover. Then on Tuesday morning, we start all over again in a nice, clean kitchen.

If this routine seems obsessive about cleaning, well, you should see Juan's side of the kitchen. Talk about obsessive!

Papa Grenn,

Sitting on top of the sand dune, feeling of beach sand under my toes, looking so far at the blue sea... the sun beaming fiercely on my raw heart. I remember we used to sit here together during those memorable summer-days, listening to your stories and laughing at your jokes. Those hot summer-days, I would hear the echoes of the fireworks in the sky,

scarlet buttons...

golden lozenges...

green... yellow... red...

Sweat on my face are the tears of my bruises that you imprint when you left me, they are not scars but signals of just how far I have been and how far I will go... with you at my side.

I miss you.

Your daughter

How to Use This Book

AT TIMES, the style of cooking practiced at Atelier Crenn can seem almost scientific in its precision: We measure ingredients in tenths of grams, we want to know the temperature at which we are incorporating certain ingredients, and so forth. And yet our cooking is ultimately more art than science, and the measurements recorded in this book should always be taken as documents of a particular time and place, and therefore subject to reinterpretation in other kitchens, under other circumstances, by other cooks. The power of a blender, the humidity in a kitchen, the crowding of a freezer—all these factors and many more can affect a recipe. Trust your judgment as to whether to keep stirring, or cooking, or chilling, and try not to be afraid of making mistakes, as it is the only true way to learn. This book offers precise instructions based on many rounds of recipe testing, but it would be misleading to suggest that every variable can be controlled and replicated. After all, even when we employ scales, thermometers, timers, and even sometimes refractometers, we know that our truest instruments in the kitchen are eyes, mouths, noses, ears, fingers, hearts, and minds. This book reflects how we really do things at Atelier Crenn. When possible, we have made suggestions for adapting professional techniques for a home kitchen, but in cases where it is simply not possible to forgo a vacuum sealer or immersion circulator, for instance, these items are not marked as optional.

Equipment

KITCHEN SCALE

Though it is not listed under every equipment list, a kitchen scale was used to produce every single recipe in this book. At Atelier Crenn, we measure our ingredients by weight rather than volume, because this is by far the best way to achieve consistent results; we use the metric system because it simplifies all our calculations. When feasible, we have provided both metric weights and the equivalent U.S. customary volume measurements, but we strongly recommend the use of a kitchen scale, particularly when it comes to using modernist ingredients like xanthan gum, gellans, and so forth, which are added in proportion to the total weight. These ingredients tend to be added in very small amounts for which volume measures are simply not very practical, and even a small difference in amount can radically change the texture of the final dish. The volume of salt, too, can differ quite a bit depending on the brand and its style of crystal. If you are using Morton's Coarse Kosher Salt, which is made by running salt crystals through rollers, you will need about 0.6 cup to get the 150 grams called for in our foie gras recipe; but if you use Diamond Crystal Kosher Salt, which is made through an evaporation process, you'll need almost twice the volume, or 1.1 cups. (Both are good-quality salts, but in the professional kitchens where I've worked, Diamond Crystal is the default brand, and cooks have all become accustomed to pinching and dashing its hollow pyramidal grains.) But no matter the brand, you will always measure the correct amount of salt by using weight rather than volume.

BLENDERS

At Atelier Crenn, we use a Vitamix Pro, which allows us to create smooth textures that a basic home blender cannot replicate. When a recipe in this book calls for a blender, it should be a powerful blender with a minimum of 2 horsepower. When the instructions call for high speed, it should be understood that one should start on low speed and gradually bring the power up to high over the course of about 3 seconds; the recommended blending time refers to the time spent at the designated speed. When adding hydrocolloids, we recommend "shearing" in the ingredient at the end of the blending process, when the mixture has formed a vortex (whirlpool) shape, and adding the hydrocolloid directly into the mixture without allowing it to touch the sides of the blender, to ensure thorough incorporation. Note that Vitamix blenders require a minimum volume of 1½ cups to work well, and that is why some of the recipes in this book call for considerably more food than will be used in the final plating.

FOOD PROCESSORS

On the savory side of the kitchen, we use Robot Coupe brand food processors, and on the pastry side, both Robot Coupe and Thermomix machines. In most cases, a powerful food processor will be able to achieve the results we are looking for with a Robot Coupe, but a

Thermomix has the added advantage of mixing, weighing, and cooking all at once. The recipes here assume access to a high-quality food processor but not a Thermomix (because they're expensive!).

SOUS VIDE

At Atelier Crenn, as in many other professional kitchens, we rely on sous-vide cooking to ensure a consistent product. To cook sous vide, we usually use a vacuum sealer to compress ingredients inside a vacuum bag and then submerge the bag in a water bath, the temperature of which is controlled with an immersion circulator; in some cases, we will cook ingredients in a vacuum bag submerged in a pot of boiling water or simply compress ingredients in the vacuum sealer without cooking them in water. In most cases, we have provided alternative instructions for sous-vide cooking, but we must acknowledge that these recipes were designed to be accomplished with a vacuum sealer and/or immersion circulator, and in a few cases, which are noted, we do not recommend attempting a recipe without the proper equipment. For what it's worth, the prices of vacuum sealers and immersion circulators have come down considerably in recent years, and it is now possible to buy a small vacuum-sealing unit and a plug-in temperature controller for less than $100 each. If you do choose to use resealable plastic freezer bags instead of vacuum bags, please use care to choose bags composed of food-safe plastic.

DEHYDRATORS

We love our dehydrators at Atelier Crenn—we currently have five in our kitchen. We are aware of the fact that they operate differently and that readers of this book will likely need to adjust our recommendations in relation to their own machines. For those who do not own a dehydrator, we offer directions for drying in the oven, which will also require some judgment calls, and will likely not produce the same kind of delicate crispiness as a dehydrator. The cost of dehydrators has also dropped recently, with the least expensive now about $35 apiece.

STRAINERS

When a recipe calls for a "fine-mesh strainer," that generally means we use a conical chinois at Atelier Crenn, though other shapes of strainer will work as well. When a recipe calls for a "coarse-mesh strainer," that generally means we use a colander at Atelier Crenn, though other shapes of strainer will work as well.

ACETATE SHEETS

We use acetate sheets for so many applications, from making thin veils to lining dehydrator trays to creating tubes. It's very useful to have a material to which food will not stick, particularly when texture is a particular concern.

Ingredients

ORGANIC SUGAR

It is a rule at Atelier Crenn that all sugar must be organic, which means the sugarcane was grown according to organic farming protocols, but not that the sugar is raw or unrefined. All our recipes were developed with organic granulated sugar, which retains more molasses than conventionally grown sugar and reacts differently to heat and other ingredients. The choice comes down to a matter of caring for our guests and their health, even when they are not aware of it. We also use some less common types of sugar, for the sake of texture, including trimoline (which creates a silkier texture), 10X confectioners' sugar (which is a very fine powdered sugar), liquid glucose (which does not crystallize as easily), and powdered glucose (which makes the sugar elastic). In the case of these exotic sugars, we have not been able to find organic alternatives.

SALT

At Atelier Crenn, our rule of thumb is to add approximately 1 percent of the total weight in salt, though there are many adjustments. The richer the dish, the less salt we will use, and the higher the water content, the more salt we will use. Fine sea salt is the default form of salt at Atelier Crenn, but it can be replaced with table salt at the same weight. Note that fine sea salt is different from fleur de sel, which is a finishing salt, like Maldon, prized for its flavor and crystal structure. Our default finishing salt is Maldon, but we use fleur de sel for applications with strong memories of my Breton roots, such as cultured butter (page 299).

WATER

In our kitchen, we always use purified water. Water is not listed among our ingredients unless it's a specialized form like seltzer water, or if it's absolutely crucial to have purified water, but it is always advisable to use the best water available in any cooking project.

SAKE KASU

Also known as sake lees, sake kasu refers to the residual yeast left after producing sake, or fermented rice wine. At Atelier Crenn, we use sake kasu as a fermentation agent for fruits, vegetables, and meats, but it is also related to amazake, which is a sweet alcoholic liquid used as a marinade or condiment in Japan. In recent years, amazake has become more popular in Western kitchens influenced by Japanese cuisine.

MODERNIST INGREDIENTS

Hydrocolloids like agar-agar and xanthan gum can seem intimidating or unappealing, but they're really just long chains of sugar or protein molecules that pull water molecules toward them in various ways, thereby thickening the texture of a liquid. Old-fashioned gelatin and pectin, for instance, are both hydrocolloids. Here is a rundown of some of the less familiar "modernist" ingredients used at Atelier Crenn, with their uses and properties:

- **AGAR-AGAR** is a seaweed-derived gelling agent and thickener that we use to make puddings and gels at concentrations of 0.1 to 0.3 percent, though it can be used at higher concentrations to make very firm gels. Agar-agar is hydrated in boiling liquids and begins to gel as it cools to about 31°C/88°F and will not lose its structure unless heated above 58°C/136°F. We usually activate agar-agar in a pot, let it cool on a sheet pan, and then blend it in a blender to create a fluid gel, because it has the stability to withstand the agitation of the blender.

- **CORN MALTODEXTRIN** is a modified carbohydrate that is useful for adding density to liquids without thickening them. So, for example, corn maltodextrin keeps our Banyuls vinegar meringue (page 89) from being too airy without necessitating the addition of sugar, which is used in most meringues. As an added bonus, it can be activated at cool temperatures.

- **GELLAN** (high and low acyl) are algae-based gelling agents, stabilizers, emulsifiers, and thickeners. Once activated in a liquid in the 80°C/175°F to 90°C/195°F range and then cooled, gellan is very stable even at high heat, which makes it perfect for making warm gels. We usually add low-acyl gellan at about 0.1 percent of the total volume, and only rarely use high-acyl gellan, which can withstand very high temperatures.

- **GUAR GUM** is an emulsifier that we like to use in conjunction with dairy because it bonds well with the proteins. Guar gum must be dissolved in cold liquid to activate it.

- **IOTA CARRAGEENAN** comes from red seaweeds and is often used in conjunction with dairy, where it is effective at very low concentrations. Iota carrageenan must be heated to 60°C/140°F and incorporated with a blender to activate.

- **KUZU (KUDZU) STARCH** is common in Japanese cuisine, but less common here. *Kuzu* offers an interestingly glutinous texture though it does not contain gluten, so it is useful for making flourless gnocchi or dumplings, such as the Comté gnocchi in our onion soup (page 71). In contrast to cornstarch and other traditional starches, *kuzu* is less processed with chemicals, is easier to hydrate in cold liquids, and will not separate when heated.

- **LECITHIN** is an emulsifier used to stabilize airs and bubbles. Like other hydrocolloids, it is water based, so it will not create air or bubbles from liquids containing alcohol or oil.
- **LOCUST BEAN GUM** is an extract of carob seed, and when used with xanthan gum, it creates an elastic yet brittle gel. It must be blended into a liquid to incorporate, but does not require heating.
- **METHOCEL** is derived from the cell walls of plants, and it helps to stabilize foams and meringues, particularly when combined with xanthan gum. It comes in many forms, but we gravitate toward Methocel F50, which can be incorporated into a hot or cold liquid with a blender and will maintain its texture in spite of being dehydrated, as in our Banyuls vinegar meringue (page 89).
- **SODIUM HEXAMETAPHOSPHATE (SHMP)** is not a hydrocolloid, but rather a sequestrant, which is used in combination with hydrocolloids to lower the temperature at which they can be activated.
- **SORBET STABILIZER** creates smoother sorbets and ice cream by reducing the size of the ice crystals. (See page 325 for more on sorbet and ice cream stabilizers.)
- **SUCRO** is an emulsifier obtained from a fatty acid called sucroester. Because it is not water based like a hydrocolloid, it can be used to aerate liquids containing alcohol or oil, like the pamplemousse bubbles in The Sea (page 123).
- **TAPIOCA MALTODEXTRIN** is a modified carbohydrate used to make oils into powders. The tapioca maltodextrin molecule can hold three times its own weight in oil without liquefying. In commercial settings, tapioca maltodextrin is used to make powdered oils for things like brownie mix, but we use it to make brown butter powder (page 224) and tangerine-oil flavored "sand" in The Sea dessert (page 261), among other textured powders.
- **VERSAWHIP** is a soy-based protein used to stabilize whipped foams. It is often used with xanthan gum in place of egg whites (because it is stronger) or gelatin (because the temperature range is greater). I like that Versawhip is vegan, but it is not effective in the presence of oils, which can limit its usefulness in recipe development.
- **XANTHAN GUM** is the most often used hydrocolloid in our kitchen, because it often enhances the efficacy of other hydrocolloids. We use xanthan gum as a thickener at very low concentrations, usually in the 0.1 to 0.2 percent range, to give sauces a tiny bit of pull to keep them from spreading across the plate, in dressings to emulsify the oils and liquids, and in purees to keep the texture nice and smooth. Xanthan gum dissolves into hot or cold liquids, and has virtually no effect on flavor, but it loses some effectiveness if it is cooked.

About Our Recipes

ORGANIZATION

Each recipe is introduced with a headnote about the inspiration and history of the dish, with notes on technique as appropriate, though most of the technical details are located within the instructions themselves. Within each dish, components are listed in order of lead time required before serving. Each component recipe is organized into ingredient list, equipment list, and instructions. When an ingredient must be added as a percentage of the total weight, which may differ in relation to evaporation or other factors, we offer instructions for calculating percentages. At the end of each dish, a section titled "To serve" lists ingredients related to garnishes intended for the dish as a whole.

SERVING SIZES

At Atelier Crenn, we serve tasting menus that can extend up to twenty-five courses, and that means each course is relatively small and refined. We simply do not serve the traditional American "entrée" that fills a dinner plate with meat and two sides. In many cases, our recipes are designed to showcase a single piece of shellfish or a poultry breast, with appropriately sized accompaniments. In the interest of honesty and authenticity, we have provided instructions for how our dishes are actually prepared and served at Atelier Crenn, but of course, these recipes may be served to fewer people in larger portions. Use the recipes however they work best for you. Some of our recipes call for large-batch kitchen projects (such as preserving lemons or making stocks) that may be used in small amounts within the finished dish; I hope that these items help you to stock your pantry with homemade ingredients that allow for further experimentation and cooking far beyond the recipes contained in these pages.

PLATING

In some cases, the plating instructions at the end of a recipe do not correspond perfectly with the accompanying image because we have allowed ourselves a bit of artistic license in the visual presentation for this book. That is, the plating instructions reflect how our dishes are prepared at Atelier Crenn.

Origin

I HAVE ALWAYS connected deeply with my family's Breton roots, even though—or perhaps because—I was adopted as a baby. When I was growing up, my family spent every summer in Brittany, where my grandparents on both sides had farms, and those farms had personalities. The farm on my father's side felt quite masculine, partly because my uncle and aunt kept cows and pigs, which they would turn into charcuterie. On my mother's side, the farm felt as warm and maternal as my grandmother, who grew potatoes, raised chickens, and kept a garden for growing vegetables that she traded with other villagers. During the summers, I spent almost every day on my grandmother's farm. She used to bring lunch out to the fields and we'd all sit down in the dirt and eat together. It was hard, sweaty work, but I swear those were the best-tasting potatoes in the world.

Brittany is a very beautiful part of France, with a lot of impressive stone architecture from the Middle Ages, and my family has a very long ancestry there, reaching back centuries. There are even rumors that we have a royal bastard somewhere on my mother's side of the family tree. Maybe that explains why my grandmother always seemed like a queen to me, in her house where she ruled over everything with a benevolent touch. The rest of the year, I lived with my parents and brother outside Paris, but those summers in Brittany really shaped me, and maybe my love for restaurants really started there, when my parents were building their house, and we spent a month living in a hotel with a bar and café-pâtisserie. It was a family-owned place in Locronan, called Au Fer à Cheval, and everybody knew my brother and me as we ran all around that place, in and out of the kitchen, the magazine shop, and the café. And of course, I loved to visit the pâtisserie next door. They had the most amazing kouign-amann, which is a traditional Breton butter cake. I probably ate one every day.

In terms of food, Brittany is known for butter, apples, potatoes, buckwheat, and seafood (especially oysters) and those ingredients are still touchstones for me, though I love to incorporate other influences as well, particularly from Japanese and Spanish sources. As a chef and as a person, I work hard to achieve a balance between memories and dreams, tradition and innovation, family and community, past and present. The recipes in this book reflect this personal push and pull. Almost every dish at Atelier Crenn pays homage to Brittany, but never in a straightforward or traditional way. In some dishes, I gravitate toward the ingredients I ate as a child, but I pair them with new flavors that I have encountered as an adult; in others, I revisit classic dishes from a modern perspective, which I believe breathes new life into the traditions I love. Our signature dish, a spherical Kir Breton, epitomizes the core philosophy of Atelier Crenn. Let it serve as an introduction to this book, just as it introduces diners to the restaurant.

I believe that when I draw on the sights, sound, tastes, and memories of my childhood, even my wildest culinary ideas carry an emotional resonance for my guests. As I prepared to open Atelier Crenn, I wanted to create a signature dish that expressed both where I come from and where I am now. On a practical level, it made sense to introduce my restaurant—and by extension, myself—with a cocktail, which would be served as the first taste of the meal. From that initial thought, I immediately realized that I had to create my own version of Kir Breton.

Kir Breton is Brittany's regional variation on the Kir Royale. We grow a lot of apples in the north, so instead of mixing crème de cassis with champagne, we use hard apple cider, which produces a cocktail that's a little sweeter and less bubbly. I was reminded of the shot of peach champagne in a bowl I'd had once at El Celler de Can Roca, in Spain, but I wanted to make a sphere for the sake of its beauty and simplicity. I talked the idea over with my indispensable pastry chef, Juan Contreras, who suggested cocoa butter shells, and we decided to put the cider inside and keep the cassis flavor on top as a dollop of fruit reduction.

Ultimately, we created a Kir Breton that splits the difference between apéritif and amuse-bouche, and which offers a first bite that I believe truly captures the spirit of Atelier Crenn. It was the first thing on the menu, and it has never left: Every single diner who has ever eaten at my restaurant has been served my Kir Breton. The flavors of apple cider and crème de cassis taste like home to me, so I think of our Kir Breton as sending a little burst of old-fashioned hospitality and modern cooking to welcome my guests. And at this point, the dish has a new meaning for me, as a symbol of my beautifully collaborative friendship with Juan, who makes about fifty Kir Bretons every day, including a few filled with nonalcoholic apple cider for guests who don't drink.

Be sure to prepare your Kir Breton in a cool place to minimize breakage and remind your guests not to nibble! Our spherical cocktail must be taken as a single shot, which explodes like a jubilant welcome, reminiscent of my mother greeting guests with a glass of Kir Breton. | *Serves 20 as an amuse*

Kir Breton

INGREDIENTS

250 grams (1 cup) apple cider
   (alcoholic or nonalcoholic)
450 grams (16 ounces) cocoa butter
60 grams (2 ounces) white chocolate
150 grams (⅔ cup) crème de cassis
22 grams Ultra-Tex 3

>>>

One day before serving:

- If you are using alcoholic apple cider, simmer it in a saucepan over low heat for 15 minutes to evaporate the alcohol and promote proper freezing.
- Pour the cider into spherical ice cube trays and freeze overnight.

At least six hours before the Kir Breton will be served:

- **TO TEMPER THE WHITE CHOCOLATE:** Fill the bottom of a double boiler or a medium pot halfway with water and bring to a boil over medium heat. In the top of the double boiler or in a large metal bowl that fits snugly over the saucepan without touching the boiling water, combine the cocoa butter and white chocolate.

EQUIPMENT

Spherical ice cube trays
    (1-inch diameter)
Double boiler or large metal bowl
    that fits snugly over a saucepan
Cooking thermometer
Sharp pin
Small squeeze bottle

- Set the top of the double boiler or the large metal bowl on the pot and attach a cooking thermometer. Heat over very low heat, stirring occasionally, until it forms a smooth syrup (38°C/100°F to 43°C/110°F).
- Prick the cider balls with a sharp pin to use as a handle to hold them. Dip each ball into the white chocolate–cocoa syrup for 1 second and remove. Smooth over the spot where you pricked the ball with your finger, then immediately place it back in the mold (leaving the top off the mold) in the refrigerator. The shell will harden in the refrigerator while the cider melts, producing a spherical white chocolate shell around liquid apple cider. Reserve any unused chocolate-cocoa syrup for another use.
- **TO PREPARE THE CRÈME DE CASSIS:** Pour the crème de cassis into a medium bowl. Whisk the Ultra-Tex 3 into the crème de cassis. Strain through a fine-mesh strainer and transfer to a small squeeze bottle. Use immediately or refrigerate until ready to serve.

TO SERVE:

- Transfer the spheres to porcelain Asian spoons and top each one with a pea-size dot of crème de cassis reduction. Advise your guests to eat the whole thing with their mouths closed around the sphere. (At Atelier Crenn, we serve our Kir Breton on small pedestals, which allows guests to pop them into their mouths in a single bite.)

PLANT

A FEW YEARS before I left France, I took a trip with my parents through the southern part of the country and we stopped in Laguiole, where renowned chef Michel Bras has developed a truly beautiful style of cooking that had an enormous influence over a whole generation of chefs. At Michel Bras's eponymous restaurant, there is no division between the cuisine and the natural environment. It's a pure reflection: His food is Laguiole and Laguiole is his food.

According to the story I heard, one day in 1978, Bras was out running in the fields of Laguiole when he was struck with the inspiration for a dish that would translate the landscape onto the plate, from the crops to the flowers to the soil. He called his dish *gargouillou*, which is a traditional dish in southern France, but what Bras made was not just an update of an old recipe, but rather a reflection of his love for the land. In a way, it was like Impressionist painting: He was showing us his vision of what he saw, rather than a Realist portrait.

At the time that I visited Michel Bras, I was obsessed with Japanese and Vietnamese food and I didn't even know I wanted to be a chef, but I believe we can carry experiences inside us until we know what to do with them. Dinner at Michel Bras was one of those moments for me: It shaped my destiny. On an unconscious level, I understood and internalized the way Bras expresses himself through food, and I started to recognize my desire to do the same for myself.

Unlike Bras, I haven't stayed in one place my whole life, and I've always felt an internal tension between my instincts for home and for travel. Even as a child, I split my time between Versailles during the school year and Brittany during the summer and winter vacations. In my twenties, I committed myself to life as an expatriate, far from my family and my past, and for a few years I even lived in Indonesia, where I encountered customs and cuisines vastly different from those of my youth. These days, of course, I am rooted in both France and the United States, and wherever I go, I carry my memories of everything I loved in the place I've left behind. When I try to communicate my sense of the natural world through my cooking, it is not an expression of the landscape outside my kitchen window, but rather of my memories and my imagination. I'm very grateful to have spent so much of my childhood on my family's farms and I feel lucky that I get to live and cook in California, one of the most fertile environments in the world, but these days, my lifestyle does not allow me to cultivate the kind of vegetable garden I would like. Instead, I garden on the plate.

In this chapter, you will find recipes that celebrate the plant kingdom. Here, plants are not relegated to supporting roles relative to fish or meat, but are the star of the show, with all of the attention they deserve. For these dishes, I try to hone in on what is really special about each plant, both in terms of flavor and emotional impact, and find a way to honor that distinctive quality, like a gardener coaxing her crops from the ground with a combination of love, patience, and hard work.

Le Jardin is my vision of a garden. The dish resembles a real garden, with its earthy quinoa soil and its array of vegetables reaching toward the sun, but it is not meant to be a literal representation as much as an emotional evocation of the wonder and surprise elicited by a beautiful garden. I am not talking about perfectly manicured plantings or even Zen rock gardens, but rather the sort of garden that allows the wildness of nature to flourish within a gardener's design. When plating Le Jardin, we strike a compromise between spontaneity and structure. We allow a pea shoot to tumble casually onto a partially unspooled ribbon of pickled beet; we control the chaos with tweezers and a trained eye, but every plate is unique.

The ingredients in Le Jardin are constantly changing with the seasons and the years, because a garden yields up its true beauty with the passage of time. No matter the season, Le Jardin incorporates raw, cooked, and pickled components and juxtaposes a colorful spectrum of vegetables with edible flowers. The following recipe is a winter variation in which the pureed parsnip may be replaced with other seasonal vegetable purees, such as the fermented yellow squash and sake kasu puree in my summer squab dish (page 203). I also love incorporating seasonal ingredients such as peas or fava beans in the spring, tomatoes and avocados in the summer, or shelling beans in the fall. Whatever the season, Le Jardin should showcase the very best produce growing in local gardens at the moment it is served. | *Serves 4*

Le Jardin

WILD RICE AND QUINOA SOIL

INGREDIENTS

50 grams (½ cup) white quinoa
Kosher salt
160 grams (¾ cup) neutral vegetable oil
Fine sea salt
20 grams (¼ cup) uncooked wild rice

EQUIPMENT

Fine-mesh strainer
Acetate sheet
Dehydrator (*optional*)
Cooking thermometer
Wire skimmer

At least 3 hours before serving:

- In a fine-mesh strainer, rinse the quinoa with cold water.
- In a small pot, bring 200 grams (scant 1 cup) water to a boil. Stir in the quinoa and a pinch of kosher salt. Cover and simmer over low heat until tender, 10 to 15 minutes. Strain the quinoa in a fine-mesh strainer to remove excess water.
- **TO DRY THE QUINOA IN A DEHYDRATOR:** Place an acetate sheet in a dehydrator tray. Evenly spread the cooked quinoa across the acetate sheet. Transfer the tray to a dehydrator set to 60°C/140°F and dry the quinoa, stirring occasionally, for 2 hours.
- **TO DRY THE QUINOA IN THE OVEN:** Preheat the oven to 60°C/140°F or the closest temperature available. Place an acetate sheet on a baking sheet. Evenly spread the cooked quinoa across the acetate sheet. Transfer the baking sheet to the oven and turn off the heat. Let the quinoa dry in the closed oven for 3 hours.

>>>

Le Jardin, *continued*

- In a frying pan with a cooking thermometer attached, heat the vegetable oil over medium-high heat to 160°C/320°F. Fry the dried quinoa for 30 seconds and remove with a wire skimmer. Spread the fried quinoa on a paper towel and let drain for about 5 minutes to remove excess oil. Season with a generous pinch of fine sea salt.
- Raise the heat under the frying pan to bring the temperature of the vegetable oil up to 190°C/375°F. Add the uncooked wild rice and fry until it puffs, 30 to 45 seconds. Remove the wild rice with a wire skimmer and spread it on a paper towel. Let drain for about 5 minutes to remove excess oil. Season with a generous pinch of fine sea salt.
- Store the quinoa and wild rice separately at room temperature in airtight containers until ready to serve.

PICKLED, PUREED, AND RAW VEGETABLES

INGREDIENTS

4 large purple-top turnips

2 large red beets

2 medium parsnips

26 grams (2 tablespoons) extra-virgin olive oil

6 grams (1 teaspoon) coarse sea salt

4 grams (1 teaspoon) granulated sugar

20 grams (4 teaspoons) champagne vinegar

20 grams (4 teaspoons) raspberry vinegar

200 grams (¾ cup plus 1½ tablespoons) whole milk

Fine sea salt

8 to 12 tiny baby carrots, assorted colors, with greens attached

8 to 12 tiny breakfast radishes with greens attached

>>>

At least 90 minutes before serving:

- Wash and peel the turnips, beets, and parsnips, discarding the stems and tips.
- Use a vegetable peeler or turning slicer to create 1-inch-wide ribbons from the center of the turnips and beets until you have 12 of each, ranging from 4 to 6 inches in length. Keep the turnip and beet piles separate and expect to lose more of the turnips to waste due to their shape.
- In a medium bowl, mix together the olive oil, coarse sea salt, and sugar.
- **TO COOK THE TURNIPS AND BEETS SOUS VIDE:** Transfer half the olive oil mixture to a vacuum bag, add the champagne vinegar and the turnip ribbons, seal the bag, and compress at 80%. Transfer the remaining olive oil mixture to another vacuum bag, add the raspberry vinegar and beet ribbons, seal the bag, and compress at 80%. Cook the turnips and beets sous vide in an immersion circulator set to 85°C/185°F until tender; remove the turnips after 45 minutes and the beets after 1 hour.

Vegetable peeler or turning slicer
Vacuum bag or resealable plastic
    freezer bag
Vacuum sealer (*optional*)
Immersion circulator or
    cooking thermometer

- **TO COOK THE TURNIPS AND BEETS ON THE STOVETOP**: Transfer half the olive oil mixture to a resealable plastic freezer bag, add the champagne vinegar and the turnip ribbons, squeeze out as much air as possible, and seal the bag. Transfer the remaining olive oil mixture to another resealable plastic freezer bag, add the raspberry vinegar and beet ribbons, squeeze out as much air as possible, and seal the bag. Fill a large pot three-quarters full with water and attach a cooking thermometer. Bring the water to 85°C/185°F over low heat and submerge both bags. Closely monitor the heat to maintain a consistent temperature and stir often. Remove the turnips after 45 minutes and the beets after 1 hour.
- Cut the peeled parsnip into small (¼-inch) dice. In a medium saucepan, combine the parsnip and the milk and simmer over low heat until the parsnip is slightly overcooked and almost all the liquid has been absorbed, about 25 minutes. Transfer the parsnip and any remaining liquid to a blender and puree until completely smooth. Season with fine sea salt.
- Gently clean the baby carrots and breakfast radishes with a damp towel and trim the greens to 1 inch in length.

INGREDIENTS
40 grams (1 cup) seasonal
    edible flowers and pea shoots
    (*optional*)

TO SERVE:

- Spoon the parsnip puree onto each plate in an asymmetric formation with 1 to 2 inches of space between dollops. Roll the turnip and beet ribbons into coils and position them in different orientations between the dollops of parsnip puree. Allow some rolls to partially unravel, if desired. Place the tiny carrots and breakfast radishes, with their greens pointing upward, on and between the dollops of parsnip puree. Carefully spoon the quinoa soil around the parsnip puree, turnip and beet ribbons, and tiny carrots and breakfast radishes to create the illusion that the soil is underneath (though it would, in fact, be too unstable as a foundation for the entire dish). Sprinkle the puffed wild rice on the quinoa soil and around the edges of the plate. Garnish with the seasonal edible flowers and pea shoots, if desired.

After all these years living in California, I like to remind myself how exotic this place seemed when I first arrived. It wasn't just the people, with their sometimes baffling manners, but also the quality of light suffusing everything and the utterly foreign flora and fauna. I was especially taken with the succulent plants that grow along the coast, sprout up in window boxes around San Francisco, and flourish in the deserts. They're like spiky little symbols of the American Southwest, which I had previously only encountered in cowboy movies.

As I fell in love with California, I particularly came to love aloe vera, a beautiful plant that is best known for its medicinal qualities, but which also offers cooks an incredible taste and texture with which to experiment. This recipe calls for unsweetened aloe juice, which is available in many health food stores and specialty Asian markets. At Atelier Crenn, we derive our aloe juice from fresh aloe leaves; although aloe is not part of the cactus family, its leaves are sharply serrated along the edges, which requires careful handling. (For more on handling fresh aloe, see page 257.)

Visually, our Carrot and Aloe dish evokes succulents growing in a red rock landscape, but it is also a study in texture, with the slipperiness of the aloe vera gel playing against the cold and the wet of the carrot sorbet and the rutabaga-grapefruit juice. At Atelier Crenn, we serve it fairly early in the tasting menu, as an invitation to embrace familiar flavors in unfamiliar forms, to wake up the palate and refresh our memories of the exoticism of everyday life. | *Serves 8*

Carrot and Aloe

CARROT SORBET

INGREDIENTS
400 grams (14 ounces) raw carrots
500 grams (2 cups plus 1½ tablespoons) fresh carrot juice
30 grams (2 tablespoons) orange juice
(At Atelier Crenn, we squeeze our own orange juice, but high-quality store-bought orange juice is fine at such a small volume.)
2 grams (scant ½ teaspoon) fine sea salt
0.2 gram xanthan gum
3.4 grams Cremodan 30

EQUIPMENT
Acetate sheet
Blender
Pacojet or home ice cream maker

At least 6 hours before serving:

• Preheat the oven to 205°C/400°F.
• Place an acetate sheet on a baking sheet. Peel the carrots and discard the shavings from the outermost section. Continue peeling the carrot into strips and spread in a single layer on the acetate sheet.
• Roast the carrot shavings until just cooked through and slightly al dente, about 5 minutes. Allow the roasted carrot shavings to cool, uncovered, for 15 minutes.
• In a blender, combine 200 grams (7.05 ounces) of the carrot shavings with 150 grams (⅔ cup) water. Add the carrot juice, orange juice, and salt and blend on high speed into a smooth puree, 30 to 60 seconds. Reduce the blender speed to low and pour the xanthan gum and Cremodan directly into the liquid without touching the sides of the blender, about 10 seconds.
• **TO MAKE THE CARROT SORBET IN A PACOJET:** Transfer the carrot mixture to a Pacojet canister and freeze until solid, at least 6 hours, and pacotize to order.

>>>

Carrot and Aloe, *continued*

- **TO MAKE THE CARROT SORBET IN A HOME ICE CREAM MAKER**: Transfer the carrot mixture to an airtight container and refrigerate until thoroughly chilled, at least 4 hours. Follow the manufacturer's instructions for your ice cream maker to process to a sorbet.

RUTABAGA-GRAPEFRUIT BROTH

Five hours before serving, prepare the Rutabaga-Grapefruit Broth (page 313) and refrigerate, uncovered, until ready to serve.

RED QUINOA SOIL

At least 3½ hours before serving:

INGREDIENTS

200 grams (2 cups) red quinoa
10 grams (2 teaspoons) fine sea salt, plus more as needed

EQUIPMENT

Fine-mesh strainer
Acetate sheet
Dehydrator (*optional*)
Cooking thermometer
Wire skimmer

- In a fine-mesh strainer, rinse the quinoa with cold water.
- In a medium pot, bring 1 liter (1 quart) water to a boil. Stir in the quinoa and salt. Cover and simmer over low heat until tender, 10 to 15 minutes. Strain the cooked quinoa in a fine-mesh strainer to remove excess water.
- **TO DRY THE QUINOA IN A DEHYDRATOR:** Place an acetate sheet in a dehydrator tray. Evenly spread the cooked quinoa across the acetate sheet. Transfer the tray to a dehydrator set to 60°C/140°F and dry the quinoa, stirring occasionally, until completely dry and crispy, about 3 hours.
- **TO DRY THE QUINOA IN THE OVEN:** Preheat the oven to 60°C/140°F or the closest temperature available. Place an acetate sheet on a baking sheet. Evenly spread the cooked quinoa across the acetate sheet. Transfer the baking sheet to the oven and turn off the heat. Let the quinoa dry in the closed oven until completely dry and crispy, about 3 hours.
- In a frying pan with a cooking thermometer attached, heat the vegetable oil over medium-high heat to 160°C/320°F. Fry the dried quinoa for 30 to 60 seconds and remove with a wire skimmer. Spread the fried quinoa on a paper towel and let drain for about 5 minutes to remove excess oil. Season with fine sea salt.
- Store at room temperature in an airtight container until ready to serve.

ALOE VERA GEL

INGREDIENTS

1 cantaloupe or other sweet melon
210 grams (1¼ cups) unsweetened
    aloe vera juice
1.1 grams locust bean gum
0.8 grams agar-agar
1.1 grams xanthan gum

EQUIPMENT

Juicer
Blender

At least 3½ hours before serving:

- Juice the cantaloupe to produce 70 grams (scant ½ cup) of juice. (The proportions in this recipe should be 3 parts aloe vera juice to 1 part melon juice, with a concentration of 0.4% locust bean gum, 0.3% agar-agar, and 0.4% xanthan gum of the total volume.)
- In a blender, combine the aloe vera juice, melon juice, locust bean gum, and agar-agar and blend into a smooth puree, 30 to 60 seconds. Reduce the blender speed to low and pour the xanthan gum directly into the liquid without touching the sides of the blender until fully incorporated, 10 seconds.
- Transfer the mixture to a medium pot and bring just to a boil over medium heat. Cook at a low boil over medium-low heat just until the liquid turns a rich gold color, 1 to 2 minutes, and remove from the heat.
- Transfer the aloe mixture to a jar and refrigerate, uncovered, until the gel sets, about 3 hours, then cover and keep refrigerated until ready to serve.

COCONUT AIR

INGREDIENTS

2 kilograms (8½ cups) canned coconut
    milk (about 5¼ cans)
20 grams (5 teaspoons) granulated sugar
20 grams (4 teaspoons) fine sea salt
18 grams (4 teaspoons) lecithin

EQUIPMENT

Blender

- In a blender, combine the coconut milk, sugar, and fine sea salt and blend on high speed for 10 seconds. Reduce the blender speed to low and pour the lecithin directly into the liquid without touching the sides of the blender until fully incorporated, about 10 seconds. Refrigerate, covered, until ready to serve.

>>>

Carrot and Aloe, *continued*

INGREDIENTS

3 or 4 raw baby carrots

15 grams (2 teaspoons) freeze-dried
    coconut pulp (*optional*)

EQUIPMENT

Aquarium pump

Mandoline slicer

TO SERVE:

Fifteen minutes before serving:

• Transfer the coconut air mixture to a large, deep container and
aerate with an aquarium pump. Adjust the settings to create
1-inch-diameter bubbles. You may continue plating while the
bubbles accumulate. Turn off the machine if the bubbles
threaten to overflow the container.

• Using a mandoline slicer set to the thinnest setting, shave the
baby carrots on an angle.

• In each bowl, spread a thin layer of quinoa soil. Sprinkle the
freeze-dried coconut on the quinoa soil, if desired. Place
1 quenelle of carrot sorbet onto the quinoa and freeze-dried
coconut to prevent slippage. Use a small spoon to arrange small
dollops of the aloe gel around the carrot sorbet.

• Garnish with the carrot shavings. (At Atelier Crenn, we also garnish this dish with dehydrated carrot chips and micro carrots.)

• Spoon 2 tablespoons of the chilled rutabaga-grapefruit juice
into each bowl to surround the rest of the dish.

• Immediately before serving, use a large spoon to cover each bowl
with the coconut air bubbles, which should remain stable for
30 to 90 seconds.

NOTE: *When we serve this dish at Atelier Crenn, the bubbles are much larger
than what is pictured here for the sake of clarity.*

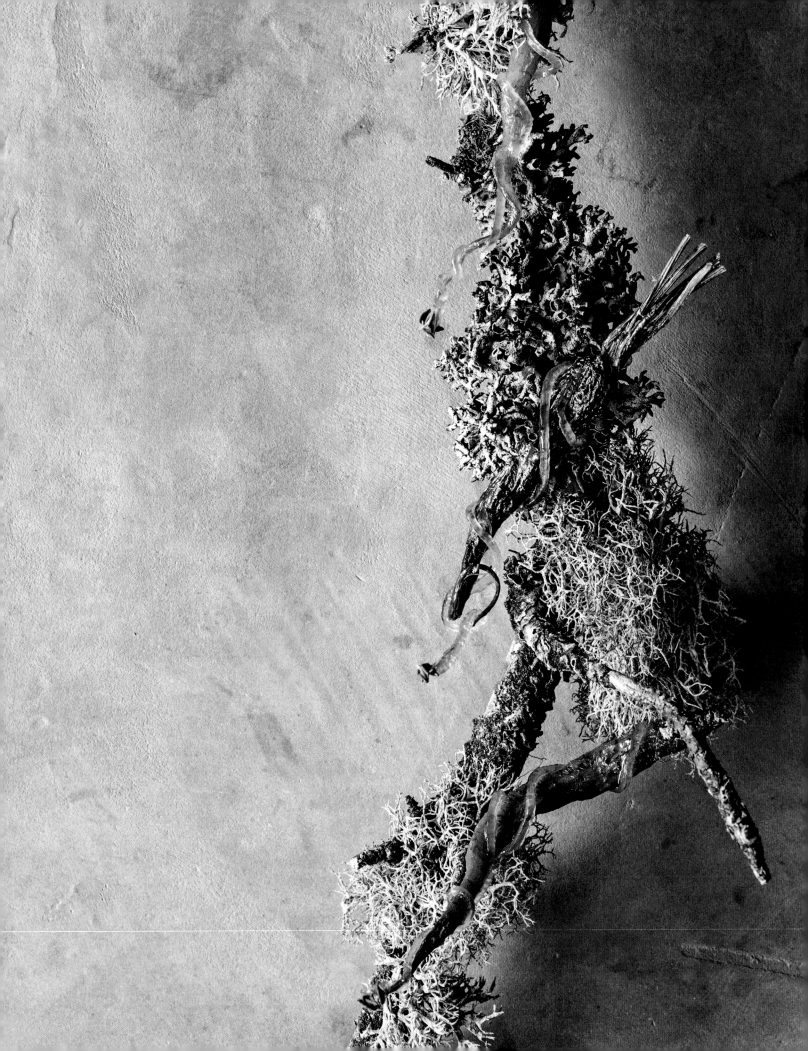

Dialogue is a central principle of our work at Atelier Crenn, because it is absolutely fundamental to our creative process. This dish arose from a fascinating discussion we had about vegetables and all that they represent for us. Over the course of the conversation, it became clear that we shared a passion for vegetables, a desire to push them into new directions, and an ambition to seize some of meat's cultural territory on behalf of vegetables. That sounds terribly serious, but the meeting ended in laughter, as we floated the idea of beef jerky being replaced by carrot jerky. The kitchen team worked together to develop this recipe for carrot jerky, and in the end, it is fun, surprising, delicious, and beautiful. There are five stages to the process: First, soak the carrots in pickling lime to create a skin; second, cure the carrots to draw out the moisture; third, brine the carrots in a flavorful liquid to rehydrate; fourth, cook the carrots; fifth, dehydrate the carrots. | *Serves 4*

NOTE: *This recipe calls for young carrots, which are available at farmers' markets in late summer and early fall. Young carrots should not be confused with so-called "baby carrots," which are in fact full-grown carrots that have been chopped and sculpted into a uniform shape and size. Look for young carrots about 8 inches in length and less than ½ inch in diameter.*

Carrot Jerky with Orange Peel

CARROT–CAYENNE JERKY

INGREDIENTS

4 liters (4.3 quarts) purified water, at room temperature

100 grams (1 cup) calcium hydroxide

20 young carrots

1,475 grams (7⅔ cups) granulated sugar

475 grams (2⅔ cups) packed brown sugar

485 grams (2 cups) fine sea salt

1 head garlic

210 grams (7.3 ounces) peeled fresh ginger

10 grams (4⅓ teaspoons) cracked black pepper

450 grams (1 pound) large carrots

400 grams (14 ounces) orange slices (from 2 to 3 oranges)

10 whole black peppercorns

Cayenne pepper

32 grams (1.1 ounces) Pure-Cote

300 grams (¾ cup) liquid glucose

>>>

At least 4½ days before serving:

- **MAKE THE PICKLING LIME:** In a large tub or pot, mix the purified water with the calcium hydroxide.
- Scrub the young carrots and trim the tips. Trim the greens of the young carrots to ⅓ inch long. Soak the young carrots in the pickling lime for 3 hours.
- **WHILE THE YOUNG CARROTS ARE SOAKING, MAKE THE DRY CURE:** In a resealable plastic freezer bag, combine 575 grams (3 cups) of the granulated sugar with the brown sugar and 450 grams (1¾ cups plus 2 tablespoons) of the fine sea salt. Peel the garlic, smash it roughly, and add to the bag. Dice 10 grams (0.35 ounce) of the peeled ginger. Add the diced ginger and cracked black pepper to the bag, seal the bag, and shake the contents well.
- When the young carrots are finished soaking, rinse them in cool water and pat dry with paper towels. Add the young carrots to the bag containing the dry cure and jostle the bag to ensure that the young carrots are thoroughly coated with the dry cure mixture. Seal the bag and allow the young carrots to cure at room temperature for 72 hours.
- When the young carrots are cured, rinse them in cool water and pat them dry with paper towels.

>>>

Carrot Jerky with Orange Peel, *continued*

EQUIPMENT

Large tub or pot

Resealable plastic freezer bag

Juicer

Acetate sheet

Dehydrator (*optional*)

Fine-mesh strainer

Spice grinder

Vacuum sealer or
     steaming rack

Small basting brush

At least 24 hours before serving:

- Clean and juice 450 grams (1 pound) of the large carrots, reserving the pulp to make carrot dust. (You do not need the juice for this recipe—drink it, reserve it for another purpose, or discard it.)
- **TO DRY THE CARROT PULP IN A DEHYDRATOR:** Place an acetate sheet in a dehydrator tray. Evenly spread the carrot pulp on the acetate sheet. Transfer the tray to a dehydrator set to 60°C/140°F and dry the pulp, stirring occasionally, for 24 hours.
- **TO DRY THE CARROT PULP IN THE OVEN:** Preheat the oven to 60°C/ 140°F or the closest temperature available. Place an acetate sheet in a baking sheet. Evenly spread the carrot pulp on the acetate sheet. Transfer the baking sheet to the oven and turn off the heat. Let the carrot pulp dry in the closed oven for 24 hours.
- Transfer the dried carrot pulp to a spice grinder and grind to a fine dust.
- Weigh the carrot dust, calculate 0.1% of the total weight, add cayenne in that amount to the carrot dust, and mix well. Set aside in an airtight container at room temperature.

At least 14 hours before serving:

- **TO BRINE THE YOUNG CARROTS:** Transfer the cured young carrots to a large, heat-resistant storage container, such as a Cambro food box. Slice the remaining peeled ginger. In a large pot, combine 5 liters (5¼ quarts) water with the remaining 900 grams (4⅔ cups) granulated sugar, the orange slices, 200 grams (7 ounces) of the ginger, the remaining 35 grams (2 tablespoons plus 1 teaspoon) fine sea salt, and the whole peppercorns. Bring to a boil over high heat. Pour 5 liters (5¼ quarts) of the hot liquid over the carrots and let cool to room temperature. Cover and let sit for 12 hours at room temperature.
- Drain the carrots in a fine-mesh strainer and discard the brining liquid.

- **TO COOK THE CARROTS SOUS VIDE:** Place the carrots in a vacuum bag, seal the bag, and compress at 99%. Fill a large pot three-quarters full with water and bring the water to a boil over medium heat. Submerge the bag and cook until the carrots are tender, about 1 hour.

- **TO COOK THE CARROTS WITHOUT A VACUUM SEALER:** Fill a medium pot with 1 inch of water and bring to a simmer. Set a steaming rack in the pot and put the carrots in the steaming rack. Steam over low heat until the carrots are overcooked inside; although the outside will look unchanged because of the skin formed by the pickling lime, the interior will be as soft as a puree.

- **TO DRY THE CARROTS IN A DEHYDRATOR:** Place an acetate sheet in a dehydrator tray. Evenly spread the carrots across the acetate sheet. Transfer the tray to a dehydrator set to 60°C/140°F and dry the carrots, stirring occasionally, for 45 minutes.

- **TO DRY THE CARROTS IN THE OVEN:** Preheat the oven to 60°C/140°F or the closest temperature available. Place an acetate sheet on a baking sheet. Evenly spread the carrots across the acetate sheet. Transfer the tray to the oven and turn off the heat. Let the carrots dry in the closed oven, stirring occasionally, for 45 minutes.

- **TO MAKE THE CAYENNE SYRUP:** In a small pot, combine 100 grams (scant ½ cup) water with the Pure-Cote and 0.8 grams (½ teaspoon) of cayenne and bring to a boil over medium heat. Add the liquid glucose to the pot and whisk to incorporate fully, about 30 seconds. Remove from the heat and set aside at room temperature.

- Once the carrots are dried, leave the acetate sheet in the dehydrator tray or on the baking sheet. Pick up each carrot to brush the entire surface with cayenne syrup and sprinkle with carrot dust while still wet, then return the coated carrots to the acetate sheet.

- Dry the coated carrots in the dehydrator or oven at 60°C/140°F, following the instructions above, for 25 minutes.

>>>

CANDIED ORANGE PEEL

INGREDIENTS

8 large navel oranges
270 grams (⅔ cup) liquid glucose
230 grams (1¼ cups) granulated sugar,
    plus more for coating

EQUIPMENT

Y-shaped vegetable peeler
Wire skimmer
Acetate sheet

At least 1 hour before serving:

- Use a Y-shaped vegetable peeler to peel the oranges in a continuous spiral, removing the least amount of white pith possible, covering the entire sphere. Ideally, each orange should produce 1 long strip of orange-colored rind.
- **TO CHIFFONADE THE PEEL:** Roll the peel into a tight coil and use a sharp knife to cut it crosswise into 1-millimeter-wide strings. Expect some breakage during handling, so it is a good idea to create 30 to 40 orange strings to yield 20 completed candied orange peels.
- **TO BLANCH THE PEEL:** In a large pot, bring 2 liters (2 quarts) water to a boil. Lay the chiffonade peels in a single layer on a wire skimmer and submerge it in the boiling water for 20 seconds. Remove from the water and immediately rinse with cold water.
- Repeat the blanching process twice more with fresh water, as the blanching water will have absorbed the bitterness of the orange peels.
- **TO MAKE STRONG SIMPLE SYRUP:** In a medium pot, combine 520 grams (2 cups plus 3¼ tablespoons) water with the liquid glucose and granulated sugar. Bring to a simmer over medium heat, stirring continuously to dissolve the sugar.
- Once the sugar has dissolved, bring the strong simple syrup to a simmer over medium heat. Add the blanched peels and simmer until the peels become translucent, about 1 minute. Remove the peels with a wire skimmer and discard the syrup.
- Place an acetate sheet on a baking sheet. Spread the orange peels in a single layer on the acetate sheet and allow to cool to room temperature.
- Fill a small, deep bowl with enough granulated sugar to cover the peels. Roll the peels in the sugar until they are well coated with crystals.
- Store at room temperature in an airtight container for up to 1 week.

>>>

Carrot Jerky with Orange Peel, *continued*

INGREDIENTS

20 mossy branches
  (foraged or sourced from a
  flower market)
40 micro thyme tips

EQUIPMENT

Acetate sheet
Dehydrator (*optional*)

TO SERVE:

At least 30 minutes before serving:

- Carefully wrap the dried carrots with candied orange peel, forming a spiral around each carrot.
- **TO DRY THE PEEL-WRAPPED CARROTS IN A DEHYDRATOR:** Place an acetate sheet in a dehydrator tray. Arrange the peel-wrapped carrots in a single layer, without touching one another, on the acetate sheet. Transfer the tray to a dehydrator set to 60°C/140°F and let dry for 25 minutes. Once dried, the carrots should not feel sticky to the touch.
- **TO DRY THE PEEL-WRAPPED CARROTS IN THE OVEN:** Preheat the oven to 60°C/140°F or the closest temperature available. Place an acetate sheet on a baking sheet. Arrange the peel-wrapped carrots in a single layer, without touching one another, on the acetate sheet. Transfer the baking sheet to the oven and turn off the heat. Let the peel-wrapped carrots dry in the closed oven for 25 minutes. Once dried, the carrots should not feel sticky to the touch.
- Place 5 mossy branches on each plate.
- Perch 1 carrot on each branch.
- Garnish each carrot with 2 micro thyme tips.

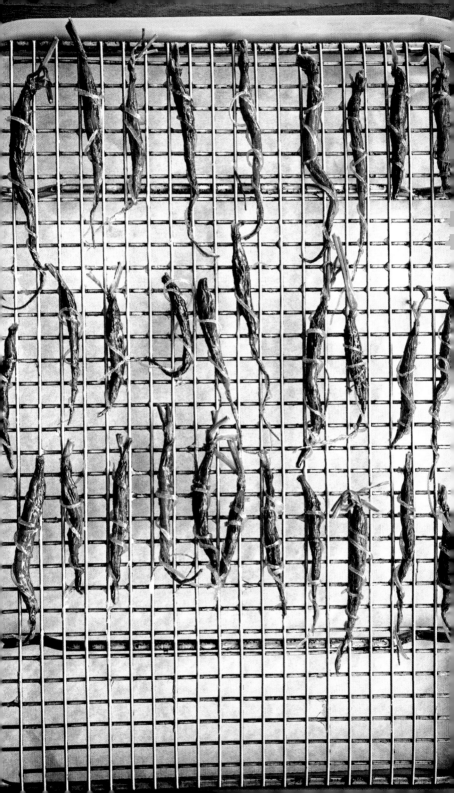

I love the look of this dish. It is meant as a kind of trompe l'oeil, which invites expectations of cinnamon and cream, but contains neither. Rather, the "cinnamon" turns out to be salsify and the "cream" is a white chocolate–cauliflower pudding topped with grated cocoa nib. Together, they offer a perfect balance of sweet and bitter flavors. And salsify is one of my favorite underappreciated ingredients. It isn't very common in the United States, but it was my father's favorite vegetable and our family ate it all year round when I was growing up. Sometimes called "oyster plant" or "poor man's oyster," salsify is a root vegetable that grows in the earth but sings of the sea; at Atelier Crenn, we serve our white chocolate salsify as part of a trio of dishes that also includes oyster (page 97) and uni with licorice (page 107). I love the way the salsify holds its own next to the seafood dishes, as it bolsters my ongoing campaign to honor vegetables as much as ingredients derived from animals.

Like other root vegetables, salsify can become mushy when overcooked, so after peeling off the tough outer layer, we create a second skin of sorts by soaking the salsify in pickling lime (water with calcium hydroxide) before cooking. For thousands of years, pickling lime has been used to make corn into masa, and haute cuisine has only recently caught up to the possibilities for its use. I first discovered pickling lime at Mugaritz, in Spain, where Chef Andoni Luis Aduriz also serves an excellent salsify dish; I talked over the idea with our former sous chef Daniel Beal, who put in a lot of work getting the technique just right. When we roast the salsify after preparing it in a lime solution, the flesh softens without losing any structural integrity; this technique works for many other vegetables, as well. | *Serves 10*

NOTE: *When buying salsify, avoid any that are woody, oversized, or particularly gnarled in favor of those that are relatively heavy for their size.*

White Chocolate Salsify

WHITE CHOCOLATE-CAULIFLOWER PUDDING

INGREDIENTS

50 grams (⅓ cup) Marcona almonds

1 cauliflower

0.7 grams calcium lactate

30 grams (1 ounce) white chocolate, preferably Valrhona Opalys, 33% cocoa

4 grams (¾ teaspoon) fine sea salt

2.8 grams low acyl gellan

0.175 gram sodium hexametaphosphate (SHMP)

>>>

At least 1 day before serving:

In a small storage container, soak the Marcona almonds in enough cool water to cover overnight.

At least 7 hours before serving:

- Drain the almonds. In a blender, combine the almonds and 1,100 grams (4⅔ cups) fresh water and blend on low speed for 2 minutes. Do not puree; the result should be almond milk rather than almond butter.
- Transfer the mixture to a large container and let settle, covered, at room temperature for 3 hours.
- Wash and trim the cauliflower, saving only the white florets and reserving the stems for another use.

>>>

White Chocolate Salsify, *continued*

EQUIPMENT

Blender

Vacuum bag or resealable plastic freezer bag

Vacuum sealer (*optional*)

Fine-mesh strainer

18 x 13-inch (half hotel) pan

- Place 250 grams (1 cup) of the cauliflower florets in a vacuum bag, seal the bag, and compress at 99%; alternatively, place 250 grams (1 cup) of the cauliflower florets in a resealable plastic freezer bag, squeeze out as much air as possible, and seal the bag.
- Fill a large pot three-quarters full with water and bring to a boil over high heat. Submerge the vacuum bag or resealable plastic freezer bag and keep at a soft boil until the cauliflower is very soft, about 2 hours.
- In a small bowl, bloom the calcium lactate with 3 grams (⅔ teaspoon) room-temperature water and set aside at room temperature. The calcium lactate will swell and thicken.
- Strain the almond milk through a fine-mesh strainer into a bowl and discard the solids.
- In a large pot, combine 1 kilogram (4¼ cups) of the almond milk with the white chocolate, fine sea salt, low acyl gellan, and SHMP. Bring the mixture to a boil over medium-high heat, stirring continuously. Add the bloomed calcium lactate, return the mixture to a boil, and remove from the heat.
- Transfer the mixture to an 18 x 13-inch (half hotel) pan and refrigerate, uncovered, until completely chilled and set to a gel, 1 to 2 hours.
- Coarsely chop the white chocolate gel into ¼-inch chunks.
- In a blender, combine the cooked cauliflower florets with the white chocolate gel and blend on high speed until smooth, about 2 minutes.
- Strain the pudding through a fine-mesh strainer into a container and refrigerate, covered, until ready to serve.

SALSIFY

INGREDIENTS
80 grams (2.8 ounces) calcium hydroxide
8 salsify roots
Fine sea salt
Extra-virgin olive oil

EQUIPMENT
Vegetable peeler
Tongs
Roasting rack
Roasting pan

At least 4 hours before serving:

- In a large storage container or pot, combine 4 liters (4.3 quarts) water with the calcium hydroxide. Stir to dissolve and set aside the pickling lime at room temperature.
- Trim the ends of the salsify, peel off the outer skin and coating, and discard.
- Cut the salsify into 4-inch lengths and then trim them into 4 x ½ x ½-inch matchsticks.
- Submerge the salsify in the lime solution and let soak at room temperature, stirring every 30 minutes, for 3 hours.
- Preheat the oven to 175°C/350°F. Fit a roasting rack in a roasting pan.
- Use tongs to remove the salsify from the lime solution and rinse well with cold water.
- Place the salsify on the roasting rack and roast until the salsify is soft, 20 to 30 minutes.
- Remove the salsify from the oven and season with fine sea salt and extra-virgin olive oil.
- Store, uncovered, at room temperature until ready to serve.

TO SERVE:

INGREDIENTS
15 grams (2 tablespoons) cocoa nib
10 grams (0.35 ounce) white chocolate,
    preferably Valrhona Opalys,
    33% cocoa
Maldon salt

EQUIPMENT
Spice grinder
Microplane grater

- Grind the cocoa nibs in a spice grinder into a very fine powder.
- In the center of each serving bowl, place 1 heaping tablespoon of white chocolate–cauliflower pudding. Sprinkle the pudding with cocoa nib powder.
- Use a Microplane grater to dust the bowl with white chocolate shavings.
- Sprinkle the bowl with a few grains of Maldon salt.
- Balance 1 piece of salsify at an angle along the edge of each bowl or dip the tip of the salsify into the pudding.

When I was a little girl, my mother used to make a simple tomato salad with three components: fresh tomatoes from our garden, simple vinaigrette, and a hunk of pain de seigle (page 335). When it appeared on the table, I felt like I couldn't see anything else. My family used to tease me about my crush on this tomato salad. They would laugh about "Dom and her tomato," but I didn't care. I feasted on all the sunshine the tomatoes had absorbed and then I drank all the vinaigrette at the bottom of the bowl. Maybe it's a little unfair, but I think French tomatoes are the best. I had never eaten beefsteak or Roma tomatoes until I came to America, and I was just slightly horrified. I was used to the regular vine-ripened cluster tomatoes, with their meaty sweetness, and it's hard to find the same taste here. Sometimes even the heirloom tomatoes don't taste like anything to me. We have incredible produce in California, but I still miss the tomatoes from my childhood. This dish is an homage to my mother's tomato salad, and a celebration of the tomato in all its glory. Too often, tomatoes are relegated to the position of accompaniment or sauce, but here the tomato is front and center, supported by the brightness of yuzu, the richness of avocado, and the aroma of basil. | *Serves 10*

Tomato

SHISO SORBET

INGREDIENTS

Kosher salt

25 grams shiso leaves

5 grams nasturtium leaves, stems,
    and flowers

60 grams (2.1 ounces) corn maltodextrin

30 grams (1¼ tablespoons) powdered
    glucose

30 grams (1 tablespoon) liquid glucose

1.2 grams (¼ teaspoon) fine sea salt

0.6 grams malic acid

0.6 grams high acyl gellan

0.6 grams xanthan gum

EQUIPMENT

Tongs

Blender

Pacojet or home ice cream maker

At least 7 hours before serving:

- Refrigerate 600 grams (2½ cups) water until well chilled.
- **TO BLANCH THE SHISO AND NASTURTIUM:** Fill a large pot with water salted at 1% of the total weight and bring to a rapid boil over high heat. Prepare an ice water bath. Use tongs to drop the shiso and nasturtium in the boiling water for 5 seconds, then immediately transfer to the ice water bath. Drain the shiso and nasturtium and discard the ice water.
- **TO MAKE SHISO WATER:** Transfer the shiso and nasturtium to a blender. Add the chilled water and blend on high speed until the herbs are completely pulverized. Add the corn maltodextrin, powdered glucose, liquid glucose, fine sea salt, and malic acid. Blend on high speed until all the solids have dissolved. Strain the liquid through a fine-mesh strainer and return to the blender. Run the blender on low speed and pour the high acyl gellan and xanthan gum directly into the liquid without touching the sides of the blender, about 1 minute.
- **TO MAKE THE SHISO SORBET IN A PACOJET:** Transfer the shiso water to a Pacojet canister and freeze until solid, at least 6 hours, and pacotize to order.

>>>

Tomato, *continued*

- **TO MAKE THE SHISO SORBET IN A HOME ICE CREAM MAKER:** Transfer the shiso mixture to an airtight container and refrigerate until thoroughly chilled. Follow the manufacturer's instructions for your ice cream maker to process to a sorbet.
- Store in an airtight container in the freezer until ready to serve.

TOMATO CONSOMMÉ

Five hours before serving, prepare Tomato Consommé (page 315) for use in the poached tomato and as a broth in the final plating.

POACHED TOMATO

INGREDIENTS
1 liter (1 quart) Tomato Consommé (page 315)
10 cherry tomatoes

EQUIPMENT
Slotted spoon or wire skimmer
Vacuum bags
Vacuum sealer
Coarse-mesh strainer

At least 4 hours before serving:

- In a large storage container, refrigerate 500 grams (2 cups) of the tomato consommé until well chilled.
- Use a sharp knife to score the bottom of the cherry tomatoes with an X.
- In a medium pot, bring the remaining 500 grams (2 cups) of tomato consommé to a simmer over medium-low heat. Add the cherry tomatoes and poach for 1 minute to loosen the skins. Plunge the cherry tomatoes into the chilled tomato consommé and remove with a slotted spoon or wire skimmer, reserving the chilled tomato consommé.
- Peel the cherry tomatoes, discarding the skins, and transfer to vacuum bags. Cover the cherry tomatoes with the chilled tomato consommé and compress at 78%.
- Strain the tomatoes through a coarse-mesh strainer and reserve the tomato consommé for the final plating. Refrigerate the tomatoes for 3 to 4 hours, until 20 minutes before serving.

YUZU PANNA COTTA

INGREDIENTS

6 grams (3 sheets) gold strength
    (200 bloom) gelatin
10 grams (2 teaspoons) yuzu juice
10 grams (2 teaspoons) tamari
160 grams (⅔ cup) whole milk
100 grams (scant ½ cup) heavy cream

EQUIPMENT

Cooking thermometer
10 small round containers to hold
    the panna cotta

At least 3½ hours before serving:

- **TO BLOOM THE GELATIN**: Submerge the gelatin sheets in enough cold water to cover until they are very pliant, 5 to 10 minutes.
- In a medium nonreactive saucepan with a cooking thermometer attached, combine the yuzu juice and tamari and cook over medium heat until just dry, about 1 minute. Add the milk and cream to the saucepan and heat to 70°C/160°F. Cook, whisking continuously, for 2 minutes, maintaining a temperature of 70°C/160°F.
- Drain the gelatin and add it to the saucepan. Continue cooking, whisking to thoroughly incorporate, for 3 minutes.
- Transfer the panna cotta mixture to 10 round glass storage containers and refrigerate, covered, until set to the consistency of sour cream, about 3 hours.

TOMATO COMPOTE

INGREDIENTS

7 heirloom tomatoes
50 grams (1.8 ounces) peeled shallot
25 grams (0.9 ounces) peeled garlic
    (4 cloves)
15 grams (3⅓ teaspoons) extra-virgin
    olive oil
Fine sea salt

EQUIPMENT

Slotted spoon or wire skimmer
Acetate sheet
Dehydrator (*optional*)

At least 3 hours before serving:

- Prepare an ice water bath. Fill a medium pot three-quarters full with water and bring to a boil over high heat.
- Use a paring knife to score a small X in the bottom of each tomato. Add the scored tomatoes to the boiling water and blanch for 20 seconds. Scoop out the tomatoes with a slotted spoon or wire skimmer and immediately plunge into the ice water bath.
- Peel the tomatoes, discarding the skins. Use a sharp knife to remove the cores, if necessary, and cut the tomatoes into fine (⅛-inch) dice, retaining the seeds and juices.
- Finely mince the shallots and garlic.
- In a medium oven-safe saucepan, heat the extra-virgin olive oil over medium-low heat. Add the shallot and garlic and sweat until softened, about 5 minutes. Add the diced tomatoes and simmer over low heat for 2 hours.
- Preheat the oven to 205°C/400°F.
- Transfer the pan with the tomatoes to the oven and roast for 30 minutes.

>>>

Tomato, *continued*

- **TO DRY THE TOMATOES IN A DEHYDRATOR:** Place an acetate sheet in a dehydrator tray. Evenly spread the tomatoes across the acetate sheet. Transfer the tray to a dehydrator set to 60°C/140°F and dry the tomatoes until completely desiccated and intensely flavorful, 30 minutes.
- **TO DRY THE TOMATOES IN THE OVEN:** Preheat the oven to 60°C/140°F or the closest temperature available. Place an acetate sheet on a baking sheet. Evenly spread the tomatoes across the acetate sheet. Transfer the sheet to the oven and turn off the heat. Let the tomatoes dry in the closed oven until they are completely desiccated and intensely flavorful, 30 minutes.
- Season with fine sea salt.

SUN-DRIED TOMATO PURÉE

INGREDIENTS

100 grams (¾ cup plus
   1¼ tablespoons) sun-dried tomatoes
4 grams (4 teaspoons) fine sea salt
0.4 gram xanthan gum

EQUIPMENT

Blender
Fine-mesh strainer

At least 3 hours before serving:

- In a large pot, combine the sun-dried tomatoes and fine sea salt with 400 grams (1⅔ cups) water and bring to a boil. Remove from the heat and let sit until the tomatoes expand, about 2 hours.
- Transfer the tomatoes and any remaining liquid to a blender and blend on high speed until smooth, about 1 minute. Reduce the blender speed to low and pour the xanthan gum directly into the liquid without touching the sides of the blender, about 10 seconds.
- Strain through a fine-mesh strainer into a storage container and refrigerate until ready to serve.

BASIL VINES

INGREDIENTS

20 grams (0.7 ounce) basil leaves

22 grams (2½ tablespoons) kuzu (kudzu) starch

1.5 grams (⅓ teaspoon) fine sea salt

EQUIPMENT

Wire skimmer

Blender

Fine-mesh strainer

Acetate sheet

Nonstick cooking spray

Pastry bag

Dehydrator (*optional*)

Desiccant (*optional*)

At least 3 hours before serving:

- **TO BLANCH THE BASIL:** Prepare an ice water bath. Fill a small pot three-quarters full with water and bring to a boil over high heat. Submerge the basil in the boiling water for 5 seconds, then remove with a wire skimmer and plunge directly into the ice water bath. Let the basil sit in the ice water until cold.

- In a blender, combine 150 grams (⅔ cup) water with the kuzu, blanched basil, and fine sea salt. Blend on high speed until pureed, about 30 seconds.

- Strain through a fine-mesh strainer and set aside at room temperature.

- Spray 1 acetate sheet with nonstick spray and wipe down with a paper towel; the residual nonstick coating will suffice.

- Transfer the basil mixture to a medium pot and bring to a boil over medium heat, stirring continuously with a whisk, until the mixture becomes thick and translucent, about 5 minutes.

- While the thickened basil mixture is still hot, transfer to a pastry bag, cut a small tip off, and pipe 10 unevenly bent vine shapes onto the acetate sheet. Let the basil vines cool to room temperature on the acetate sheet.

- **TO DRY THE BASIL VINES IN A DEHYDRATOR:** Place the acetate sheet in a dehydrator tray. Transfer the tray to a dehydrator set to 60°C/140°F and dry the basil vines until crisp, about 2 hours.

- **TO DRY THE BASIL VINES IN THE OVEN:** Preheat the oven to 60°C/ 140°F or the closest temperature available. Place the acetate sheet on a baking sheet. Transfer the baking sheet to the oven and turn off the heat. Let the basil vines dry in the closed oven until completely dry and crisp, about 2 hours.

- Store in an airtight container at room temperature until ready to serve. Store with a desiccant, if desired.

>>>

Tomato, *continued*

SMOKED AVOCADO

INGREDIENTS

3 Hass avocados

80 grams (6 tablespoons) extra-virgin
    olive oil

75 grams (5 tablespoons) fresh lime juice

60 grams (2 tablespoons plus
    I teaspoon) liquid glucose

0.65 grams fine sea salt

EQUIPMENT

Blender

Fine-mesh strainer

30 grams (1 ounce) applewood chips

Metal roasting pan

Kitchen torch

At least 30 minutes before serving:

- Split the avocados, remove the pits, and scoop the flesh from
  the peel.
- In a blender, combine 450 grams (scant 2 cups) of the avocado
  with the extra virgin olive oil, lime juice, liquid glucose, and
  fine sea salt. Blend on high speed until smooth, about I minute.
- Strain the puree through a fine-mesh strainer over a bowl; discard the liquid in the bowl.
- **TO SMOKE THE AVOCADO:** Line a metal roasting pan with
  aluminum foil. Place the avocado puree in a shallow bowl on
  one side of the pan and the wood chips on the other side of
  the pan. Ignite the wood chips with a kitchen torch and cover
  with foil. Smoke the avocado for 15 minutes.
- Store the smoked avocado in an airtight container in the
  refrigerator until ready to serve.

INGREDIENTS

Tomato consommé (reserved from
    poached tomato component)
Extra-virgin olive oil
Maldon salt
Micro basil
Micro chamomile

EQUIPMENT

Vacuum bags (*optional*)
Vacuum sealer (*optional*)
Immersion circulator (*optional*)
Cooking thermometer

Twenty minutes before serving:

- **TO WARM THE POACHED TOMATO SOUS VIDE:** Place the poached tomatoes in vacuum bags and seal without compressing. Cook the tomatoes sous vide in an immersion circulator set to 72°C/162°F for 15 to 20 minutes.
- **TO WARM THE POACHED TOMATO ON THE STOVETOP:** Place the poached tomatoes in a small pot with a cooking thermometer attached and cook over low heat, closely monitoring the heat and turning the tomatoes often to maintain a consistent temperature of 72°C/162°F, for 15 to 20 minutes.
- In a small pot with a cooking thermometer attached, warm the tomato consommé reserved from the poached tomato over low heat until it reaches 72°C/162°F to 80°C/176°F.
- Run a paring knife along the edge of the yuzu panna cotta containers to help release them. Invert 1 yuzu panna cotta into the center of each small serving bowl.
- Spoon 1 spoonful of the tomato compote on top of the yuzu panna cotta. Spoon 1 small spoonful of smoked avocado and 1 small spoonful of sun-dried tomato puree on top of the tomato compote. Place 1 poached tomato on top of the smoked avocado.
- Drizzle the poached tomato with extra-virgin olive oil and a small pinch of Maldon salt. Garnish the plate with micro basil leaves and micro chamomile.
- Balance 1 basil branch on top of the tomato compote.
- Serve 1 small scoop of shiso sorbet in a teacup or very small bowl as an accompaniment.
- Pour the warm tomato consommé around the poached tomato tableside.

Given my longstanding Francophilia, it seems obvious that I should love French onion soup, but in fact, the traditional dish has always been too heavy for me, and I rarely order it because I don't want to feel that my lunch has punched me in the stomach. But I do admire the way French onion soup offers a moment of exploration and discovery, as you push through the thick layer of cheese toward the steaming broth and onions below. The Onion Soup at Atelier Crenn is a bit of a topsy-turvy version of the classic, with the cheese lingering below the surface instead of floating above, but my hope is that dipping through a vinegar veil into the richness of Comté gnocchi and onion marmalade will provide the same rush of delight. | *Serves 10*

Onion Soup

ONION BROTH

Five hours before serving, prepare Onion Broth (page 309).

ONION MARMALADE

At least 2 hours before serving:

INGREDIENTS

1 large red onion
300 grams (1¼ cups) red wine vinegar
100 grams (½ cup) granulated sugar
2 grams (scant ½ teaspoon) fine sea salt

- **TO BRUNOISE THE ONION:** Halve the onion through the root, cut off the stem but not the root, and peel back the tough outer layer. Cut slices horizontally toward the root at ⅛-inch intervals, and then again vertically at ⅛-inch intervals to make matchsticks attached at the root. Then cut against the grain of the matchsticks at ⅛-inch intervals to create ⅛-inch cubes.
- In a medium nonreactive pot, combine 250 grams (8.8 ounces) of the onion brunoise with 300 grams (1¼ cups) water and the vinegar, sugar, and salt. Simmer over low heat for 2 hours.
- Transfer to an airtight container and set aside until ready to serve.

COMTÉ GNOCCHI

At least 90 minutes before serving:

INGREDIENTS

220 grams (7.75 ounces) Comté cheese
8 grams (0.3 ounces) black truffle
90 grams (½ cup) kuzu (kudzu) starch
15 grams (3¼ teaspoons) truffle oil

>>>

- Cut 50 grams (1.75 ounces) of rind from the Comté and set aside. Use a Microplane grater to grate the remaining Comté and the black truffle into a medium bowl.
- **TO MAKE THE CHEESE WATER:** In a medium pot, bring 1 liter (1 quart) water to a simmer, add the reserved Comté rind, and simmer over low heat for 30 minutes.
- Strain the liquid through a fine-mesh strainer and discard the solids.

>>>

Onion Soup, *continued*

EQUIPMENT

Microplane grater

Fine-mesh strainer

Blender

Pastry bag

Silicone half-sphere molds
(3-centimeter diameter)

- In a blender, combine 280 grams (9.9 ounces) of the warm cheese water with the kuzu and mix on medium speed until viscous, about 3 minutes.
- Transfer the mixture to a medium pot and bring to a simmer over medium heat. Add the grated Comté and grated truffle and stir until incorporated. Remove from the heat. Working quickly, while the mixture is still hot, stir in the truffle oil, transfer the mixture to a pastry bag, and pipe it into 3-centimeter silicone half-sphere molds.
- Refrigerate, uncovered, for 1 hour, then cover and refrigerate until ready to serve.

ONION PUREE

At least 30 minutes before serving:

INGREDIENTS

2 large red onions

15 grams (1 tablespoon) unsalted butter

40 grams (2 tablespoons plus
2 teaspoons) apple cider vinegar

1 lemon

5 grams (1¼ teaspoons) granulated
sugar

5 grams (1 teaspoon) fine sea salt

Xanthan gum

EQUIPMENT

Fine-mesh strainer

Blender

Squeeze bottle with a cap

- Peel and brunoise the onions (see page 71).
- In a heavy-bottomed pan, melt the butter over medium heat. Add 500 grams (3⅓ cups) of the diced onion and brown over medium-high heat, stirring occasionally to prevent sticking and burning, for 10 to 12 minutes.
- **TO DEGLAZE THE PAN:** Pour the vinegar into the pan and scrape the bottom with a wooden spatula while the liquid simmers and reduces by half, about 20 minutes.
- Juice half the lemon and reserve the rest for another use. Strain the lemon juice through a fine-mesh strainer and discard the solids.
- Weigh the blender canister on a kitchen scale and record the weight. Transfer the onions to the blender and add 10 grams (2 teaspoons) of the strained lemon juice, the salt, and the sugar. Blend on medium speed until the mixture becomes a smooth puree, about 20 seconds. Weigh the blender canister again to calculate the total weight of the mixture. Calculate 0.1% of the total weight, record that amount, and return the canister to the blender. Weigh out the recorded amount of xanthan gum and with the blender running on low speed, pour the xanthan gum directly into the liquid without touching the sides of the blender until fully incorporated, about 10 seconds.
- Transfer the mixture to a squeeze bottle with a cap and store at room temperature until ready to serve.

VINEGAR VEIL

INGREDIENTS
235 grams (scant 1 cup) sherry vinegar
2 grams agar-agar
1 gram low acyl gellan

EQUIPMENT
Immersion blender or whisk
Fine-mesh strainer
Shallow 9 x 13-inch or 10 x 12-inch
    container
Silicone mat

INGREDIENTS
Truffle oil
Fresh lemon balm leaves

EQUIPMENT
Small round cookie cutter
    (4-centimeter diameter)
Fine-mesh strainer

At least 20 minutes before serving:

- In a small nonreactive pot, combine 100 grams (6¾ table-spoons) water with the vinegar, agar-agar, and gellan. Use an immersion blender or whisk to fully incorporate the gellan. Bring the mixture to a boil over medium-high heat and remove from the heat.
- Strain the liquid through a fine-mesh strainer into a shallow 9 x 13-inch or 10 x 12-inch container lined with a silicone mat.
- Allow to cool, uncovered, on a level surface at room temperature until the gel sets, about 10 minutes.
- Without removing the gel from the container in which it has set, cover with plastic wrap and refrigerate until ready to serve.

TO SERVE:

- Use the cookie cutter to punch out vinegar veil discs and set aside.
- In a small pot, combine the broth and the gnocchi and keep warm over low heat until ready to serve.
- In each bowl, pipe a 4-inch-diameter ring of onion puree.
- Strain the broth through a fine-mesh strainer, reserving both the liquid and the gnocchi.
- Place 1 gnocchi in the center of each plate, within the circle of onion puree. Coat the gnocchi with 1 drop of truffle oil. Cover each of the gnocchi with 1 vinegar veil.
- Decorate the ring of onion puree with 5 drops of onion marmalade and 3 lemon balm leaves in an alternating pattern.
- Ladle the warm broth into each bowl tableside.

At Atelier Crenn, we don't name our dishes the way most other restaurants do. When our guests are first seated, we present them with a menu of sorts, but it offers a poem encompassing the entire tasting menu, not a list of options from which to choose. In the kitchen, we fall back on very short descriptions, so this dish is called "Grains" or "Grains and Seeds," but the truth is, buckwheat and quinoa are both technically grains that are seeds—unless they've been sprouted. On an emotional level, they seem more like cereals, and we often refer to this dish as "cereal for grown-ups," because it is simple, cozy, and filling. I grew up eating buckwheat, and it carries strong maternal associations for me, and that feeling carries through this dish, even to people who have never eaten buckwheat before. We emphasize the earthiness of the buckwheat with flax, sunflower, and pumpkin seeds and then we add sturgeon pearls and trout roe for contrast. There is something so satisfying about the balance of this dish, which combines salty and sweet, crunchy and creamy, and warm and cool sensations. Everything comes together in the bowl: land and sea, comfort and excitement, home and nature. It's what life is all about. | *Serves 4 as an entrée*

Grains and Seeds

RED QUINOA SOIL

One day before serving, prepare Red Quinoa Soil (see page 46) concurrently with the smoked buckwheat, below.

SMOKED BUCKWHEAT

One day before serving:

INGREDIENTS
Fine sea salt
500 grams (3 cups) buckwheat, preferably Anson Mills
625 grams (3 cups) neutral vegetable oil

EQUIPMENT
Fine-mesh strainer
Acetate sheet
Dehydrator (*optional*)
Cooking thermometer
Wire skimmer
Metal roasting pan
30 grams (1 ounce) applewood chips
Kitchen torch

- Bring 3 liters (3.2 quarts) water and 10 grams (2 teaspoons) of fine sea salt to a boil. Add the buckwheat and simmer until tender, about 15 minutes. Strain through a fine-mesh strainer.
- **TO DRY THE BUCKWHEAT (CONCURRENTLY WITH THE RED QUINOA) IN A DEHYDRATOR:** Place an acetate sheet in a dehydrator tray. Evenly spread the cooked quinoa across the acetate sheet. Transfer the tray to a dehydrator set to 60°C/140°F and dry the quinoa, stirring occasionally, until completely dry and crispy, about 3 hours.
- **TO DRY THE BUCKWHEAT (CONCURRENTLY WITH THE QUINOA) IN THE OVEN:** Preheat the oven to 60°C/140°F or the closest temperature available. Place an acetate sheet on a baking sheet. Evenly spread the cooked buckwheat on the acetate sheet and dry in the closed oven with the heat off for 3 hours.
- **TO FRY THE BUCKWHEAT:** Line a baking sheet with paper towels. In a medium pot with a cooking thermometer attached, heat the vegetable oil to 205°C/400°F. Add the dried buckwheat and fry until crispy, 30 to 60 seconds. Remove the buckwheat with a wire skimmer, transfer to the paper towel–lined baking sheet, and allow to cool to room temperature. Season with fine sea salt.

>>>

Grains and Seeds, *continued*

- **TO SMOKE THE BUCKWHEAT:** Line a metal roasting pan with aluminum foil. Spread the fried buckwheat on one side and the wood chips on the other side. Ignite the wood chips with a kitchen torch and cover with foil. Smoke the buckwheat for 15 minutes.
- Store the smoked buckwheat and red quinoa separately in air-tight containers at room temperature until ready to serve.

SMOKED STURGEON PEARLS

INGREDIENTS

200 grams (7 ounces) smoked sturgeon loin

20 grams (0.7 ounces) peeled shallot (1 to 2 bulbs) (*optional*)

400 grams (1¾ cups) heavy cream (*optional*)

5 grams (0.2 ounce) thyme (*optional*)

6 grams (3 sheets) gold strength (200 bloom) gelatin (*optional*)

Fine sea salt (*optional*)

EQUIPMENT

Microplane grater (*optional*)

Strainer (*optional*)

Small squeeze bottle (*optional*)

Insulated gloves (*optional*)

Safety glasses (*optional*)

Liquid nitrogen (*optional*)

Acetate sheet (*optional*)

If you do not have access to liquid nitrogen, at least 6 hours before serving:

- Tightly wrap the smoked sturgeon loin in plastic wrap and freeze until solid, at least 6 hours.

If you do have access to liquid nitrogen, at least 1 hour before serving:

- Cut the shallot into ⅛-inch rings.
- In a small pot, bring the heavy cream, sturgeon loin (not frozen), shallot, and thyme to a light simmer. Reduce the heat to low, cover, and let steep, stirring occasionally to avoid scorching the bottom, until the cream tastes strongly like smoked sturgeon, 30 to 60 minutes.
- To bloom the gelatin, submerge it in enough cold water to cover until it is very pliant, 5 to 10 minutes.
- Strain the cream through a fine-mesh strainer; discard the thyme and shallot and reserve the fish for another use.
- Return the cream to the small pot and bring back up to a light simmer.
- Drain the water from the gelatin and add the gelatin to the pot, whisking gently to incorporate the gelatin for 30 to 60 seconds. Remove the cream from the heat, allow to cool to 38°C/100°F, season with fine sea salt, and transfer to a small squeeze bottle.
- Put on insulated gloves and safety glasses. Working in batches of 20 drops, squeeze the sturgeon cream into the liquid nitrogen. Scoop out with a slotted spoon and place in a single layer on an acetate sheet. Transfer the acetate to the freezer to keep cold until ready to serve.

BONITO DASHI

Two and a half hours before serving, prepare Dashi (page 316) with bonito and katsuobushi.

TOASTED SEEDS

One hour before serving:

INGREDIENTS

100 grams (¾ cup) golden flaxseeds
50 grams (scant ½ cup) pumpkin seeds
50 grams (½ cup) sunflower seeds

- Working in batches, toast each type of seed individually in a pan over medium heat until golden brown, 30 to 60 seconds.
- Let cool and set aside together in an airtight container at room temperature until ready to serve.

SMOKED TROUT ROE

At least 15 minutes before serving:

INGREDIENTS

55 grams (2 ounces) steelhead trout roe
5 (1-foot) eucalyptus branches

EQUIPMENT

Large metal roasting pan
Kitchen torch

- **TO SMOKE THE TROUT ROE:** Line a large metal roasting pan with aluminum foil. Place the trout roe on one side and the eucalyptus on the other side. Ignite the eucalyptus with a kitchen torch and cover with foil. Smoke the trout roe for 15 minutes.
- Store the smoked trout roe in an airtight container and refrigerate until ready to serve.

TO SERVE:

INGREDIENTS

20 grams (0.7 ounce) micro herbs, such as sorrel, chervil, tarragon, cilantro
30 grams (1 ounce) yuzu kosho

- In a small pot, warm 2 cups of the dashi over low heat. Bring up to a low simmer and remove from the heat.
- Pick the herbs from their stems.
- Place a small amount (equivalent to three grains of rice) of yuzu kosho on one side of each shallow bowl and spread into a thin layer.
- In a medium bowl, mix together the buckwheat, quinoa, and toasted seeds. Place 3 tablespoons of the mixture onto the yuzu kosho in each bowl. Garnish the grains and seeds with the smoked trout roe, followed by the sturgeon pearls (if you did not use liquid nitrogen, use a Microplane grater to grate the frozen sturgeon into the bowl), and finally, the micro herbs. Present the bowls to your guests and gently pour ½ cup of the hot dashi into each bowl tableside. The broth should lap at the grains and seeds without washing them apart.

In keeping with all the signature dishes at Atelier Crenn, A Walk in the Forest offers emotional access to memories of the natural world. Neuroscientists have confirmed Proust's famous insights into the sensory component of memory, and this dish taps into our senses of smell and taste to trigger intense feelings. The earthy scents and flavors of pine, mushrooms, rye, and herbs transport us to the forest, which is such a rich symbolic space. There is a reason that so many fairy tales and myths feature heroes venturing into the forest to discover themselves: The forest is full of mystery and surprise. Of course, the forest means different things to different people, but for me, the most immediate associations are foraging for blackberries with my father in the forest of Locronan, and finding myself in the woods of San Francisco's Buena Vista Park, which has been kept as a natural forest in the midst of the city that grew up around it.

A Walk in the Forest should be plated as a trail, with the burnt pine meringue and pumpernickel soil forming a path from which the mushrooms and herbs spring up. The hazelnut creates the sense of rocks and plants crunching underfoot and the accents of vinegar and wine contribute a subtle undercurrent of rot and regeneration. A Walk in the Forest has been on the menu from the very beginning of Atelier Crenn, and it continues to evolve. Ideally, this recipe should be considered a path into the unknown, rather than a destination in itself, and I would love to think anyone making a version of A Walk in the Forest would arrive at his or her own woodland memories. | *Serves 10*

NOTE: *To save time, the basil soil, pumpernickel soil, and mushroom whims should be dehydrated or oven-dried concurrently, on separate trays or baking sheets.*

A Walk in the Forest

MUSHROOM BROTH

At least 5 hours before serving, prepare Mushroom Broth (page 312) for use in the mushroom puree and pickled mushroom components. Any unused mushroom stock may be kept covered in the refrigerator for up to 1 week or frozen for use in another recipe.

PUMPERNICKEL SOIL

At least 3½ hours before serving, while preparing recipes for basil soil and mushroom whims:

INGREDIENTS

400 grams (14 ounces) pumpernickel bread, homemade (see page 331) or store-bought

Fine sea salt

>>>

- Cut the pumpernickel bread into ¼-inch pieces.
- **TO DRY THE PUMPERNICKEL IN A DEHYDRATOR:** Place an acetate sheet in a dehydrator tray. Evenly spread the pumpernickel pieces across the acetate sheet. Transfer the tray to a dehydrator set to 60°C/140°F and dry the pumpernickel until crisp, about 3 hours.

>>>

EQUIPMENT

Acetate sheet

Dehydrator (*optional*)

Food processor

- **TO DRY THE PUMPERNICKEL IN THE OVEN:** Preheat the oven to 60°C/ 140°F or the closest temperature available. Place an acetate sheet on a baking sheet. Evenly spread the pumpernickel pieces across the acetate sheet. Transfer the baking sheet to the oven and turn off the heat. Let the pumpernickel dry in the closed oven with the heat off until crisp, about 3 hours.
- Transfer the dried pumpernickel to a food processor and pulse in 2-second bursts until the bread has broken down to crumbs about the size of quinoa. Season with fine sea salt.
- Transfer to an airtight container and store at room temperature until ready to serve.

MUSHROOM WHIMS

INGREDIENTS

50 grams (4¼ tablespoons) isomalt sugar

10 small king trumpet mushrooms

EQUIPMENT

Mandoline slicer

Acetate sheet

Dehydrator (*optional*)

At least 3½ hours before serving, while preparing recipes for basil soil and pumpernickel soil:

- In a medium pot, mix together the isomalt sugar and 100 grams (scant ½ cup) water and bring to a boil over medium heat. Once at a boil, remove the pot from the heat but keep warm.
- Cut the bottom off the mushrooms and reserve them to make the mushroom puree.
- Using a mandoline slicer, shave the mushrooms into very thin lengthwise slices and reserve at least 20 of the best looking intact slices for drying into whims. Use the rest of the mushroom slices in the mushroom puree.
- Dip the perfect mushroom slices in the isomalt solution and lay them in a single layer on an acetate sheet.
- **TO DRY THE MUSHROOM SLICES IN A DEHYDRATOR:** Place the mushroom-covered acetate sheet on a dehydrator tray. Transfer the tray to a dehydrator set to 60°C/140°F and dry the mushrooms, without stirring, until crisp, about 3 hours.
- **TO DRY THE MUSHROOM SLICES IN THE OVEN:** Preheat the oven to 60°C/140°F or the closest temperature available. Place the mushroom-covered acetate sheet on a baking sheet. Transfer the baking sheet to the oven and turn off the heat. Let the mushroom slices dry in the closed oven with the heat off, without stirring, until crisp, at least 3 hours.

- Store the mushroom whims in the closed oven with the heat off or in an airtight container with a paper towel enclosed at room temperature until ready to serve.

BASIL SOIL

INGREDIENTS

400 grams (14 ounces) brioche, homemade (see page 331) or store-bought
4 bunches fresh basil
625 grams (3 cups) neutral vegetable oil
Fine sea salt

EQUIPMENT

Acetate sheet
Dehydrator (*optional*)
Wire skimmer
Food processor

At least 3½ hours before serving, while preparing recipes for pumpernickel soil and mushroom whims:

- Cut the brioche into ¼-inch pieces.
- **TO DRY THE BRIOCHE IN A DEHYDRATOR:** Place an acetate sheet in a dehydrator tray. Evenly spread the brioche pieces across the acetate sheet. Transfer the tray to a dehydrator set to 60°C/140°F and dry the brioche until crisp, about 3 hours.
- **TO DRY THE BRIOCHE IN THE OVEN:** Preheat the oven to 60°C/140°F or the closest temperature available. Place an acetate sheet on a baking sheet. Evenly spread the brioche pieces across the acetate sheet. Transfer the baking sheet to the oven and turn off the heat. Let the brioche dry in the closed oven with the heat off until crisp, about 3 hours.
- Remove and discard the stems from the basil leaves.
- In a medium pot with a cooking thermometer attached, heat the vegetable oil until it reaches 175°C/350°F. Working in batches, set the basil leaves in a wire skimmer and submerge in the oil to fry until the basil leaves are bright green and brittle. Remove the basil with the wire skimmer and transfer to a paper towel. Repeat the frying process with the remaining basil leaves. Allow the basil leaves to cool to room temperature, about 10 minutes.
- Transfer the dried brioche and 80 grams (2.8 ounces) of the fried basil to a food processor and pulse in 2-second bursts until the brioche looks completely green and the crumbs are about the size of quinoa grains. Season with fine sea salt.
- Transfer to an airtight container and store at room temperature until ready to serve.

>>>

MUSHROOM PUREE

INGREDIENTS

1 large white onion

2.5 grams (0.1 ounce) garlic

18 grams (0.65 ounce) peeled shallot

25 grams (2 tablespoons) neutral
    vegetable oil

200 grams (7 ounces) king trumpet
    mushroom trimmings (reserved from
    mushroom whims; supplement with
    more king trumpet mushrooms if
    necessary)

7.5 grams (½ tablespoon) fine sea salt

3.5 grams (0.1 ounce) fresh sage

25 grams (5 teaspoons) sherry vinegar

500 grams (2 cups plus 2 tablespoons)
    mushroom broth

EQUIPMENT

Blender

At least 3½ hours before serving:

- Cut the onion into small (¼-inch) dice. Mince the garlic. Brunoise the shallot into fine (⅛-inch) dice (see page 71).
- In a sauté pan, heat the vegetable oil over medium heat. Add the mushroom trimmings and cook until they are caramelized on one side, about 2 minutes. Add 135 grams (scant 1 cup) of the diced onion and continue cooking for 5 minutes. Add the shallot brunoise, minced garlic, fine sea salt, and sage and cook until tender, stirring occasionally to avoid browning and sticking, 1 to 2 minutes. Deglaze the pan with the sherry vinegar and a splash of mushroom broth as needed to keep the mushrooms from sticking to the pan, stirring, for 30 seconds.
- Transfer the contents of the pan to a blender and puree into a very smooth paste, about 30 seconds. Add more mushroom broth to the blender as needed to achieve the consistency of ketchup.
- Set aside 100 grams (3.5 ounces) of mushroom puree for use in the mushroom paper component and refrigerate the rest, covered, for up to 1 week. Any unused mushroom puree may be reserved for use as a fantastic spread on toasted or grilled bread.

MUSHROOM PAPER

INGREDIENTS

100 grams (3.5 ounces)
    mushroom puree

50 grams (4¼ tablespoons)
    isomalt sugar

EQUIPMENT

Acetate sheet
Dehydrator *(optional)*

At least 3½ hours before serving:

- **TO MAKE THE MUSHROOM PAPER BASE:** In a small pot, mix together the mushroom puree, isomalt sugar, and 10 grams (1 tablespoon) water. Bring to a boil and remove from the heat.
- **TO DRY THE MUSHROOM PAPER IN A DEHYDRATOR:** Place an acetate sheet in a dehydrator tray. Evenly spread a paper-thin layer of the mushroom paper base across the acetate sheet. Transfer the tray to a dehydrator set to 60°C/140°F and dry until crisp, about 3 hours.
- **TO DRY THE MUSHROOM PAPER IN THE OVEN:** Preheat the oven to 60°C/140°F or the closest temperature available. Place an acetate sheet on a baking sheet. Evenly spread a paper-thin layer of the mushroom paper base across the acetate sheet. Transfer the baking sheet to the oven and turn off the heat. Let the mushroom paper dry in the closed oven until crisp, about 3 hours.

PICKLED MUSHROOMS

INGREDIENTS

I clove garlic
10 royal trumpet mushrooms
10 pioppini mushrooms
10 maitake mushrooms
10 oyster or chanterelle mushrooms
Vegetable oil
5 fresh sage leaves
5 grams (1 teaspoon) Madeira wine
5 grams (1 teaspoon) sherry vinegar
30 grams (2 tablespoons) mushroom
    broth
15 grams (1 tablespoon) unsalted butter

EQUIPMENT

Oven-safe saucepan
Tongs

Ninety minutes before serving:

• Preheat the oven to 190°C/375°F.
• Mince the garlic.
• Clean and trim the ends from all the mushrooms, breaking up the larger mushrooms but leaving smaller mushrooms whole.
• In an oven-safe saucepan, heat a thin layer of vegetable oil over medium heat. Once the oil is hot, add a single layer of mushrooms and a proportionate amount of garlic and sage, using tongs to remove the mushrooms once they begin to brown, about 10 minutes per batch. Use tongs to transfer the mushrooms to paper towels to absorb any excess oil. Scrape out and discard the cooked garlic and sage. Repeat the browning process with more vegetable oil, garlic, and sage until all the mushrooms have been browned. Return all the mushrooms to the saucepan.
• Add the Madeira and simmer over medium heat until the volume has reduced by half. Add the sherry vinegar and simmer over medium heat until the volume has reduced by half again. Add the mushroom stock and the butter and transfer the saucepan to the oven for 7 minutes.
• Keep warm until ready to serve.

FLUTED CREMINI MUSHROOMS

INGREDIENTS

30 grams (1.1 ounce) peeled shallot
    (2 cloves)
10 grams (0.35 ounce) peeled garlic
    (1 to 2 cloves)
10 cremini mushrooms
Neutral vegetable oil
200 grams (¾ cup plus
    1½ tablespoons) Madeira wine
300 grams (1¼ cups) white wine

EQUIPMENT

Paring knife
Kitchen torch

NOTE: *Fluting is a classical French mushroom preparation that has largely fallen out of fashion in haute cuisine, but I find the shape quite beautiful and evocative of the natural world.*

One hour before serving:

• Mince the shallot and garlic.
• **TO FLUTE A MUSHROOM:** Use a paring knife to peel the outer layer from each cremini mushroom, pulling upward from the stem toward the top. Holding the paring knife in the center of the blade, rather than the handle, cut a shallow groove, with the blade entering the mushroom at an angle, running from the center of the mushroom top toward the edge. Twist your wrist to follow the curve of the mushroom and peel off a small slice of mushroom. Turn the mushroom and repeat the cutting motion, moving all the way around the mushroom. If the center of the mushroom looks messy, press the flat edge of the knife tip around the center to create a star pattern, if desired.

>>>

A Walk in the Forest, *continued*

- Coat a large saucepan with vegetable oil and sauté the shallot and garlic over low heat for 2 minutes.
- Raise the heat to medium and add the Madeira wine and white wine. Burn off the alcohol with a kitchen torch.
- Add the mushroom broth and bring to a simmer, then add the fluted cremini mushrooms to the saucepan. Cook over low heat until the mushrooms are tender but not losing their shape, about 20 minutes. Remove the cremini mushrooms from the pan and discard the liquid.
- Return the cremini mushrooms to the pan and keep warm until ready to serve.

PINE MERINGUE

INGREDIENTS

125 grams (4.4 ounces) egg whites
(from about 4 eggs)
200 grams (1 cup) granulated sugar
7 drops pine extract

EQUIPMENT

Stand mixer with whisk attachment
Pastry bag

Up to 5 hours before serving:

- Working in a cool place, in the bowl of a stand mixer fitted with the whisk attachment, combine the egg whites with the sugar and 50 grams (3 tablespoons plus 1 teaspoon) water and whip the meringue base until stiff peaks form. Turn off the mixer and fold in the pine extract.
- Transfer the mixture to a pastry bag and refrigerate until ready to serve.

HAZELNUT PRALINE

INGREDIENTS

300 grams (10.6 ounces) hazelnuts
200 grams (scant 1 cup) neutral
    vegetable oil
1 gram (scant ¼ teaspoon) fine sea salt

EQUIPMENT

Blender
Squeeze bottle

INGREDIENTS

Foraged herbs
20 hazelnuts

EQUIPMENT

Microplane grater
Kitchen torch

At least 20 minutes before serving:

- Preheat the oven to 190°C/350°F.
- On a baking sheet, spread the hazelnuts in a single layer and bake until browned but not burned, about 15 minutes.
- Transfer the nuts to a blender and add the oil and salt. Blend on high speed until very smooth, about 1 minute. The praline should be the consistency of a very loose peanut butter, as this is a soft "praline."
- Transfer the praline to a squeeze bottle and set aside at room temperature until ready to serve.

TO SERVE:

- Wash, dry, and pick the leaves from the foraged herbs.
- Grate the hazelnuts with the Microplane grater.
- Cut a corner from the pastry bag and pipe the pine meringue in a broad stripe across the plate. Use a spoon to spread the pine meringue 4 inches wide and up to ½ inch deep across each plate. This "meringue path" should not be smooth, but should have some peaks and valleys. (Think of Van Gogh rather than Ingres.)
- Brown the meringue path with a kitchen torch.
- Sprinkle the pumpernickel soil in a wandering trail along the meringue path. Sprinkle the basil soil in a wandering trail, criss-crossing the pumpernickel soil trail, along the meringue path.
- Use a small spoon to drizzle the praline in another wandering trail along the meringue path. Use a small spoon to drop small dots of mushroom puree along the meringue path.
- Arrange the mushrooms on top of the other components, evenly distributing each type of mushroom on each plate, with 1 fluted cremini mushroom per person.
- Garnish the plate with the mushroom whims.
- Garnish the sides of the plate, alongside the meringue path, with grated hazelnuts and foraged herbs.

In the United States, salad is served at the beginning of a meal; in France, salad is served near the end, as a cleansing bite before the cheese course. At Atelier Crenn, we conclude the savory portion of our tasting menu with a "salad" viewed through the looking glass; instead of dressing greens with vinaigrette, we dress a vinegar meringue with greens. For those accustomed to American dining conventions, our salad can be a bit disorienting, but I welcome that moment of surprise as another way of refreshing and resetting the palate before the conclusion of the tasting menu. | *Serves 40 as an hors d'oeuvre or palate cleanser*

NOTE: *Banyuls vinegar is the best vinegar in the world. It is made from vin doux (sweet wine) made from Grenache grapes grown in Banyuls-sur-mer, and it retains the wine's complex range of flavors, from licorice to coffee, orange peel to nuts. If you cannot find Banyuls vinegar, substitute sherry vinegar, but be sure to use the very best, as vinegar is the undisputed star of this "salad."*

NOTE: *Because the blender requires a minimum volume to make the recipe workable, there may be some unused meringue material if you are not serving 40 people.*

Salad

BASIL SOIL

INGREDIENTS
80 grams (5 tablespoons) Banyuls vinegar
6.2 grams Methocel F50 or
 Methocel A4M Food Grade
1.2 grams xanthan gum
0.9 gram sodium hexametaphosphate
 (SHMP)
58 grams (2¼ tablespoons)
 liquid glucose
9 grams (2¼ teaspoons) granulated sugar
58 grams (6½ tablespoons) corn
 maltodextrin
1 gram (scant ¼ teaspoon) fine sea salt

EQUIPMENT
Stand mixer with a whisk attachment
Acetate sheet
Nonstick cooking spray
Pastry bag
Dehydrator (*optional*)

At least 5½ hours before serving:

- In the bowl of a stand mixer fitted with the whisk attachment, combine 205 grams (¾ cup plus 1¾ tablespoons) water with the vinegar and whip on medium speed. With the mixer running, working one ingredient at a time, add the Methocel, xanthan gum, and SHMP, whipping each for 20 seconds to incorporate before adding the next ingredient. Add the liquid glucose and whip for 2 minutes. With the mixer running, working one ingredient at a time, add the sugar, corn maltodextrin, and fine sea salt, whipping each for 1 minute to incorporate before adding the next ingredient.
- Raise the mixer speed to high and continue to whip until the meringue mixture will hold a peak, 10 to 15 minutes.
- Spray an acetate sheet with nonstick cooking spray and wipe down with a paper towel; the residual nonstick coating will suffice. Place the acetate sheet on a dehydrator tray or baking sheet.
- Transfer the meringue mixture to a pastry bag. Pipe 1-inch-diameter meringue hemispheres onto the acetate sheet, leaving a ½-inch space between each meringue.
- **TO DRY THE MERINGUES IN A DEHYDRATOR:** Place the acetate-lined dehydrator tray in the dehydrator. Transfer to a dehydrator set to 60°C/140°F and dry the meringues for 5 hours.

>>>

Salad, *continued*

- **TO DRY THE MERINGUES IN THE OVEN**: Preheat the oven to 60°C/140°F or the closest temperature available. Transfer the acetate-lined baking sheet to the oven and turn off the heat. Let the meringues dry in the closed oven with the heat off for 5 hours.

OLIVE OIL JAM

INGREDIENTS
100 grams (3.5 ounces) egg yolks
  (from about 5 eggs)
150 grams (6 tablespoons) liquid glucose
50 grams (2 tablespoons) trimoline
  inverted sugar syrup
12 grams (¾ teaspoon) fine sea salt
450 grams (2 cups) olive oil

EQUIPMENT
Robot Coupe or food processor
Small nonreactive pot
Cooking thermometer
Stand mixer
Vacuum sealer (*optional*)
Pastry bag

NOTE: *A former employee learned a version of this recipe when he was chef de partie at Alinea in Chicago and modified it for use as pastry chef at Benu here in San Francisco, and again as chef de cuisine at Atelier Crenn.*

- In a Robot Coupe or food processor, beat the egg yolks on medium speed for 2 minutes.
- In a small, nonreactive pot with a cooking thermometer attached, mix together the glucose and trimoline inverted sugar syrup over medium heat until the temperature reaches 115°C/235°F, about 3 minutes. Remove from the heat.
- With the stand mixer set to medium speed, gradually drizzle the warm sugar mixture into the egg yolks. Continue mixing on medium speed while adding the fine sea salt. Gradually incorporate the olive oil, which will turn the mixture cloudy, about 1 minute.
- To clarify the color, turn off the mixer and sprinkle in up to 2 teaspoons water and stir with a spatula. (The water helps the yolks to emulsify.)
- To further remove suspended air bubbles, transfer the mixture to a vacuum bag, seal, and compress at 85% in a vacuum sealer, if desired.
- Transfer to a pastry bag and refrigerate until ready to serve.

BANYULS VINEGAR PUDDING

INGREDIENTS
80 grams (5 tablespoons) Banyuls vinegar
20 grams Ultra-Tex 8

EQUIPMENT
Blender
Fine-mesh strainer
Pastry bag

- In a blender, combine 120 grams (½ cup) water with the vinegar and blend on high speed for 2 minutes.
- Reduce the blender speed to low and gradually pour the Ultra-Tex directly into the liquid without touching the sides of the blender until it is fully incorporated, about 20 seconds.
- Pass the pudding mixture through a fine-mesh strainer to ensure a smooth texture.
- Transfer the pudding mixture to a pastry bag and refrigerate for up to 2 days until ready to serve.

INGREDIENTS
Micro herbs, lettuces, and flowers,
    as seasonally available
Additional lettuces (*optional*)

EQUIPMENT
Miniature ball cutter
    (1-centimeter diameter)

TO SERVE:

- One at a time, insert a miniature ball cutter into the meringues and rotate to create a hollow. Cut a small corner from the pastry bag containing the Banyuls vinegar pudding and pipe ½ teaspoon into the hollow of each meringue. Cut a small corner from the pastry bag containing the olive oil jam and pipe 1 teaspoon of the olive oil jam onto the vinegar pudding.
- Arrange a bouquet of micro herbs, lettuces, and flowers peeking out of the hollow of each meringue.
- Serve as a passed hors d'oeuvre or serve with additional lettuces on individual plates as a formal palate cleanser.

SEA

WHEN I WAS a little girl, my father used to take me to the early-morning fish market at the Port de Douarnenez de Cornouaille, near our house in Brittany. It was a very special time for me, in part because it gave me a chance to be alone with my dad, without my brother. Although he was very strict about my staying close by his side, loved being out in the misty morning air, surrounded by the smell of fish and the noises of the market. I was only about three or four years old when we started going, so I felt terribly out of place amid the chaos of yellow-booted fishermen calling to one another as they threw fish and cracked jokes. I used to withdraw into myself and observe how the fishermen moved so purposefully across the slippery ground, and imagine their lives from the lines on their faces. And of course, I watched my father as he navigated the huge open-air market, and I learned from him how to spot the best fish, how to talk with the fishermen, and how to respect the sea.

In French, we call this kind of commercial market *la criée*—the word is derived from the "cry" of voices at an auction. As a kid, I was captivated by these ancient sounds: For centuries, Breton fishermen have pulled their boats up to this port and used their voices to sell their fish, exactly the way that I saw in the 1970s, and *la criée* was like a time machine that transported me back through the history of Brittany and helped me understand why our culture is so deeply entwined with the sea. I'm sorry to say it, but there's no equivalent to *la criée* here in San Francisco, even for chefs. It's all been mediated by fish distributors and middlemen, which is a shame—and yet I do feel that I recapture some of that wonder and immediacy every time I taste really fresh shellfish, especially the lobster and langoustines that used to wag their claws at my younger self.

The sea has always been an incredible resource for humanity, but something has changed in the last half century, as fishing technology has extended our reach deeper, farther, and wider. A recent United Nations report found that the annual catch of fish removed from the ocean every year is now almost 40 percent larger than it was fifty years ago, even though the fish populations have declined. According to Seafood Watch, the latest estimates suggest that "we have removed as much as 90 percent of the large predatory fish such as shark, swordfish and cod from the world's oceans." Meanwhile, climate change and pollution have threatened our oceans with acidification, overwhelming algae blooms, petroleum spills, and all manner of other threats to sea creatures—and by extension, to seafood.

At Atelier Crenn, we steer away from serving large fish like tuna in favor of smaller fish and shellfish, but there is always more to learn about seafood and the sea, so we strive to keep up with the science, which can be a challenge. In the end, we always try to research the most sustainable and delicious options, but many of the restaurant's seafood choices correspond to my personal preferences. Luckily for me, as a child of Brittany, oysters are a responsible choice since oyster farms actually play a restorative role in ocean ecology.

I don't pretend to be a perfect oceanic steward, but I do try to cultivate an appreciation of the sea. Our seafood dishes try to capture some of my own awe when I contemplate the incredible diversity and the bracing simplicity of the sea. The seafood dishes at Atelier Crenn draw widely and respectfully from the traditions of Brittany, California, and Asia, traveling among continents like the ocean currents that connect them.

Brittany is home to the best oysters in the world. "You are eating the sea," writes Eleanor Clark in *The Oysters of Locmariaquer*, her book-length ode to Breton oysters. "You are on the verge of remembering you don't know what, mermaids or the sudden smell of kelp on the ebb tide or a poem you read once, something connected with the flavor of life itself." Oysters express their surroundings the way wine expresses *terroir*, and the rich nutrients and minerals of the Belon river in southern Brittany are so highly revered in France that thousands of tons of oysters are transplanted there to complete their *affinage* (or "refinement"). I will always be loyal to Belon oysters, but in recent years I've also come to love the Kumamoto and Kusshi varieties grown in northern California and the Pacific Northwest, which are both small varieties.

For this dish, we lightly poach the oysters, which allows us to preserve the texture of raw oyster; each of the accompaniments draws attention to the slippery, ephemeral, life-affirming glory of a freshly shucked oyster. I love the way it situates the oyster in the blue of the coconut-algae water, which looks like the sea itself. | *Serves 6*

Oyster Wheatgrass Coconut

WHEATGRASS PUREE

INGREDIENTS

5 grams low acyl gellan

0.4 gram sodium hexametaphosphate (SHMP)

1.3 grams calcium lactate

30 grams wheatgrass leaves

5 grams (1 teaspoon) fine sea salt

0.4 gram ascorbic acid

EQUIPMENT

Blender

Squeeze bottle

- In a large pot, combine 500 grams (2 cups plus 5½ teaspoons) water with the low acyl gellan and SHMP and bring to a boil over medium-high heat. Stir in the calcium lactate and return the mixture to a boil.
- Transfer the mixture to a shallow container and refrigerate until set to a gel. Transfer the gel to a blender and add the wheatgrass, fine sea salt, and ascorbic acid and blend until smooth.
- Transfer the wheatgrass puree to a squeeze bottle and refrigerate, covered, until ready to serve.

>>>

Oyster Wheatgrass Coconut, *continued*

ALGAE COCONUT WATER

INGREDIENTS

4 young coconuts
2 grams (0.7 ounce) agar-agar
15 grams (0.5 ounce) blue-green algae
5 grams (1 teaspoon) fine sea salt
2 grams (0.7 ounce) granulated sugar
0.75 gram xanthan gum

EQUIPMENT

Coffee filter
Blender

- Crack the young coconuts open and collect the coconut water.
- In a large pot, combine 500 grams (2 cups) of the coconut water with the agar-agar. Bring to a boil, then immediately remove from the heat.
- Transfer the coconut water mixture to a shallow container and refrigerate until set to a gel.
- Whisk the gel until it liquefies, then strain it through a coffee filter.
- In a blender, combine 500 grams of the filtered coconut water gel with the algae, fine sea salt, sugar, and xanthan gum and blend on high speed until emulsified, about 20 seconds.
- Refrigerate, covered, until all the bubbles have dissipated, at least 1 hour or until ready to serve.

POACHED OYSTER

INGREDIENTS

12 small oysters

EQUIPMENT

Oyster knife
Vacuum bag or resealable plastic freezer bag
Vacuum sealer (*optional*)
Immersion circulator or cooking thermometer

- Scrub the oyster shells.
- **TO OPEN AN OYSTER:** Wrap the oyster in a kitchen towel with the flat side up and the hinge facing you. Brace the oyster against a countertop, carefully insert an oyster knife into the hinge, and gently but firmly torque the knife to open the shell. Discard the top shell.
- After opening each oyster, pour the oyster liquor into a small cup. Scrape along the inside of the bottom shell with the oyster knife to sever the flesh from the shell. Use the oyster knife or your finger to remove any broken shell fragments or debris.
- **TO COOK THE OYSTERS SOUS VIDE:** Transfer the oyster flesh and oyster liquor to a vacuum bag, discarding the shells. Seal the bag and compress at 99%. Cook the oysters in an immersion circulator set to 55°C/130°F for 2 minutes.
- **TO COOK THE OYSTERS ON THE STOVETOP:** Transfer the oyster flesh and oyster liquor to a resealable plastic freezer bag, discarding the shells. Squeeze out as much air as possible and seal the bag. Fill a large pot three-quarters full with water and attach a cooking thermometer; bring the water to 55°C/130°F over medium heat and submerge the bag, closely monitoring the heat and stirring often to maintain a consistent temperature, for 2 minutes.
- Serve immediately. Discard the oyster liquor or drink as a treat.

INGREDIENTS

8 grams freeze-dried coconut

1 finger lime

6 stems fresh sea grape

6 oyster leaves (*optional*)

Fresh seaweed (*optional*)

Seasonal flowers (*optional*)

- In each shallow bowl, arrange 2 oysters. Squeeze 3 small dollops of wheatgrass puree around each bowl. Spoon 6 small spoonfuls of freeze-dried coconut around each bowl. Ladle in the algae coconut water. Squeeze an equal amount of finger lime cells onto each oyster. Garnish with 1 stem of sea grape. Garnish with 1 oyster leaf, fresh seaweed, and seasonal flowers, if desired.

This one-bite dish is a great example of what happens when modernist technique intersects with culinary tradition, but the truth is, we didn't set out to make a modern version of fish and chips. In fact, it all started with pommes soufflé. In the classic French recipe, the potatoes are sliced very thin and fried twice—first in hot oil and then in very hot oil—but the potatoes do not always puff up properly, so we started to experiment with modern methods because we wanted a more consistent product. Our former chef de cuisine took the lead on the pommes soufflé project. At first, he made pommes soufflés from a potato batter, which worked well, but we preferred to keep the integrity of the potato, so he developed a kind of hybrid system, in which two slices of potato are sandwiched together with a batter made of potato starch and egg white. Using a ring mold to create perfect circles is not merely cosmetic in this case: The pressure of the ring mold seals the batter in a layer of potato, so that when it hits the hot frying oil, a crust quickly traps the relatively moist batter inside. As the temperature rises, the batter steams up, which in turn puffs the potato into a soufflé. And unlike the classic French method, it works every time.

Once we had our perfect pommes soufflés, the question was what to do with them. Our chef de cuisine had an idea inspired by his own memories of growing up in Boston and eating fish and chips, which was a big part of his childhood, even though he didn't particularly like fried fish. The dish was designed to highlight all the best aspects of fish and chips with some additional culinary tecnique: In Atelier Crenn's version, one can really taste the fish because is not coated in oil and bread crumbs, and the flavors of our tartar sauce are isolated and balanced against the fish. We serve our version without utensils, like the traditional fish and chips, and I love the immediacy of the experience. Even though fish and chips are not touchstones of my own memory, our dish allows me taste a hot summer night in New England and really imagine what it would feel like to grow up with a different relationship to seafood. In the end, I believe this dish tells a story about the ways that inventive cooking can help us reimagine our childhoods, wherever we lived and whatever we ate. | *Serves 10*

Fish and Chips

POMMES SOUFFLÉS

INGREDIENTS
8 unpeeled Yukon Gold potatoes
10 large eggs
300 grams (1⅔ cups) potato starch
Neutral vegetable oil

>>>

Two hours before serving:

- Slice the potatoes as thinly as possible on a mandoline slicer, stacking the slices in piles of 10 and discarding the smaller end pieces.
- Separate the eggs, place the whites in a deep vessel such as a deli-style quart container, and reserve the yolks for use in the tartar sauce component.
- Place the potato starch in a medium bowl.
- Fill a medium pot halfway with vegetable oil and attach a cooking thermometer. Heat the oil over medium-high heat to 165°C/325°F.

>>>

Fish and Chips, *continued*

Mandoline slicer

Cooking thermometer

Basting brush

1-inch ring mold

Offset spatula

Wire skimmer

Acetate sheet

Dehydrator (*optional*)

- Working in batches of 10, lay the potato slices on a paper towel and pat dry with another paper towel.
- Dip 5 potato slices into the potato starch and use your fingers to smooth the starch to create an even coating on one side. Lay the slices on a paper towel starch-side up.
- Use a basting brush to coat the other 5 potato slices with an even coating of egg white. Lay the slices on the paper towel egg white–side up.
- Firmly press the potato starch–dredged side of 1 potato slice down onto the egg white–coated side of another slice. Repeat with the remaining slices to create 5 pressed potato slice "sandwiches."
- Use a 1-inch ring mold to punch out perfectly circular discs. Without lifting the slices, check that the edges are sealed firmly, with no batter leaking out. (When the potatoes touch the hot vegetable oil, they should form a shell around the wet batter, which will expand in the heat and puff up the potato.)
- Repeat with the remaining potato slices, working in batches of 5, until you have dredged, coated, sandwiched, and punched out all the slices.
- **TO FRY THE POTATOES:** Use an offset spatula to lift the potato discs off the work surface and check again that the edges are firmly sealed.
- Fill a deep pot halfway with neutral vegetable oil and attach a cooking thermometer. Heat the oil over high heat to 165°C/325°F, then lower the heat to maintain a consistent temperature. Working in batches of 5, transfer the potato discs to the hot vegetable oil and fry until they turn golden brown and puff up, about 15 seconds, then immediately remove with a wire skimmer and transfer to a paper towel.
- **TO DRY THE POMMES SOUFFLÉS IN A DEHYDRATOR:** Place an acetate sheet in a dehydrator tray. Arrange the fried pommes soufflés on the acetate sheet in a single layer without touching one another. Transfer the tray to a dehydrator set to 95°C/200°F and dry the pommes soufflés for at least 1 hour. Hold them in the dehydrator until ready to serve.
- **TO DRY THE POMMES SOUFFLÉS IN THE OVEN:** Preheat the oven to 95°C/200°F. Place an acetate sheet on a baking sheet.

Arrange the pommes soufflés on the acetate sheet in a single layer without touching one another. Transfer the baking sheet to the oven and turn off the heat. Let the pommes soufflés dry in the closed oven with the heat off for at least 1 hour. Hold them in the oven until ready to serve.

CURED RED SNAPPER

INGREDIENTS
2 red snapper fillets
1 lemon
1 bunch fresh flat-leaf parsley
900 grams (4¾ cups) granulated sugar
900 grams (2 pounds) kosher salt

EQUIPMENT
Vegetable peeler
Blender

At least 1 hour before serving:

- Clean the red snapper fillets and remove any remaining scales or imperfections. Skin the fillets and halve them lengthwise.
- Use a vegetable peeler to separate the yellow zest from the lemon, removing as little of the bitter white pith as possible. Set aside 10 fingernail-size curls of zest for use as a garnish; store the curls in an airtight container with a damp paper towel. Reserve the rest of the zest for use in the cure mixture and reserve the flesh for use in the tartar sauce.
- Remove and discard the parsley stems. Coarsely chop the parsley leaves.
- In a large storage container, mix together the lemon zest, chopped parsley, sugar, and salt. Dip the snapper fillets into the cure mixture, making sure the entire surface of each fillet is covered in the cure. Cover with plastic wrap pressed against the contents of the container and refrigerate for 25 minutes.
- Remove the cured snapper fillets, rinse with cool water, and pat dry with paper towels. Discard the cure mixture.
- Cut the cured snapper into slices ⅛-inch thick, then trim the slices into scant 1½ x 1-inch squares, so that they will not overhang the potato soufflés when stacked on top. Reserve the snapper scraps for use in the tartar sauce component.
- Cover and keep cool until ready to serve.

  >>>

Fish and Chips, *continued*

INGREDIENTS

35 grams (1.25 ounces) egg yolk
(reserved from pommes soufflés
component)

18 grams (3½ teaspoons) fresh
lemon juice (from lemon flesh
reserved from cured red snapper
component)

6 grams (heaping 1 teaspoon)
Dijon mustard

5 grams (1 teaspoon) fine sea salt

4 grams (1 teaspoon) granulated sugar

0.8 gram xanthan gum

430 grams (scant 2 cups) grapeseed oil

100 grams whole gherkin pickle
with juice

40 grams (1.4 ounces) peeled shallot
(3 to 4 cloves)

10 grams (0.4 ounces) fresh flat-leaf
parsley leaves

100 grams (3.5 ounces) red snapper
scraps (reserved from cured red
snapper component)

EQUIPMENT

Food processor
Squeeze bottle

At least 30 minutes before serving:

- **TO MAKE THE MAYONNAISE:** In a food processor, combine 60 grams (¼ cup) water with the egg yolk, lemon juice, Dijon mustard, fine sea salt, sugar, and xanthan gum. Process until the texture is thick and creamy, about 20 seconds. Slowly drizzle in the grapeseed oil until fully emulsified, about 1 minute.
- Transfer to an airtight container and refrigerate.
- Dice the pickles, reserving the juice.
- Mince the shallots.
- Remove and set aside 10 of the smallest, best-looking parsley leaves. Remove and discard the stems. Roughly chop the rest of the parsley leaves.
- Finely dice the red snapper scraps.
- In a large bowl, mix together the pickles, shallots, parsley, snapper, and 24 grams (0.85 ounce) of pickle juice. Add 300 grams (10.6 ounces) of the mayonnaise and mix gently. Reserve the remaining mayonnaise for use in the final plating.
- Transfer the tartar sauce to a squeeze bottle and refrigerate until ready to serve.

INGREDIENTS

4 Fresno chiles

200 grams (2 cups) malt vinegar powder

10 lemon rind curls (reserved from cured
red snapper component)

10 small fresh parsley leaves (reserved
from tartar sauce component)

Maldon salt

EQUIPMENT

Sharp tool such as tweezers or cake tester

Parchment paper (*optional*)

Small sieve

- Cut very thin slices from the Fresno chile tips, yielding 3 or 4 slices before the rings become hollow. Transfer the chile slices to the container with the lemon zest.
- Remove the pommes soufflés from the dehydrator or oven and use a sharp tool such as a tweezer or cake tester to poke a hole in the top of each one. Squeeze tartar sauce into each pomme soufflé until full, about 2 grams of tartar sauce each.
- Arrange 10 pommes soufflés close together on a plate or a disposable surface, such as parchment paper. Fill a small sieve with malt vinegar powder. Tap the sieve lightly to dust the top of the soufflés with a small sprinkling of malt vinegar powder.
- Lay 1 slice of cured red snapper, centered, on top of each pomme soufflé.
- Place 1 dot of mayonnaise on each serving plate. Place 1 pomme soufflé on top of each dot of mayonnaise. Top each piece of cured red snapper with 1 lemon rind curl, 1 Fresno chile slice, and 1 small parsley leaf. Season with a small pinch of Maldon salt.
- Advise your guests to eat the entire dish as a single bite.

Licorice is a flavor with a strange history. Most of what we think of as licorice is made from aniseed and anise oil, while true licorice is a mild-tasting edible root with no anise flavor. But both licorice and anise are used to make pastis, a lovely French liqueur that first became popular after absinthe (another anise-flavored drink) was outlawed in 1932. (I love the drama of drinking pastis, because it starts clear but is diluted with water in the glass to become elegantly cloudy.) In France, licorice-related flavors such as anise and fennel are very classic accompaniments to seafood, and that is the inspiration for this dish, which balances the subtle sweetness of licorice, sea urchin, and sunchoke in relation to the acidity of the yuzu bubbles, which create some of the mysterious energy of a glass of pastis. I love the way this dish creates a dialogue between French and Japanese seafood traditions; I grew up eating sea urchin in Brittany, but for most people, the ingredient is closely associated with sushi and often referred to as "uni." By framing the sea urchin with licorice on one side and yuzu on the other, this dish draws on both the complexity of French cuisine and the delicacy of Japanese cuisine in a simple and gratifying composition. | *Serves 10*

Sea Urchin with Licorice

SOUS-VIDE SEA URCHIN

INGREDIENTS
150 grams (⅓ pound) sushi-grade
    sea urchin (uni)
8 grams (4 sheets) gold strength
    (200 bloom) gelatin
190 grams (¾ cup plus 2½ teaspoons)
    white wine
165 grams (scant ¾ cup) heavy cream
125 grams (½ cup plus ½ tablespoon)
    mirin
50 grams (scant ¼ cup) whole milk
30 grams (2 tablespoons) tamari
2.5 grams whey protein
1 gram agar-agar
1 gram xanthan gum

>>>

At least 1 day before serving:

- **TO COOK THE SEA URCHIN SOUS VIDE:** Place the sea urchin in a vacuum bag, seal the bag, and compress at 98%. Cook the sea urchin sous vide in an immersion circulator set to 55°C/130°F for 25 minutes.

- **TO COOK THE SEA URCHIN ON THE STOVETOP:** Place the sea urchin in a resealable plastic freezer bag, squeeze out as much air as possible, and seal the bag. Fill a large pot three-quarters full with water and attach a cooking thermometer; bring the water to 55°C/130°F over medium heat and submerge the bag, closely monitoring the heat to maintain a consistent temperature and stirring often, for 25 minutes.

- While the sea urchin is cooking, bloom the gelatin: Submerge the gelatin in enough cold water to cover until it is very pliant, 5 to 10 minutes. Drain the water and transfer the gelatin to a large, deep container.

- Meanwhile, in a medium pot, simmer the white wine over medium-low heat until it has reduced by half, about 15 minutes. Add the heavy cream, mirin, milk, and tamari and return the mixture to a simmer. With the mixture at a simmer, whisk in the whey protein, agar-agar, and xanthan gum until fully incorporated, then remove from the heat.

>>>

Sea Urchin with Licorice, *continued*

EQUIPMENT

Vacuum bag or resealable plastic
 freezer bag

Vacuum sealer (*optional*)

Immersion circulator (*optional*)

Blender

Cooking thermometer

Fine-mesh strainer

2 acetate sheets

9 x 13 (quarter-sheet) pan

1-inch ring mold

- While the sea urchin is still hot, remove it from the vacuum bag or resealable plastic freezer bag and transfer to a blender. Add the hot wine-cream mixture and blend on high for 1 minute.
- Turn off the blender and use the cooking thermometer to check the temperature of the sea urchin mixture. If it is below 60°F/140°F, return the mixture to the pot in which you heated the cream and heat over medium-low heat until it reaches 60°F/140°F (gelatin is activated at this temperature).
- Pour the hot sea urchin mixture on top of the gelatin while whisking to incorporate. Strain through a fine-mesh strainer.
- Trim 2 acetate sheets to fit a 9 x 13-inch (quarter-sheet) pan. Place 1 sheet in the pan and set the other aside.
- Pour 425 grams (15 ounces) of the strained sea urchin mixture into the acetate-lined baking pan. Tamp the pan on the counter to remove any bubbles and cover with the second acetate sheet.
- Cover the pan with plastic wrap and refrigerate overnight.
- Use a 1-inch ring mold to punch out 10 circles of sea urchin.
- Cover with plastic wrap and refrigerate until ready to serve.

LICORICE CONSOMMÉ

INGREDIENTS

30 grams (1.05 ounces) unsweetened
 black licorice stick

25 grams (1 tablespoon) liquid glucose

0.5 gram fine sea salt

Xanthan gum

EQUIPMENT

Vacuum bags or resealable plastic
 freezer bags

Vacuum sealer (*optional*)

Immersion circulator or cooking
 thermometer

Kitchen scale

Fine-mesh strainer

Blender

At least 3 hours before serving:

- **TO COOK THE LICORICE CONSOMMÉ SOUS VIDE:** In a vacuum bag, combine 300 grams (1¼ cup) water with the licorice, liquid glucose, and fine sea salt and compress at 90%. Cook the vacuum bag in an immersion circulator set to 55°C/130°F for 2 hours.
- **TO COOK THE LICORICE CONSOMMÉ ON THE STOVETOP:** In a resealable plastic freezer bag, combine 300 grams (1¼ cup) water with the licorice, liquid glucose, and fine sea salt. Squeeze out as much air as possible and seal the bag. Fill a large pot three-quarters full with water and attach a cooking thermometer; bring the water to 55°C/130°F over low heat and submerge the bag, closely monitoring the heat to maintain a consistent temperature and stirring often, for 2 hours.
- Open the vacuum bag or resealable plastic freezer bag and strain the liquid through a fine-mesh strainer.

- Weigh the liquid on a kitchen scale and calculate 0.15%, which will be the amount of xanthan gum to add. Transfer the liquid to a blender and blend low speed, pouring the xanthan gum directly into the liquid without touching the sides of the blender, for about 10 seconds.
- Transfer to a storage container and refrigerate, uncovered, for 1 hour, then cover and refrigerate until ready to serve.

SUNCHOKE PUDDING

INGREDIENTS

550 grams (19 ounces) sunchoke
400 grams (1¾ cups) heavy cream
100 grams (scant ½ cup) whole milk
Fine sea salt
Iota carrageenan
Guar gum

EQUIPMENT

Vacuum bags or resealable
    plastic freezer bags
Vacuum sealer (*optional*)
Immersion circulator or
    cooking thermometer
Blender
Kitchen scale
Fine-mesh strainer

At least 2 hours before serving:

- Peel and dice the sunchokes, holding them in a large pot or bowl filled with cold water, submerged, as you work, to prevent oxidation.
- **TO COOK THE SUNCHOKES SOUS VIDE:** In a vacuum bag, combine 375 grams (13.25 ounces) of the diced sunchoke with the heavy cream and milk and compress at 98%. Cook the sunchoke sous vide in an immersion circulator set to 55°C/130°F for 1 hour.
- **TO COOK THE SUNCHOKES ON THE STOVETOP:** In a resealable plastic freezer bag, combine 375 grams (13.25 ounces) of the diced sunchoke with the heavy cream and milk, squeeze out as much air as possible, and seal the bag. Fill a large pot three-quarters full with water and attach a cooking thermometer; bring the water to 55°C/130°F over medium heat and submerge the bag, closely monitoring the heat to maintain a consistent temperature and stirring often, for 1 hour.
- Set the blender canister on a kitchen scale and tare to zero. Transfer the contents of the vacuum bag or resealable plastic freezer bag to the blender canister and weigh. Calculate 0.7% of the total weight and add that much in fine sea salt while running the blender at low speed. Calculate 0.8% of the total weight and add that much in iota carrageenan while running the blender at low speed. Calculate 0.1% of the total weight and add that much in guar gum while running the blender at low speed, pouring it directly into the liquid without touching the sides of the blender, about 10 seconds. Raise the speed to high and puree for 1 minute.
- Strain the sunchoke puree through a fine-mesh strainer into a storage container.
- Refrigerate the sunchoke pudding, covered, until ready to serve.

>>>

Sea Urchin with Licorice, *continued*

POTATO SKIN GEL

INGREDIENTS

3 medium unpeeled
    Yukon Gold potatoes
Agar-agar

EQUIPMENT

Vacuum bags or resealable
    plastic freezer bags
Vacuum sealer (*optional*)
Immersion circulator or
    cooking thermometer
Fine-mesh strainer
Glass jar with lid
30 grams (1 ounce) cedar chips
Kitchen torch
Aluminum foil

At least 2 hours before serving:

- Preheat the oven to 190°C/375°F.
- Scrub the potatoes and prick each with a fork several times.
- On a baking sheet, roast the potatoes until the skins are dark brown, 35 to 40 minutes.
- Halve the potatoes and scoop out their flesh; reserve it for another use. Weigh the potato skins and measure out twice the weight in water.
- **TO COOK THE POTATO SKIN WATER SOUS VIDE:** Transfer the water and roasted potato skins to a vacuum bag, seal the bag, and compress at 90%. Cook the potato skins sous vide in an immersion circulator set to 55°C/130°F for 1 hour.
- **TO COOK THE POTATO SKIN WATER ON THE STOVETOP:** Transfer the water and roasted potato skins to a resealable plastic freezer bag, squeeze out as much air as possible, and seal the bag. Fill a large pot three-quarters full with water and attach a cooking thermometer; bring the water to 55°C/130°F over low heat and submerge the bag, closely monitoring the heat to maintain a consistent temperature and stirring often, for 1 hour.
- Open the vacuum bag or resealable plastic freezer bag and strain the liquid through a fine-mesh strainer. Discard the solids.
- Weigh the liquid on a kitchen scale and transfer to a bowl. Calculate 0.2% of the weight and whisk in that much in agar-agar.
- Transfer the mixture to a glass jar and refrigerate, uncovered, until set to a gel, about 1 hour.
- Place the jar in a roasting pan and surround with the cedar chips. Light the cedar chips with a kitchen torch and cover the roasting pan with aluminum foil. Let the cedar chips smoke for 15 minutes, then close the glass jar and refrigerate until ready to serve.

YUZU BUBBLES

INGREDIENTS
50 grams (scant ¼ cup) yuzu juice
10 grams (2½ teaspoons)
    granulated sugar
1 gram xanthan gum
0.5 gram fine sea salt
5 grams Versawhip

EQUIPMENT
Blender
Fine-mesh strainer

INGREDIENTS
15 grams (0.53 ounces) caviar
Fennel tips

EQUIPMENT
Aquarium pump
Blender

Thirty minutes before serving:

- In a blender, combine 450 grams (scant 2 cups) water with the yuzu juice, sugar, xanthan gum, and salt and blend on high speed until fully incorporated, about 1 minute. Reduce the blender speed to low and add the Versawhip without touching the sides of the blender, blending on low until fully incorporated, about 1 minute.
- Pass the liquid through a fine-mesh strainer.

TO SERVE:

Fifteen minutes before serving:

- Transfer the yuzu bubble mixture to a large, deep container and aerate with an aquarium pump. Adjust the settings to create 1-inch-diameter bubbles. You may continue plating while the bubbles accumulate. Turn off the machine if the bubbles threaten to overflow the container.
- While the bubbles are accumulating: Transfer the sunchoke pudding to a blender and puree on medium speed until the texture loosens, about 1 minute.
- **TO PLATE:** In each shallow bowl, spoon ¼ cup of the liquid sunchoke pudding and refrigerate, uncovered, until the pudding sets again, about 5 minutes. Top the pudding with 1 circle of sea urchin. Spoon the licorice consommé in a circle around the sea urchin each bowl. Use a spoon to top with 1.5 grams of caviar and 1.5 grams of potato skin gel.
- Garnish each bowl with fennel tips.
- Immediately before serving, use a large spoon to cover each bowl with the yuzu bubbles, which should remain stable for 30 to 90 seconds.

Tasting abalone is like plunging into the sea, but cooking it is not as simple. If abalone is cooked improperly, it can be unpleasantly chewy, so proper technique is crucial. The abalone we serve at Atelier Crenn is delivered alive, and I always tell my cooks that we have to be careful not to kill it twice; that is, we want to ease it very slowly from life to death by steaming the abalone in the shell, roasting the trimmed muscle over low heat, and then returning the abalone to its shell for the final plating. It's a beautiful presentation, as the play of colors on the pearlescent shell enhances and reflects the balanced flavors of the entire dish.

Abalone is much more plentiful in the Pacific than the Atlantic, and in fact, I'd only tasted abalone once or twice before I emigrated from France. In honor of the abalone's natural environment, we accompany the shellfish with sun-dried tomatoes and yuzu, which allude to Californian and Japanese cuisine, respectively. At the last moment before serving, we baste the abalone with a bit of butter. The overall effect is delicate yet gratifying. | *Serves 4*

Abalone

MILK SKIN

At least 6 hours before serving:

INGREDIENTS
240 grams (1 cup) whole milk
24 grams (2 tablespoons plus
    2 teaspoons) kuzu (kudzu) starch
2.4 grams (scant ½ teaspoon)
    fine sea salt

EQUIPMENT
Blender
2 large acetate sheets
Nonstick cooking spray
Rolling pin
Dehydrator (*optional*)

- In a blender, combine the milk, kuzu, and fine sea salt. Blend on high until the kuzu is fully hydrated, about 1 minute. Pour the milk mixture into a medium pot and bring to a boil over medium-high heat, stirring vigorously, until the milk mixture thickens, 2 to 3 minutes.
- Spray 2 large sheets of acetate with nonstick cooking spray. Spread the milk mixture evenly on the sprayed side of 1 sheet, and press the top with the sprayed side of the other acetate sheet, to sandwich the milk mixture between the sprayed sides of the acetate sheets. Use a rolling pin to spread the milk skin mixture very evenly into a thin sheet. Refrigerate for 1 hour.
- **TO DRY THE MILK SKIN IN A DEHYDRATOR:** Transfer the acetate sheets to a dehydrator tray and remove the top acetate sheet. Transfer the tray to a dehydrator set to 60°C/140°F and dry the milk skin until crispy, about 6 hours.
- **TO DRY THE MILK SKIN IN THE OVEN:** Preheat the oven to 60°C/140°F or the closest temperature available. Transfer the acetate sheets to a baking sheet and remove the top acetate sheet. Let the milk skin dry in the closed oven with the heat off until crispy, about 6 hours.

YUZU PANNA COTTA

At least 3½ hours before serving, prepare Yuzu Panna Cotta (see page 65).

>>>

Abalone, *continued*

SUN-DRIED TOMATO
PUREE

At least 1 hour before serving, prepare Sun-Dried Tomato Puree (page 66).

YUZU AIR

Up to 2 days before serving:

INGREDIENTS

50 grams (3 tablespoons plus
    2 teaspoons) lecithin
50 grams (2 tablespoons) liquid glucose
100 grams (⅓ cup plus 1¼ tablespoons)
    yuzu juice
Fine sea salt

- **TO PREPARE THE LECITHIN SYRUP:** In a small pot, combine the lecithin, liquid glucose, and 65 grams (¼ cup) water and cook just below a simmer until it thickens, about 1 minute.
- Pour the mixture into a blender and blend on high until it is emulsified, about 20 seconds.
- Transfer to an airtight container and refrigerate.

Up to 3 hours before serving:

EQUIPMENT
Blender
Fine-mesh strainer
Kitchen scale

- In a blender, combine 10 grams (0.35 ounce) of the lecithin syrup with the yuzu juice and 565 grams (2⅓ cups) water and blend until incorporated, about 30 seconds.
- Strain the liquid through a fine-mesh strainer and weigh on a kitchen scale. Add 1% of the weight in fine sea salt and stir well.
- Refrigerate, covered, until ready to serve.

ABALONE

One hour before serving:

INGREDIENTS

4 small abalone (about 50 grams/
    1.75 ounces each), preferably live

- Prepare an ice water bath.
- Heat a deep heavy-bottomed pot on the stove over medium heat for 5 minutes.
- Reduce the heat to low and add the abalones to the pan shell-side down. Pour water up to the edge of the abalone shells and gently bring up to a simmer over the course of 2 minutes. Simmer for 10 to 15 seconds, remove the abalones from the pan with tongs, and plunge into the ice water bath. (This process will subdue the abalones and kill them gradually so that their flesh is not tough from rigor mortis.)

EQUIPMENT
Tongs
Wooden spatula or other blunt
    kitchen tool
Clean sponge

>>>

- **TO REMOVE THE ABALONES FROM THEIR SHELLS:** For each abalone, use a wooden spatula or other blunt kitchen tool to pry apart the muscle and shell, gently working all the way around while keeping the abalone whole. Scrub the shells thoroughly and reserve for plating.
- **TO CLEAN THE ABALONES:** Hold each abalone with the viscera hanging downward over a sink or bowl and use a sharp knife to slice the viscera from the muscle. Discard the viscera. Use a clean sponge to scrub off the black film along the edges of the muscle, as it is bitter to taste and ugly to look at. Slice off the curled "lips" and the pointed tip, because these parts will be tough no matter how gently you cook them.
- Serve immediately.

TO SERVE:

INGREDIENTS
2 grams (½ teaspoon) neutral vegetable oil
15 grams (1 tablespoon) unsalted butter
15 grams (1 tablespoon) fresh lemon juice

EQUIPMENT
Aquarium pump
Metal skewer

Fifteen minutes before serving:

- Transfer the yuzu-lecithin mixture to a large, deep container and aerate with an aquarium pump. Adjust the settings to create 1-inch-diameter bubbles. You may continue plating while the bubbles accumulate. Turn off the machine if the bubbles threaten to overflow the container.
- While the bubbles are accumulating: In a sauté pan, heat the vegetable oil over medium heat. Add the abalone flesh and sear over medium heat until browned, about 1 minute on each side.
- Pour off the oil, reduce the heat to low, and add the butter and lemon juice to deglaze the pan. Pan baste the abalone with a spoon until a metal skewer inserted into the flesh feels warm to the touch, about 2 minutes.
- Remove the abalone from the pan and slice very thin while still hot.
- **TO PLATE:** Place a clean abalone shell, pearly side up, on each plate and arrange the abalone slices on each shell. Spoon 1 teaspoon of yuzu panna cotta and ½ teaspoon of tomato coulis into each shell. Use your hands to break the milk skin into rustic ½ x ½-inch shards, and top each shell with milk skin.
- Immediately before serving, use a large spoon to cover each bowl with the yuzu air bubbles, which should remain stable for 30 to 90 seconds.

This dish is about showing respect for the life of the fish. At Atelier Crenn, we serve *shima aji* (also known as striped jack) from Japan, where the traditional *ike jime* method of killing with a sharp spike not only ensures a painless death but also prevents the flesh from souring. And *shima aji* is one of my favorite fish to cook with, because it is very rich, like other members of the mackerel family, but less pungent; in some ways, it is most similar to yellowtail, though amberjack, snapper, or Spanish mackerel would work well as substitutes for *shima aji* in this dish as well.

When I imagine our *shima aji* swimming in their natural home, I am inspired to surround the fish with Southeast Asian flavors and fashion an environment in which the fish "lives" again on the plate, swimming among the white-capped waves.

We cure and smoke the *shima aji* to bring out the full complexity of the flavor, but the latter process is optional, and there is no need to cook the fish after curing. In fact, we want to serve the fish below room temperature to present a contrast with the hot tempura, like warm tropical air hanging over cool ocean waters. | *Serves 4*

Shima Aji with White Beets and Turnip Leaf Tempura

TURNIP PUREE

At least 4½ hours before serving:

INGREDIENTS

1 kilogram (2.2 pounds) peeled turnip
2.5 grams (0.9 ounce) calcium lactate
10 grams (2 teaspoons) fine sea salt
10 grams (0.35 ounce) low acyl gellan
0.7 gram sodium hexametaphosphate
  (SHMP)

EQUIPMENT

Vacuum bag or resealable
  plastic freezer bag
Vacuum sealer (*optional*)
Blender
Cooking thermometer
Squeeze bottle

- Clean and peel the turnips, then chop into small (¼-inch) dice.
- Fill a large pot three-quarters full with water and bring to a boil over medium heat.
- Transfer 1 kilogram of the diced turnip to a vacuum bag or resealable plastic freezer bag, seal the bag, and compress at 99%; alternatively, transfer 1 kilogram of diced turnip to a resealable plastic freezer bag, squeeze as much air as possible, and seal the bag. Submerge the vacuum bag or resealable plastic freezer bag in the boiling water and boil until the turnip is very soft, about 2 hours.
- Open the vacuum bag or plastic freezer bag and transfer the cooked turnip to a blender. Puree until smooth, about 30 seconds.
- In a small bowl, bloom the calcium lactate with 11 grams (2¼ teaspoons) room-temperature water and set aside at room temperature. The calcium lactate will swell and thicken.

>>>

Shima Aji with White Beets and Turnip Leaf Tempura, *continued*

- Transfer the pureed turnip to a pot and attach a cooking thermometer. Add the salt, low acyl gellan, and SHMP and bring to 100°C/210°F over medium heat.
- Add the calcium lactate to the turnip mixture. Cook over medium heat until the mixture returns to 100°C/210°F. (At Atelier Crenn, we use a Thermomix to blend the ingredients at the appropriate temperatures.)
- Transfer the mixture to a storage container and refrigerate until cold, about 2 hours.
- Transfer to a blender and blend on high speed until the texture of pudding, about 1 minute.
- Transfer the turnip puree to a squeeze bottle and refrigerate until ready to serve.

BEET ICE

At least 3½ hours before serving:

INGREDIENTS

1,800 grams (4 pounds) white beets
Ascorbic acid solution (reserved from pickled albino beet component)
10 grams (2 teaspoons) fine sea salt
0.2 gram xanthan gum
0.2 gram ascorbic acid
0.2 gram malic acid

EQUIPMENT

Blender
Fine-mesh strainer
Robot Coupe or food processor
Coarse-mesh strainer

- Peel the white beets and immediately submerge them in the ascorbic acid solution to prevent them from turning brown.
- Roughly chop the beets into small (¼-inch) dice, keeping the other peeled pieces in the ascorbic acid solution as you work.
- Transfer the beets to a blender and blend on high speed for 5 minutes. Pass through a fine-mesh strainer and discard the solids.
- In the blender, combine the beet juice, fine sea salt, xanthan gum, ascorbic acid, and malic acid and blend until incorporated, about 30 seconds.
- Transfer to a cold-safe storage container and freeze until frozen solid, about 3 hours.
- Once frozen, transfer to a Robot Coupe or food processor and blend into a fine white powder. (At Atelier Crenn, we also use liquid nitrogen.) Pass the ice through a coarse-mesh strainer and transfer to a cold-safe storage container. Freeze until ready to serve.

PICKLED ALBINO BEETS

INGREDIENTS

2 grams (0.7 ounce) ascorbic acid
1,125 grams (2.5 pounds) white beets
250 grams (1 cup) rice wine vinegar
35 grams (2 tablespoons plus
    1 teaspoon) mirin
2.55 grams (½ teaspoon) fine sea salt

EQUIPMENT

Mandoline or meat slicer
¾-inch ring mold
Vacuum bag
Vacuum sealer

At least 2½ hours before serving:

- In a large bowl, mix 2 kilograms (8½ cups) water with the ascorbic acid.
- Peel the beets and immediately submerge them in the ascorbic acid solution to prevent them from turning brown. When all the beets are peeled, remove each beet from the ascorbic acid solution, reserving the ascorbic acid solution. Slice the beets into thin rounds on a mandoline or meat slicer and punch each slice with a ¾-inch ring mold to form perfect circles. Return the beet slices to the ascorbic acid solution.
- In a large bowl, combine the rice wine vinegar with 400 grams (1⅔ cups) water, the mirin, and the fine sea salt.
- Transfer the beet slices to a vacuum bag, reserving the ascorbic acid solution for use in the beet ice component. Cover the beets with the vinegar mixture and compress at 99%.
- Refrigerate for at least 2 hours until ready to serve.

CURED AND SMOKED SHIMA AJI

INGREDIENTS

150 grams (5.25 ounces) peeled
    fresh ginger
40 grams (1.4 ounces) fresh lemongrass
600 grams (1.3 pounds) kosher salt
600 grams (3 cups plus 2 tablespoons)
    granulated sugar
1 fillet (at least 100 grams or ¼ pound)
    sashimi-grade shima aji, yellowtail,
    amberjack, snapper, or Spanish
    mackerel

EQUIPMENT

Food processor
Aromatic wood chips (*optional*)

NOTE: *This is a very short curing process, so it is absolutely imperative that you start with very fresh sashimi-grade fish.*

At least 90 minutes before serving:

- Grate the ginger and chop the lemongrass in a food processor.
- In a large nonreactive bowl, combine the ginger and lemongrass with the kosher salt and sugar and mix well. Spread the curing mixture over the entire surface of the fish fillet and cover tightly with plastic wrap. Refrigerate for at least 40 minutes.
- **OPTIONAL**: Once the fish is cured, smoke the fish over aromatic wood chips for 25 minutes. (At Atelier Crenn, we use cedar charcoal and smoking bricks from Japan.)
- Slice the fish very thin (about 5 mm/0.2 inch) and refrigerate.

Shima Aji with White Beets and Turnip Leaf Tempura, *continued*

TEMPURA BABY TURNIPS

INGREDIENTS

8 baby turnips with greens attached

215 grams (1⅓ cups) white rice flour

105 grams (¾ cup plus 1 heaping tablespoon) cornstarch

460 grams (2 cups) seltzer water

1.6 grams lye

1 gram xanthan gum

12 grams (2½ teaspoons) fine sea salt

1,400 grams (1½ quarts) neutral vegetable oil

EQUIPMENT

Wire rack

Blender

Cooking thermometer

Wire skimmer

INGREDIENTS

8 baby turnips (reserved from turnip leaf tempura component)

Red amaranth (*optional*)

EQUIPMENT

Mandoline

Up to 20 minutes before serving:

- Remove and clean the turnip greens, reserving the baby turnips for garnish.
- Line a wire rack with a double layer of paper towels.
- In a blender, combine the rice flour, cornstarch, seltzer water, lye, xanthan gum, and salt and blend on medium-high speed for 10 seconds. (At Atelier Crenn, we aerate our tempura batter with soda chargers, but in a home setting, I suggest seltzer water in the batter.)
- In a deep pot with a cooking thermometer attached, heat the vegetable oil over high heat to 175°C/350°F to 190°C/375°F.
- Dredge the turnip leaves in the tempura batter. In batches of 3, fry until puffy and golden brown, 1 to 2 minutes. You may need to adjust the heat to keep the oil in the 175°C/350°F to 190°C/375°F range. Use a wire skimmer to remove the tempura turnip leaf. Transfer to the wire rack lined with paper towels. The tempura can be held for up to 10 minutes in a warm (95°C/200°F) oven but should be served hot to preserve the crisp texture.

TO SERVE:

Thirty minutes before serving, remove the fish from the refrigerator and allow to temper until just slightly cooler than room temperature.

- Slice the turnips on a mandoline.
- On each plate, arrange the fish slices upright in a staggered pattern to create a shape like a fence. Balance a piece of tempura turnip leaf on top. Working quickly, squeeze 5 dots of turnip puree around the central ingredients. Sprinkle slices of white beet and sliced baby turnip across the entire plate. Spoon 2 spoonfuls of beet ice onto each plate, being careful not to let it touch the tempura. (At Atelier Crenn, we serve the beet ice tableside, to keep it very cold.)

In Brittany, the sea has always signified bounty and camaraderie, so seafood platters (or *plateaux de fruits de mer*) are a natural expression of hospitality. When I was a child, my mother would offer our guests a gorgeous array of shellfish, from lobster all the way to sea snails, along with a choice of homemade mignonette, clarified butter, and herbed mayonnaise. I still love these simple flavors, but I have adapted the impulse behind those seafood platters into my own sampling of the sea, accompanied by squid ink meringue, juniper-lime foam, and a powder made of anchovy, lemon, and sesame oils. The specific components in this dish have ranged from tai snapper to sea urchin, and I particularly love to highlight fish and bivalves such as mussels and clams, as in the recipe that follows, but feel free to substitute freely, as the important principle is to procure whatever is absolutely best at the precise moment in any particular market. After all, seafood is a snapshot in time, so mix and match according to local and seasonal availability, and remember to serve a nice fresh bread as well. In Brittany, we eat *plateaux de fruits de mer* with a pain de seigle (see page 337), and it is quite appropriate alongside this dish as well. | *Serves 10*

The Sea

SQUID INK MERINGUE

INGREDIENTS

150 grams (5.3 ounces) egg whites
(from about 5 eggs)
100 grams (½ cup) granulated sugar
50 grams (2 tablespoons) liquid glucose
10 grams (0.4 ounce) squid ink powder
10 grams (2 teaspoons) fine sea salt

EQUIPMENT

Stand mixer with whisk attachment
Cooking thermometer
Acetate sheet
Nonstick cooking spray
Offset spatula
Dehydrator (*optional*)

At least 24 hours in advance:

- In the bowl of a stand mixer fitted with the whisk attachment, whip the egg whites on medium speed until frothy, 4 to 5 minutes.
- In a small pot with a cooking thermometer attached, mix together the sugar and liquid glucose and cook over medium heat until the syrup reaches 121°C/250°F.
- With the stand mixer running on high speed, drizzle the warm syrup into the egg whites. The mixture should appear glossy. Continue to run the mixer on high and gradually sprinkle in the squid ink powder and salt to incorporate.
- Spray an acetate sheet with nonstick cooking spray and wipe down with a paper towel; the residual nonstick coating will suffice.
- Use an offset spatula to spread the squid ink meringue in a thin, even layer across the acetate sheet.
- **TO DRY THE MERINGUE IN A DEHYDRATOR:** Place the acetate sheet in a dehydrator tray. Transfer the tray to a dehydrator set to 50°C/120°F and dry the meringue until crispy, 24 hours.
- **TO DRY THE MERINGUE IN THE OVEN:** Preheat the oven to 50°C/120°F or the closest temperature available. Place the acetate sheet on a baking sheet. Transfer the baking sheet to the oven and turn off the heat. Let the meringue dry in the closed oven with the heat off until crispy, 24 hours.
- Store in an airtight container at room temperature until ready to serve.

>>>

The Sea, *continued*

JUNIPER-LIME FOAM

INGREDIENTS

20 grams (0.7 ounce) juniper berries
50 grams (3 tablespoons plus
   1 teaspoon) fresh lime juice
   (from about 2 limes)
300 grams (10.6 ounces) egg whites
   (from about 10 eggs)
10 grams (2 teaspoons) fine sea salt
2 grams Versawhip

EQUIPMENT

Roasting pan
Fine-mesh strainer
Blender

At least 24 hours in advance:

- Preheat the oven to 175°C/350°F.
- In a roasting pan, spread the juniper berries in an even layer and toast in the oven until fragrant, about 10 minutes.
- In a large bowl or storage container, combine the lime juice and toasted juniper berries and refrigerate for 24 hours to steep.

Within 1 hour of serving:

- Strain the lime juice through a fine-mesh strainer and discard the juniper berries.
- Transfer the lime juice to a blender and add the egg whites and fine sea salt and blend on high speed for 5 seconds. Pour the Versawhip directly into the liquid without touching the sides of the blender, and blend to incorporate, about 10 seconds.
- Transfer to an airtight container and refrigerate.

HAMACHI SASHIMI AND KOMBU-CURED SEA BASS

INGREDIENTS

200 grams (7 ounces) kombu
200 grams (7 ounces) sashimi-grade
   sea bass fillet
200 grams (7 ounces) sashimi-grade
   hamachi loin

At least 4½ hours before serving:

- In a large pot or container, mix together 1 liter (1 quart) water with the kombu. Clean the sea bass fillet and submerge it in the kombu solution. Refrigerate for 4 hours.
- While the sea bass is curing, clean the hamachi loin and cut it into 20 slices, approximately ½ an inch thick and weighing 10 grams each. Refrigerate until ready to serve.
- When the sea bass is cured, cut it into 20 slices resembling the shape of the hamachi loin slices and refrigerate until ready to serve.

PICKLED MUSSELS

INGREDIENTS
20 mussels
200 grams (¾ cup plus 1½ tablespoons)
    champagne vinegar
4 grams fine sea salt

EQUIPMENT
Kitchen scissors
Vacuum bag
Vacuum sealer

At least 3 hours before serving:

- **TO STEAM THE MUSSELS:** Prepare an ice water bath. In a medium pot, combine 200 grams (¾ cup plus 1½ tablespoons) cold water with the mussels. Cover and bring to a simmer over medium heat. Steam until the mussel shells just open, 1 to 2 minutes, then transfer to the ice water bath. Use your fingers to remove the meat from the shells. Use kitchen scissors to remove the tongue and beard from each mussel. Discard any mussels that do not open.
- **TO PICKLE THE MUSSELS:** In a vacuum bag, combine the cleaned mussels with the vinegar and fine sea salt, seal the bag, and compress at 99%.
- Refrigerate for at least 2 hours.

SAFFRON AIOLI

INGREDIENTS
20 grams (4 teaspoons) champagne
    vinegar
5 grams (0.18 ounce) saffron
2 egg yolks
10 grams (2 teaspoons) fine sea salt
400 grams (1¾ cups plus
    1¼ tablespoons) grapeseed oil

EQUIPMENT
Fine-mesh strainer
Blender
Squeeze bottle

- In a small pot, bring the champagne vinegar to a boil over medium heat.
- Place the saffron in a small heat-safe container and pour the champagne vinegar over it. Let sit for 1 hour at room temperature.
- Refrigerate the container until cold, about 2 hours.
- Once cold, strain the saffron vinegar through a fine-mesh strainer into a blender.
- Add the egg yolks and salt. Blend on low speed for 5 seconds. With the blender running on low speed, slowly pour in the oil to emulsify until completely combined, about 1 minute.
- Transfer to a squeeze bottle and refrigerate until ready to serve.

The Sea, *continued*

FENNEL PUREE

INGREDIENTS

2 large fennel bulbs

5 grams low acyl gellan

0.3 grams sodium hexametaphosphate (SHMP)

1.25 grams calcium lactate

5 grams (0.18 ounce) fresh flat-leaf parsley leaves

5 grams fine sea salt

0.5 gram xanthan gum

EQUIPMENT

Vacuum bag or resealable plastic freezer bag

Vacuum sealer (*optional*)

Blender

Cooking thermometer

Tongs

Fine-mesh strainer

Squeeze bottle

Three hours before serving:

- Wash the fennel bulbs and cut against the grain into ½-inch slices, reserving 15 grams (0.53 ounce) of the fennel fronds.
- Fill a large pot three-quarters full with water and bring to a boil.
- **TO COOK THE FENNEL SOUS VIDE**: Transfer 500 grams (17.6 ounces) of the fennel to a vacuum bag, seal the bag, and compress at 99%; alternatively, transfer 500 grams (17.6 ounces) of the fennel to a resealable plastic freezer bag, squeeze out as much air as possible, and seal the bag.
- Submerge the vacuum bag or resealable plastic freezer bag in the boiling water to cook sous vide until tender, about 2 hours.
- While the fennel is still hot, transfer to a blender and puree on high for 30 seconds. Reduce the blender speed to low and pour the low acyl gellan and SHMP directly into the liquid without touching the sides of the blender and blend to incorporate, about 20 seconds.
- In a small bowl, bloom the calcium lactate with enough water to cover and set aside at room temperature. The calcium lactate will swell and thicken; add more water, if necessary.
- Transfer the fennel mixture to a medium pot with a cooking thermometer attached and heat over medium heat to 100°C/210°F. Strain the calcium lactate and add it to the pot. Bring the mixture to a boil, then remove from the heat.

CANDIED
LEMON PEEL

INGREDIENTS

2 lemons
100 grams (½ cup) granulated sugar
100 grams (¼ cup) liquid glucose

EQUIPMENT

Y-shaped peeler
Fine-mesh strainer

At least 1 hour before serving:

- Use a Y-shaped vegetable peeler to peel the lemons in a continuous spiral, removing the least amount of white pith possible and covering the entire sphere. Ideally, each lemon should produce 1 long strip of rind.
- **TO CHIFFONADE THE PEEL**: Roll the peel into a tight coil and use a sharp knife to cut it crosswise into 1-millimeter strings. Expect some breakage during handling, so it is a good idea to create 30 to 40 lemon strings to yield 20 completed candied lemon peels.
- **TO BLANCH THE PEEL**: Fill a small pot three-quarters full with cold water and add the lemon peels. Bring the water to a boil over high heat, then strain through a fine-mesh strainer and discard the water.
- Repeat the blanching process 3 times, starting with fresh cold water each time, as the blanching water will have absorbed the bitterness of the lemon peels.
- In a small pot, combine 200 grams (¾ cup plus 1½ tablespoons) cold water with the sugar and liquid glucose. Add the lemon peels and bring to a simmer over medium heat. Reduce the heat to low and simmer until the peels are translucent, about 30 minutes.
- Refrigerate, covered, until ready to serve.

The Sea, *continued*

SMOKED TROUT ROE

INGREDIENTS
55 grams (2 ounces) trout roe
4 fresh eucalyptus leaves

EQUIPMENT
Small tray
Roasting pan
Kitchen torch

At least 1 hour before serving:

- Line a small tray with parchment paper. Spread the trout roe in an even layer across the parchment paper. Place the small tray in a roasting pan and add the eucalyptus leaves on the other side of the pan. Light the eucalyptus leaves with a kitchen torch and cover the pan with aluminum foil. Smoke the trout roe until aromatic, 30 to 45 minutes. Extinguish the leaves, cover the small tray with plastic wrap, and refrigerate until ready to serve.

SEA POWDER

INGREDIENTS
20 grams (1½ tablespoons) anchovy packing oil
20 grams (1½ tablespoons) lemon oil
20 grams (1½ tablespoons) sesame oil
5 grams (1 teaspoon) fine sea salt
50 grams (1.8 ounces) tapioca maltodextrin

EQUIPMENT
Robot Coupe or food processor

- In a small bowl, mix together the anchovy oil, lemon oil, sesame oil, and fine sea salt.
- Wipe the chamber of the Robot Coupe or food processor with a paper towel to ensure that it is completely dry.
- Add the tapioca maltodextrin, turn on the machine, and slowly drizzle in the oil mixture until fully incorporated. The mixture should become a fluffy powder.
- Store in an airtight container at room temperature until ready to serve.

STEAMED CLAMS

INGREDIENTS
20 medium clams
20 grams (4 teaspoons) fresh lemon juice (from about 1 lemon)
Maldon salt

- In a small pot, bring 400 grams (1⅔ cups) water to a boil over medium heat. Add the clams and lemon juice, cover with a lid, and bring to a boil again. Steam the clams until the shells just begin to open, 3 to 4 minutes; do not wait until they are fully open, or they will be overcooked. Discard any clams that do not open.
- Use your fingers to remove the clam meat from the shells.
- Season with Maldon salt and set aside until ready to serve.

>>>

TO SERVE:

EQUIPMENT

Blender or immersion blender

Thirty minutes before serving:

- Chill the plates in the refrigerator.

Ten minutes before serving:

- Take the hamachi loin and kombu-cured sea bass out of the refrigerator to temper until just slightly cooler than room temperature.

Five minutes before serving:

- Dust 1 side of each plate with sea powder. Arrange 2 pickled mussels, 2 steamed clams, 2 slices of hamachi loin, and 2 slices of kombu-cured sea bass on top of the sea powder on each plate.
- Squeeze 5 dots of fennel puree among the shellfish and fish slices. Squeeze 5 dots of saffron aioli among the dots of fennel puree. Arrange 2 candied lemon peels among the other components. Use a small spoon to drop 3 small (5.5-gram/0.2-ounce) dollops of smoked trout roe among the other components.
- Break the squid ink meringue into small (½ x ½-inch) shards and arrange among the other components.

Immediately before serving:

- Blend the juniper-lime foam for 30 seconds to generate bubbles, then allow to settle and use a large spoon to drop 3 large spoonfuls on top of the other components.
- Serve immediately.

This dish was inspired by a trip I took to Spain in 2010, when I had the pleasure of visiting incredible restaurants in the company of incredible chefs. On that trip, I was inspired by the full range of Spanish cuisine, from innovative modernism to classical technique, and I was particularly taken by the culinary tradition of pairing seafood and pork. The food near San Sebastián, a beach town on the northern coast of Spain, manages to be both bold and balanced, exciting and comforting, refreshing and earthy. There's something about it that reminds me of that moment when you first step into the ocean and half of your consciousness belongs to the heat of the air and the other to the cold of the water. In this dish, we slice squid and lardo into identical shapes, to create that frisson of cognitive dissonance between land and sea. | *Serves 10*

NOTE: *We serve our Squid with Lardo on a large piece of black slate with Buckwheat Flatbread (page 329) as an accompaniment.*

Squid with Lardo

HAM BROTH

At least 5 hours before using, prepare Ham Broth (page 322), to be served tableside.

CREAMED POTATO

About 3 hours before serving:

INGREDIENTS

400 grams (1¾ cups) unsalted butter
575 grams (1¼ pounds) Yukon Gold
    potatoes (4 medium)
200 grams (¾ cup plus 1½ tablespoons)
    heavy cream
Fine sea salt

EQUIPMENT

Vacuum bag or resealable
    plastic freezer bag
Vacuum sealer (*optional*)
Tamis
Bowl scraper
Silicone spatula

- Cut the butter into small (¼-inch) dice and let sit at room temperature to soften.
- Place each potato in its own vacuum bag, seal the bags, and compress at 99%; alternatively, place the potatoes in individual resealable plastic freezer bags, squeeze out as much air as possible, and seal the bags.
- Fill a large pot three-quarters full with water and bring to a boil over high heat. Submerge the bags and cook for 2 hours.
- Remove the potatoes from the bags and peel off the skins. While the potatoes are still hot, press through a tamis with a bowl scraper into a small pot.
- In a separate pot, bring the cream just to a boil and immediately remove from the heat.
- Transfer a small amount of cream to the pot with the potato and combine with a silicone spatula, just enough that the potato will stick to the side of the pot when stirring. Start to incorporate the butter, about 10 grams at a time, stirring continuously with the rubber spatula. If the potatoes start to break, add more heated cream; if the potatoes become too thick, incorporate more butter. Repeat this process until the potatoes are smooth and creamy.
- Season with fine sea salt and keep warm until ready to serve.

>>>

Squid with Lardo, *continued*

SQUID AND LARDO NOODLES

INGREDIENTS

400 grams (14.1 ounces) kosher salt
2 bigfin reef squid (aori ika) fins
400 grams (2¼ cups) lardo
1 lemon
White truffle oil
Extra-virgin olive oil

EQUIPMENT

Clean kitchen towel
Fine-mesh strainer

- **TO SALT-CURE THE SQUID:** Pour half the kosher salt into a shallow medium container. Lay the squid fins on top of the kosher salt and pour the remaining kosher salt over the squid fins, making sure that the entire surface is covered.
- Refrigerate the container, uncovered, for 6 minutes.
- Remove the squid fins from the kosher salt and rinse with cool water.
- Use a clean kitchen towel to pat the squid fins dry. Rub the squid fins with the towel to remove the skin and sinew, which are unpleasantly chewy.
- Use a sharp knife to slice the squid as thin as possible (about ⅛ inch) across the fin, to create shapes resembling noodles.
- Use a sharp knife to slice the lardo into shapes resembling the sliced squid (about 2 x ⅛ x ⅛ inches). Reserve any imperfect pieces for use in the squid ink–lardo emulsion.
- In a medium storage container, mix together the sliced squid and lardo.
- Squeeze the lemon and strain the juice through a fine-mesh strainer.
- Dress the sliced squid and lardo with lemon juice, truffle oil, and olive oil to taste.
- Refrigerate, covered, until 5 minutes before serving.

SQUID INK—LARDO EMULSION

INGREDIENTS

600 grams (3⅓ cups) lardo, plus any
   lardo reserved from the squid and
   lardo noodles component
2 egg yolks
15 grams (0.6 ounce) squid ink powder
10 grams (2 teaspoons) fresh lime juice
4 grams (¼ tablespoon) fine sea salt
0.4 gram xanthan gum

EQUIPMENT

Blender
Pastry bag

- Cut the lardo into rough dice.
- In a medium pot, cook the lardo over low heat until the fat has rendered.
- Drain off the rendered fat into a heatproof bowl and keep warm. (The fat must be liquid to emulsify properly.)
- In a blender, combine the egg yolks, squid ink powder, lime juice, and fine sea salt and blend on low speed to incorporate. With the blender running on low speed, drizzle in 400 grams (14.1 ounces) of the rendered lardo fat until completely emulsified. Add 10 grams (2 teaspoons) water and the xanthan gum and blend for 10 seconds more.
- Transfer the emulsification to a pastry bag and refrigerate until ready to serve.

PARSLEY CHIPS

INGREDIENTS

400 grams (1¾ cups) neutral
    vegetable oil
40 fresh flat-leaf parsley leaves
Fine sea salt

EQUIPMENT

Cooking thermometer
Wire skimmer
Acetate sheet (*optional*)
Dehydrator (*optional*)

- In a medium pot with a cooking thermometer attached, heat the vegetable oil over high heat to 205°C/400°F. Add the parsley leaves and fry until crisp, about 20 seconds, then remove the parsley with a wire skimmer.
- Season the parsley chips with fine sea salt.
- Hold the parsley chips on an acetate sheet on a dehydrator tray in a dehydrator set to 50°C/120°F or store in an airtight container at room temperature; alternatively, preheat the oven to 50°C/120°F, turn off the oven, and hold the parsley chips in the closed oven with the heat off until ready to serve.

GARLIC CHIPS

INGREDIENTS

2 heads elephant garlic
1 kilogram (4¼ cups) cold whole milk
400 grams (1¾ cups) neutral
    vegetable oil
Fine sea salt

EQUIPMENT

Meat slicer or mandoline
Cooking thermometer
Wire skimmer

- Separate the elephant garlic into cloves and peel the cloves. Slice the garlic cloves as thin as possible on a meat slicer or mandoline. The sliced garlic should be so thin that it is almost translucent.
- **TO BLANCH THE GARLIC:** In a small pot, combine the sliced garlic and 330 grams (1⅓ cups) cold milk. Bring to a boil over medium heat, then immediately strain off the milk.
- Repeat the blanching process 2 more times with fresh cold milk.
- In a medium pot with a cooking thermometer attached, heat the vegetable oil over medium-high heat to 160°C/300°F to 163°C/325°F. Add the sliced garlic and fry until the garlic begins to crisp but does not yet brown. (If the garlic is allowed to brown, it will taste bitter.) Remove the garlic chips with a wire skimmer and transfer to paper towels to drain excess oil.
- Season the garlic chips with fine sea salt.
- Store in an airtight container at room temperature until ready to serve.

    >>>

Squid with Lardo, *continued*

TO SERVE:

INGREDIENTS
Black truffle (*optional*)
Buckwheat Flatbread
  (page 329; *optional*)

EQUIPMENT
Offset tweezers
Microplane grater (*optional*)

Five minutes before serving:

- Bring the squid and lardo out of the refrigerator to come to room temperature.
- Spoon ½ tablespoon of the creamed potato onto the far right side of each plate or shallow bowl. Use offset tweezers to pinch about one-tenth of the squid and lardo noodles. Cup the squid and lardo noodles with the palm of one hand and rotate the tweezers with the other hand to roll the noodles into a tight nest shape. Place the nest on top of the creamed potato. Squeeze a squiggle of lardo emulsion onto the nest.
- Garnish the top of the nest with 1 parsley chip and 1 garlic chip.
- Immediately before serving, warm 200 grams (7.05 ounces) of ham broth and pour 20 grams per person tableside.
- Grate black truffle into the ham broth, if desired. (At Atelier Crenn, we also sprinkle the plate with a ham powder we make in house.)
- Serve with buckwheat flatbread broken into irregular, rustic shapes, if desired.

Whenever possible, I love to champion overlooked ingredients, like sunchoke and rutabaga, because they are gastronomic underdogs that deserve more respect. Sunchokes, which are also called Jerusalem artichokes in English or *topinambours* in French, have started to pop up on a few restaurant menus in recent years, but rutabagas are still waiting for haute-cuisine recognition. Of course, the cultural meaning of sunchokes and rutabaga is more striking in France, where they carry deeply negative historical associations: My grandparents' generation ate a lot of them during World War II because they are hardy and nutritious, but then rejected them as symbols of wartime deprivation and hardship. Ultimately, they became *légumes oubliés*, or forgotten vegetables, which scarcely anyone eats in France, but both are quite delicious. Likewise, many Americans see grapefruit and rice crackers as unappealing diet foods, but they are truly some of my favorite ingredients. Crab, in contrast, is widely appreciated, so on some level it just tickles me to pair a delicacy like crab with underestimated ingredients, because the ultimate result is so unexpectedly delicious and forces a reconsideration of our culinary prejudices. (And really, there are so many ways to serve crab beyond the butter-and-lemon clichés.) The truth is, almost anything can taste beautiful if you cook it properly. | *Serves 4*

Crab with Sunchoke

RICE CRACKER

At least 4 hours and up to 1 day before serving:

INGREDIENTS

160 grams (1 cup) wild rice

5 grams (1 teaspoon) fine sea salt,
    plus more as needed

Neutral vegetable oil

EQUIPMENT

Fine-mesh strainer

Blender

Acetate sheet

Dehydrator (*optional*)

Cooking thermometer

Wire skimmer

- In a large saucepan, bring 1.5 liters (6⅓ cups) water to a boil. Add the wild rice and fine sea salt and keep at a low boil until the wild rice is overcooked and mushy, about 1 hour. Strain through a fine-mesh strainer and reserve the rice and the cooking liquid separately.
- Transfer the cooked wild rice to a blender and puree until very smooth. Add a small amount of the cooking liquid as needed to achieve a consistency slightly thicker than heavy cream.
- **TO CRISP THE RICE IN A DEHYDRATOR:** Place an acetate sheet in a dehydrator tray. Evenly spread the rice puree across the acetate sheet as thinly as possible while maintaining complete coverage. Transfer the tray to a dehydrator set to 60°C/140°F, until the rice is crisp, flipping the rice sheet over once the top is dry, at least 3 hours. If the rice sheet breaks in the process of flipping, just rearrange it as a single layer on the acetate sheet.
- **TO CRISP THE RICE IN THE OVEN:** Preheat the oven to 60°C/ 140°F or the closest temperature available. Place an acetate sheet on a baking sheet. Evenly spread the rice puree across the acetate sheet as thinly as possible while maintaining complete coverage.

>>>

Crab with Sunchoke, *continued*

- Let the rice dry in the closed oven with the heat off until the rice is crisp, flipping the rice sheet over once the top is dry, at least 3 hours. If the rice sheet breaks in the process of flipping, just rearrange it as a single layer on the acetate sheet.
- Cool the rice sheet to room temperature, uncovered on the dehydrator tray or baking sheet, then transfer to an airtight container, if serving the next day.

Up to 4 hours before serving:

- Fill a small pot three-quarters full with vegetable oil and attach a cooking thermometer. Heat the oil to 175°C/350°F. Working in batches, break off 3-inch pieces of the dried rice crisp and drop into the oil. The rice should puff up like a rice cracker. Remove the rice crackers with a wire skimmer, transfer to a paper towel, and let sit for 2 minutes.
- Season the rice crackers with fine sea salt.
- Store in an airtight container at room temperature until ready to serve.

SUNCHOKE PUREE

INGREDIENTS
340 grams (¾ pound) sunchokes
600 grams (2½ cups) whole milk
Fine sea salt

EQUIPMENT
Blender

One to two hours before serving:

- Peel the sunchokes, holding them in a large pot or bowl filled with cold water, submerged, while peeling and cutting, to prevent oxidization. Cut the sunchokes into ¼-inch cubes.
- In a small pot, combine 225 grams (7.9 ounces) of the diced sunchokes with the milk and heat over low heat, without boiling, until the sunchoke is very soft, about 20 minutes.
- Transfer the sunchoke and milk to a blender and puree until smooth. Season with fine sea salt. Return the sunchoke puree to the small pot and keep warm until ready to serve.

RUTABAGA-GRAPEFRUIT BROTH

One to two hours before serving, prepare Rutabaga-Grapefruit Broth (page 313), but do not chill after straining; instead, return the broth to the pot in which it was cooked and keep warm.

SPIDER CRAB

INGREDIENTS
1 large white onion
1 fennel bulb
2 lemons
Fine sea salt
4 cloves garlic
8 grams (1 tablespoon)
    whole black peppercorns
4 sprigs fresh thyme
3 bay leaves
2 spider crabs

EQUIPMENT
Cooler
Fine-mesh strainer
Small kitchen scissors

INGREDIENTS
115 grams (½ cup) unsalted butter
1 bunch celery

EQUIPMENT
Y-shaped peeler

One hour before serving:

- Peel the onion and cut it into 1-inch pieces. Trim the fennel and cut it into 1-inch pieces. Quarter the lemons.
- Fill a large pot three-quarters full with generously salted water. Add the onion, fennel, lemon, garlic, black peppercorns, thyme, and bay leaves and bring to a simmer over medium-low heat. Submerge the crabs in the water and simmer until they have just turned red, 6 to 7 minutes, then remove the crabs and place in a cooler to rest.
- Strain 3 cups of the poaching liquid through a fine-mesh strainer into a small pot and set aside.
- Once the crab has cooled to room temperature, remove from the cooler and detach the legs from the body.
- **TO EXTRACT THE CRABMEAT:** Work from the tip toward the base, dislocating the segments and pulling them apart to cleanly remove the cartilage. Use a pair of small kitchen scissors to carefully cut the edges of each shell segment until you can pry it open and remove the flesh in chunks. Set aside the cleaned crabmeat at room temperature until ready to serve.

TO SERVE:

- Cut the butter into large (½-inch) dice.
- In a medium saucepan, whisk half the diced butter into the rutabaga-grapefruit broth over low heat until fully incorporated, about 2 minutes, then immediately remove from the heat.
- Gently warm the reserved poaching liquid until it is hot to the touch but well below a simmer. Whisk in the remaining diced butter over low heat until it is fully incorporated, about 2 minutes. Add the crabmeat to the poaching liquid to warm, about 1 minute.
- **TO PLATE:** Spoon the sunchoke puree onto the bottom of each shallow bowl. Arrange the warm crab pieces on top of the puree. Plant the rice cracker into the puree at diagonal angles among the crab pieces.
- Peel curls from the celery stalks and use as garnish.
- To finish, spoon 2 tablespoons of the rutabaga-grapefruit broth in each bowl to surround the rest of the dish.

I grew up eating beautiful *homards bleus*, the bright blue lobsters that live off the coast of Brittany. I love lobster in any form, from steamed to grilled, but I was always especially fond of the lobster bisque my mother used to make, full of fresh cream from my uncle's cows and tomatoes from our garden. At my age, I finally know enough about cooking and memory to recognize that I could never re-create my mother's lobster bisque, even if she gave me the most detailed recipe (and to be honest, she keeps all her recipes in her head, or perhaps her heart). Instead, I try to capture the feelings of lobster bisque, particularly the sense of indulgence born of slurping a rich soup on a warm summer night. My own version of lobster bisque transfers the tomato from the broth to a delicate veil that one must penetrate to discover bone marrow custards, which stand in for the rich cream of the original. Each spoonful transforms the diner into a kind of fisherman who plunges in to discover the gifts of the sea. | *Serves 10*

Lobster Bisque

BONE MARROW CUSTARDS

INGREDIENTS

1,800 grams (4 pounds) marrow
    bones, cut into cylinders
Kosher salt
420 grams (1¾ cups) nonfat milk
6 grams (1¼ teaspoons) fine sea salt
2 grams (scant ½ teaspoon)
    champagne vinegar
50 grams (7 tablespoons) kuzu
    (kudzu) starch
1.2 grams agar-agar

>>>

One day before serving:

- While wearing kitchen gloves, use a metal skewer to scrape the marrow out of the bones. Discard the bones.
- **TO BRINE THE BONE MARROW:** Put the bone marrow in a storage container with a lid. Using a 20:1 ratio of water to kosher salt, mix enough brine to cover the bone marrow completely. Refrigerate, covered, overnight to draw out the blood.

The next day:

- Strain the marrow and discard the brining liquid.
- In a large pot, render the bone marrow pieces over medium-low heat until they start to brown and liquefy, about 30 minutes.
- Push the bone marrow through a fine-mesh strainer to remove any remaining sinewy pieces. Let the bone marrow cool, uncovered, at room temperature.
- Bring the milk out of the refrigerator to warm up to room temperature.
- **TO PREPARE THE ACETATE MOLDS:** Cut the acetate sheets into three 20 x 5-inch rectangles. Roll each rectangle of acetate lengthwise into a 20-inch cylinder and use painter's tape or masking tape to secure the seam. Wrap the bottom of the tube in two layers of plastic wrap.

>>>

Lobster Bisque, *continued*

EQUIPMENT

Kitchen gloves

Metal skewer

Fine-mesh strainer

4 Acetate sheets

Painter's tape or masking tape

Blender

Rondeau or similar wide-bottomed pot

Flat wooden spatula

Pastry bag

Bain-marie or large heat-resistant
    measuring cup

- In a blender, combine the milk, salt, and champagne vinegar and blend on high for 10 seconds. Add the kuzu and blend on high, scraping down the sides if necessary, until the kuzu is incorporated, about 20 seconds. Add the agar-agar and blend on high for 10 seconds. Add 170 grams (6 ounces) of the rendered bone marrow and blend on high for 20 seconds.

- Transfer the milk-kuzu mixture to a rondeau or similar wide-bottomed pot and bring to a simmer over medium-high heat until the milk mixture starts to thicken, about 30 minutes. Stir with a flat wooden spatula, scraping along the bottom of the pan to prevent burning, until the mixture begins to pull away from the sides of the pot, about 10 minutes.

- Place a pastry bag in a small bain-marie or large heat-resistant measuring cup and fold the sides over the edges. Pour the milk-kuzu mixture into the pastry bag and secure with a tight knot.

- Using a towel or kitchen gloves to handle the hot pastry bag, pipe the mixture into the acetate tubes until they are full. Chill the acetate tubes in the refrigerator until set to a firm gel, at least 1 hour.

- Line a tray with an acetate sheet. Remove the tape and slice the cylinder into ¼-inch discs, reminiscent of bone marrow. Arrange the slices of bone marrow custard in a single layer on the acetate sheet, cover with plastic wrap, and refrigerate until ready to serve.

POACHED LOBSTER
AND LOBSTER BISQUE
BROTH

INGREDIENTS
5 whole Maine lobsters

1 large fennel bulb

1 white onion

1 carrot

1 clove garlic

120 grams (½ cup) white wine

5 sprigs fresh thyme

1 bay leaf

Fine sea salt

125 grams (½ cup) unsalted butter

500 grams (2 cups plus 2½ tablespoons)
Lobster Stock (page 317)

1,350 grams (5½ cups) nonfat milk

2 grams guar gum

EQUIPMENT
Stockpot with lid

Steaming rack

Fine-mesh strainer

Powerful blender

Eight hours before serving:

- **TO PREPARE THE LOBSTERS:** Plunge a sharp knife directly behind each lobster head. Cut the heads from the bodies. Remove the gills from the bodies and discard. Remove the antennae from the heads and discard. Rinse with cool water.

- **TO POACH THE LOBSTER IN COURT BOUILLON (QUICK VEGETABLE STOCK):** Roughly chop the fennel bulb, reserving the fennel fronds. Peel and roughly chop the onion. Roughly chop the carrot, discarding the top. Finely chop the garlic. In a stockpot with a fitted lid, combine 500 grams (2 cups plus 2 tablespoons) water with the white wine, fennel, onion, carrot, garlic, thyme, bay leaf, and a pinch of fine sea salt. Bring to a simmer over high heat and simmer, uncovered, for 8 minutes. Place a steaming rack at the bottom of the pot. Place the lobsters head-downward in the pot and steam until the shells turn bright red, 7 to 10 minutes. Depending on the size of your pot, you may need to work in batches and replenish the water as necessary. Reserve the remaining court bouillon in the refrigerator; court bouillon should be brought to a boil every time it is reused.

- Once the lobsters are cooked, rinse them with cold water. Separate the meat from the shells and the brains from the heads. Reserve the brains to make lobster brain–tomato gel and reserve the meat to cook with sweetbreads immediately before serving.

- Cut the butter into large (½-inch) dice and set aside to soften at room temperature.

- Use the lobster shells to prepare Lobster Stock (page 317).

- Transfer 500 grams (2 cups plus 2 tablespoons) of the hot lobster stock to a powerful blender and freeze or reserve the remaining stock for another use.

- While the lobster stock is still hot, add the softened butter to the blender and blend on high until fully incorporated, about 15 seconds. Add the nonfat milk and 2 grams of fine sea salt and blend on high until fully incorporated, about 15 seconds. Reduce the blender speed to low and pour the guar gum directly into the liquid without touching the sides of the blender, about 10 seconds.

- Season with fine sea salt and keep warm.

>>>

Lobster Bisque, *continued*

LOBSTER BRAIN— TOMATO GEL

INGREDIENTS

1 fennel bulb

1 leek

2 stalks celery

5 grams (½ tablespoon) whole black peppercorns

5 grams fennel seed

1 bay leaf

100 grams (scant ½ cup) unsalted butter

6 lobster brains (reserved from poached lobster component)

250 grams (1 cup) dry vermouth

500 grams (2 cups plus 2½ tablespoons) Tomato Consommé (page 315)

22.5 grams agar-agar

0.75 gram fine sea salt

EQUIPMENT

Fine-mesh strainer

10 x 10-inch shallow square container

At least 4 hours before serving:

- Wash and cut 50 grams (1.75 ounces) of the fennel, 50 grams (1.75 ounces) of the leek, and 50 grams (1.75 ounces) of the celery against the grain into ½-inch pieces.
- In a medium bowl, mix together the peppercorns, fennel seed, and bay leaf.
- In a medium pot, melt the butter over medium-high heat until it just begins to brown, about 90 seconds. Add the lobster brains and pan roast, turning occasionally, for about 5 minutes. Add the fennel, leek, celery, peppercorns, fennel seed, and bay leaf and cook over medium heat for 10 minutes.
- Pour the vermouth into the pot to deglaze. Simmer over medium heat, scraping the bottom to release residual bits of lobster brain, until the liquid reduces by half, about 2 minutes.
- Add 1.5 liters (6⅓ cups) water to the pot and simmer over medium-low heat until the volume reduces to one-sixth, about 2 hours.
- Strain the contents of the pot through a fine-mesh strainer, discarding the strained solids.
- Prepare Tomato Consommé (page 315), but do not season with fine sea salt.
- In a medium pot, combine 500 grams (1 pint) of the tomato consommé and 250 grams (1 cup) of the reduced lobster brain broth together with the agar-agar and fine sea salt. Bring the mixture to a boil over medium heat and stir for 10 seconds. Remove from the heat.
- Strain the mixture through a fine-mesh strainer into a shallow square container approximately 10 x 10 inches to yield a ½-inch depth, and discard the solids. Refrigerate the strained mixture, uncovered, until completely set to a gel, about 1 hour.
- Without removing the gel from the container, cut it into ½-inch squares. Wrap the container in plastic wrap and refrigerate until ready to serve.

FRIED SWEETBREADS

INGREDIENTS
1,850 grams (2 quarts) cold whole milk
5 veal sweetbreads

EQUIPMENT
Cooking thermometer

At least 24 hours before serving:

- In a large pot with a cooking thermometer attached, combine the cold milk and sweetbreads and bring to 71°C/160°F over medium-high heat. Cook the sweetbreads in the milk, adjusting the heat as needed to keep the temperature at 71°C/160°F, for 20 minutes.
- Remove the sweetbreads and discard the milk.
- **TO PRESS THE SWEETBREADS**: Arrange the sweetbreads in a single layer on a dinner plate and cover with another dinner plate. Place a 1-kilogram (2.2-pound) weight on top of the upper plate. Refrigerate until firm, about 24 hours.
- **TO TRIM THE SWEETBREADS**: Using your fingers, remove the skin, ducts, and outer membrane from the sweetbreads.
- Cut the sweetbreads into thin slices and keep refrigerated until 1 hour before serving, then remove from the refrigerator and let come to room temperature before frying to order.

DEHYDRATED SEAWEED

INGREDIENTS
200 grams (7 ounces) mermaid's
    hair seaweed

EQUIPMENT
Acetate sheet
Dehydrator (*optional*)

At least 3 hours before serving:

- Cut the seaweed into 4-inch strips.
- **TO DRY THE SEAWEED IN A DEHYDRATOR**: Place an acetate sheet in a dehydrator tray. Evenly spread the seaweed across the acetate sheet. Transfer the tray to a dehydrator set to 60°C/140°F and dry the seaweed until completely dry and crispy, about 3 hours.
- **TO DRY THE SEAWEED IN THE OVEN**: Preheat the oven to 60°C/140°F or the closest temperature available. Place an acetate sheet on a baking sheet. Evenly spread the seaweed across the acetate sheet. Transfer the baking sheet to the oven and turn off the heat. Let the seaweed dry in the closed oven with the heat off until completely dry and crispy, about 3 hours.
- Hold in the dehydrator or in an airtight container at room temperature until ready to serve.

>>>

Lobster Bisque, *continued*

VEGETABLE DASHI VEIL

INGREDIENTS

25 grams (0.9 ounces) daikon
10 grams (0.35 ounces) peeled
    fresh ginger
3.5 grams (¼ tablespoon) fine sea salt
3.5 grams kombu
5 grams agar-agar
10 grams low acyl gellan

EQUIPMENT

Stockpot
Fine-mesh strainer
Three 13 x 18-inch (half-sheet) pans
    or baking sheets
4-inch ring mold

NOTE: *This vegetable dashi recipe is adapted from our regular vegetable dashi recipe (see page 316) to yield an appropriate amount.*

Two hours before serving:

• Peel the daikon and cut it into ¼-inch cubes. Julienne the ginger.
• In a stockpot, bring 1 liter (1 quart) water to a boil. Add the daikon, ginger, and salt. Cover, remove from the heat, and let sit for 20 minutes.
• Strain the vegetable dashi through a fine-mesh strainer and reserve the daikon for another use.
• In a medium pot, bring 500 grams (2 cups plus 2 tablespoons) of the vegetable dashi to a boil, reserving the remaining vegetable dashi for use in the plankton gel component. Whisk in the agar-agar and low acyl gellan and remove from the heat.
• Strain the mixture through a fine-mesh strainer and discard the solids.
• Pour the mixture into three 18 x 13-inch (half-sheet) pans, dividing it evenly. Refrigerate, uncovered, until set to a gel, about 1 hour.
• Use a 4-inch ring mold to cut circular veils of the gel. Refrigerate, covered, in the pans until ready to plate.

>>>

Lobster Bisque, *continued*

PLANKTON GEL

INGREDIENTS

280 grams (1 cup plus 3 tablespoons) vegetable dashi (reserved from vegetable dashi veil component)

1.4 grams locust bean gum

1.4 grams xanthan gum

0.6 gram low acyl gellan

0.3 gram high acyl gellan

0.3 gram powdered plankton

EQUIPMENT

Blender

Vacuum bag or resealable plastic freezer bag

Vacuum sealer (*optional*)

3-centimeter half-sphere molds

One hour before serving:

- In a blender, combine the vegetable dashi, locust bean gum, xanthan gum, low acyl gellan, high acyl gellan, and powdered plankton and blend on high to incorporate, about 1 minute.
- **TO COOK THE GEL**: Fill a large pot three-quarters full with water and bring to a boil. Transfer the mixture to a vacuum bag, seal, and compress at 99%; alternatively, transfer the mixture to a resealable plastic freezer bag, squeeze out as much air as possible, and seal the bag. Submerge the bag in the boiling water and cook for 30 minutes.
- Open the bag and transfer the contents to 3-centimeter half-sphere molds. Refrigerate, uncovered, until the gel has set, about 1 hour.
- Cover with plastic wrap and refrigerate until ready to serve.

PICKLED PEARL ONIONS

INGREDIENTS

150 grams (⅔ cup) red wine vinegar

150 grams (¾ cup plus ½ tablespoon) granulated sugar

1.5 grams (¼ teaspoon) fine sea salt

20 white pearl onions

At least 30 minutes before serving:

- In a small pot, combine 150 grams (⅔ cup) water with the red wine vinegar, sugar, and fine sea salt and bring to a simmer over medium heat.
- Meanwhile, cut off the base of each onion and quarter them lengthwise. Peel off and discard the outer petals.
- Transfer the onions to a medium bowl and pour the pickling liquid on top, shifting the onions to submerge them. Allow to cool, uncovered, at room temperature, then cover and refrigerate until ready to serve.

INGREDIENTS

100 grams (3.5 ounces) egg whites
   (from about 3 eggs)
20 grams (2½ tablespoons) cornstarch
1.5 grams (¼ teaspoon) fine sea salt
50 grams (1.75 ounces) panko
   bread crumbs
50 grams (⅓ cup) rice flour
Neutral vegetable oil
Fine sea salt
Fennel fronds (reserved from lobster
   bisque component)
10 stems Japanese sea grapes

EQUIPMENT

Vacuum bag (*optional*)
Immersion circulator (*optional*)
Cooking thermometer
Spice grinder

TO SERVE:

- **TO WARM EACH SERVING SOUS VIDE:** For each diner, fill 1 vacuum bag with 25 grams (0.9 ounces) of lobster bisque, 3 chunks of lobster meat (reserved from lobster bisque component), 1 plankton gel, 1 lobster brain, and 2 bone marrow dumplings. Seal the bags and cook together sous vide in an immersion circulator set to 72°C/160°F for 15 minutes. Open each bag and transfer the contents of each bag to its own shallow bowl.
- **TO WARM THE BISQUE ON THE STOVETOP:** In a large pot, combine 150 grams (⅔ cup) of broth, 18 chunks of lobster meat (reserved from lobster bisque component, above), 6 plankton gels, 6 lobster brain gels, 12 bone marrow dumplings, and 6 sea grape stems. Warm over medium heat to 72°C/160°F, then divide among shallow bowls, with each serving containing 25 grams (0.9 ounces) of lobster bisque, 3 chunks of lobster meat, 1 plankton gel, 1 lobster brain gel, and 2 bone marrow dumplings.

While the bisque is warming:

- **TO MAKE THE SLURRY:** In a large bowl, whisk together the egg whites, cornstarch, and fine sea salt.
- **TO MAKE THE BREADING:** In a spice grinder, grind the panko until it is slightly less coarse, about 30 seconds. In a large bowl, mix together the ground panko and rice flour.
- **TO BATTER THE SWEETBREADS:** Coat each sweetbread in the slurry and immediately dip in the panko breading, making sure that the entire surface is encrusted with the breading.
- Fill a small pot three-quarters full with vegetable oil and attach a cooking thermometer. Bring the oil to 175°C/350°F over high heat. Add the battered sweetbreads and fry for 2 minutes, then remove with a slotted spoon and let rest on a paper towel. Season the sweetbreads with fine sea salt.
- Place 1 slice of fried sweetbread in each bowl of lobster bisque.
- Float 1 vegetable dashi veil on top of each bowl.
- Place 1 small fennel frond on top of each veil.
- Top each bowl with dehydrated seaweed.
- Decorate each bowl with a few petals of pickled pearl onion and 1 sea grape stem.

LAND

I WAS JUST six years old when I first understood where meat comes from. My uncle Jean Fagot raised pigs and cows on his farm in Brittany, and one day my brother and I were sleeping in the farmhouse when we were awakened by the sound of inhuman screaming. I looked out the window and saw my uncle and his men chasing a little pig around the yard, which was already covered with blood. In retrospect, I realize that the scene I found so frightening at the time was actually much better than what one would find these days in an industrial slaughterhouse. My uncle's farm practiced a responsible orientation to meat: That pig was raised humanely with plenty of fresh air and wholesome food, and every last bit of its body was used, starting with blood sausage made right in the yard that day, and extending to rillettes, head cheese, *saucisson*, and pâté. There is an incredible tradition of charcuterie in France, and my family made practically everything you can make from a pig. My father even aged his own ham in a cave, just like generations and generations before him.

But pigs these days are often raised in cramped crates, crowded into filthy pens, and flooded with antibiotics, which still fail to protect their health and the health of people who eat their meat. I have come to the conclusion that my conscience will not permit me to participate in the mainstream pork industry. So while you may see lardo or pork belly as an accent at Atelier Crenn, we are very, very careful with the sourcing, and you will never see a big pork chop at the center of the plate, even though I know that some people may miss that sort of dish.

Trust me, I am aware that there are snippy comments floating around the Internet that our tasting menu is light on meat, but the truth is, I do it intentionally. I design my menus as a conscious effort to move toward a new cultural orientation that acknowledges and celebrates the joys of eating meat, but doesn't perpetuate the false belief that the center of our diet—or the culmination of the tasting menu—should be a large slab of meat.

When it comes to beef, I have serious concerns about the ethical, environmental, health, and culinary consequences of industrial ranching. We have come distressingly far from the kind of beef raised on my uncle's ranch in Brittany, where beef was delicious and wholesome, without hormones or antibiotics. I remember watching the cattle head out to the pasture in the morning and back to their spacious barn at night, and feeling that we knew and loved the individual cow who gave us our milk and our meat. That way of life may be lost forever, but Japanese Wagyu is the closest approximation that I have found, and so that is what we serve at Atelier Crenn. Wagyu cattle are treated kindly and not overmedicated; not coincidentally, their flavor is also far superior, so I prefer to serve it uncooked. I understand that completely raw beef is less appreciated in the United States than in France, and so our kitchen has developed a curing and fermenting process that "cooks" the beef while retaining the intense natural flavor and some of the texture of raw beef.

Several of the recipes in this chapter feature poultry, and one includes foie gras, which deserves an explanation in light of what I have written about animal cruelty. Intellectually, I oppose foie gras, and we stopped serving it at Atelier Crenn years ago, but my happy childhood memories of visiting another aunt, Madeleine Quelennec, at her foie gras farm in Lot-et-Garonne in southwestern France have left me with an emotional attachment to foie gras that I cannot deny. I remember playing in the farmyard filled with noisy ducks and geese, and they seemed very happy to me, though perhaps that was the naiveté of youth. The birds I saw certainly roamed freely, but I understand now that they must have been force-fed and that the practice is cruel. And yet and yet and yet: I still love foie gras. When I imagine seeing just one more of my aunt's foie gras terrines, I know I would devour it with joy in my heart. In the end, I decided to include a foie gras dish (page 183) from the early days of Atelier Crenn as an acknowledgment of my own evolution as an eater and a chef. After all, if this book is about the "metamorphosis of taste," then I must honor the ways our menu has changed over the years.

But I draw the line at chicken. You will never see chicken at Atelier Crenn, in the kitchen, the dining room, staff meal, or even chicken stock. We happily serve other breeds of poultry, like duck, pintade, and squab (see pages 159, 189, 197, and 203), but we make pintade consommé (page 318) for use as a cooking liquid. The smaller market for specialty poultry breeds means that the birds tend to be raised more thoughtfully and ethically than chicken, and perhaps as a result, they offer more flavor and character than the washed-out chicken sold in this country. To be clear, I am not opposed to eating chicken in principle, but I have not yet found a chicken supplier that meets the standards of Atelier Crenn. We do use chicken eggs in our recipes quite a bit, because there is really no viable substitute for the classic chicken egg, but they are raised ethically, organically, and locally. (For what it's worth, I'm quite skeptical of the term "free range," which seems to have been drained of any specific meaning, if it ever had one. I want an egg farmer who loves his or her chickens and raises them according to his or her conscience, not some arbitrary certification.) As the chef of a forty-seat restaurant, I recognize that I have a very small effect on the gargantuan poultry industry, yet I hope to teach the cooks who pass through my kitchen how to work with better birds and perhaps even cultivate a new orientation among diners.

In the end, it's not just the ethics of meat that concern me, but the environmental consequences as well. I truly believe in moving meat to the side of the plate, along the lines advocated by Chef Dan Barber in his book *The Third Plate*. If we are going to eat animals, we should limit ourselves to humane, sustainable, organic farms, and we simply must eat less meat. To be perfectly honest, I am very moderate in my personal meat consumption. I cook with meat and I relish the flavors, but I believe we must treat animals respectfully and to do so, we must consider meat with our eyes open—even if it makes us uncomfortable. It is no accident that this is the shortest chapter in my book. As an animal lover and a chef, this is my stance: We must eat less meat, we must eat it more thoughtfully, and we must make it so delicious that our cooking becomes a way of showing respect for the animal that has given up its life for us.

One windy day in the summer of 2012, I was walking with a friend in San Francisco's Buena Vista Park. Our dogs were running ahead of us, and we were rambling after them, deeply engrossed in a discussion of the politics and ethics of California's recent ban on foie gras (which was later lifted). I was concentrating hard, listening to her point of view, but conscious of clinging to my own happy memories of eating foie gras made by my aunt Madeleine. By chance, I looked up into the canopy and saw a little bird's nest nestled on the lowest branch of a live oak. Suddenly, I was inspired. At Atelier Crenn, we use a nest as our logo, because it symbolizes the conjunction of art and nature, but in that moment, I understood the nest as a powerful emblem of rebirth as well. I saw that it was time to let go of one of my favorite dishes, which envisioned foie gras as a fallen log (see page 183). It was time to build a nest and cultivate something new. I immediately sketched my vision of a dish called Birth, with a nest filled with eggs and surrounded by branches, though I did not know at first how to execute the idea. It took quite a bit of experimentation to develop a good nest from corn silk, until we learned to keep the nest in the dehydrator until right before plating the dish, but that kind of painstaking creative process is exactly what this dish is all about. It's a matter of evolution. I pay homage to my memories of foie gras with a foundational layer of duck liver pâté, which literally and figuratively underlies my corn silk nest filled with corn "eggs" flavored with duck fat and garnished with dark chocolate branches. Ultimately, I want this dish to communicate the way that a chef is indebted to culinary tradition, that every inspiration is a reinvention, and that every birth is a rebirth. | *Serves 20*

Birth

DUCK LIVER PÂTÉ

INGREDIENTS
225 grams (8 ounces) duck liver
Whole milk, to cover
6 grams (1¼ teaspoons) fine sea salt
3 grams (¼ tablespoon) granulated sugar
3 grams (1½ teaspoons) pink curing salt
Vegetable oil
75 grams (½ cup) peeled green apple
50 grams (1.8 ounces) peeled shallot
10 grams (0.35 ounces) peeled garlic
 (1 to 2 cloves)
100 grams (6¾ tablespoons) Madeira
 wine
400 grams (1½ cups plus 3 tablespoons)
 heavy cream
0.5 gram guar gum
0.5 gram xanthan gum

>>>

At least 1 day before serving:

- In a storage container with a tight-fitting lid, combine the duck liver with enough whole milk to cover. Refrigerate, covered, for 24 hours.

The next day:

- In a small bowl, mix together the fine sea salt, sugar, and pink curing salt.
- Rinse the duck liver with cool water.
- **TO COOK THE DUCK LIVER SOUS VIDE:** In a vacuum bag, combine the duck liver with the salt-and-sugar mixture. Seal the bag and shake to ensure that the entire surface of the duck liver is covered in the salt-and-sugar mixture. Cook the duck sous vide in an immersion circulator set to 68°C/155°F until the duck liver is light pinkish-brown, similar in color to a camel-hair coat, about 20 minutes.

>>>

Birth, *continued*

EQUIPMENT

Vacuum bag or resealable plastic
    freezer bag
Vacuum sealer (*optional*)
Immersion circulator or
    cooking thermometer
Blender
Fine-mesh strainer
Pastry bag

- **TO COOK THE DUCK LIVER ON THE STOVETOP:** In a resealable plastic freezer bag, combine the duck liver with the salt-and-sugar mixture. Seal the bag and shake to ensure that the entire surface of the duck liver is covered in the salt-and-sugar mixture. Squeeze out as much air as possible and seal the bag again.
Fill a large pot three-quarters full with water and attach a cooking thermometer; bring the water to 68°C/155°F over medium heat and submerge the bag, closely monitoring the heat to maintain a consistent temperature and stirring often, until the duck liver is light pinkish-brown, similar in color to a camel-hair coat, about 20 minutes.
- Set the duck liver aside in the bag at room temperature to cool.
- Peel and chop the apple into small (¼-inch) dice. Mince the shallot and garlic.
- Coat a large pan with a thin layer of vegetable oil and sweat the apple, shallot, and garlic over medium-low heat until tender, about 2 minutes.
- **TO DEGLAZE THE PAN:** Add the Madeira wine and raise the heat to medium, scraping the bottom of the pan with a flat spoon or spatula, until the volume reduces by half, about 2 minutes. Add the cream and simmer, scraping the bottom occasionally, for 10 minutes. Add the duck livers and continue to simmer the liquid for 2 minutes.
- Transfer the duck livers and deglazing liquids to a blender. Puree on high speed until completely smooth, about 1 minute. Reduce the blender speed to low and pour the guar gum and xanthan gum directly into the liquid without touching the sides of the blender, about 20 seconds.
- Strain the puree through a fine-mesh strainer and transfer to a pastry bag.
- Refrigerate until ready to serve.

CORN SILK NEST

INGREDIENTS
10 whole ears sweet corn
Neutral vegetable oil

EQUIPMENT
Acetate sheet
Dehydrator (*optional*)
Cooking thermometer
Slotted spoon or wire skimmer

At least 3½ hours before serving:

- Use a sharp knife to cut the top and bottom off each ear of corn. Use the corn silk in this recipe and reserve the corn on the cob for the corn pearls component. Discard the ends and husks.
- **TO DRY THE CORN SILK IN A DEHYDRATOR:** Place an acetate sheet in a dehydrator tray. Evenly spread the corn silk across the acetate sheet. Transfer the tray to a dehydrator set to 60°C/140°F until completely dry and crispy, about 3 hours. Reserve the acetate sheet for further dehydration.
- **TO DRY THE CORN SILK IN THE OVEN:** Preheat the oven to 60°C/140°F or the closest temperature available. Place an acetate sheet on a baking sheet. Evenly spread the corn silk across the acetate sheet. Transfer the baking sheet to the oven and turn off the heat. Let the corn silk dry in the closed oven with the heat off until completely dry and crispy, about 3 hours. Reserve the acetate sheet for further drying.
- **TO FRY THE CORN SILK:** Fill a deep medium pot with 6 inches of vegetable oil and attach a cooking thermometer. Heat the oil to 150°C/300°F over medium-high heat. For each nest, add 1 small handful of corn silk and fry until lightly golden brown, about 45 seconds. Remove the corn silk with a slotted spoon or wire skimmer and transfer to paper towels. Let sit on paper towels for 10 minutes to drain excess oil.
- Shape the fried corn silk into 20 circular, 1-inch diameter nests.
- **TO CRISP THE CORN SILK NESTS IN A DEHYDRATOR:** Transfer the corn silk nests to the acetate-lined dehydrator tray. Transfer the tray to a dehydrator set to 60°C/140°F to crisp and hold until ready to serve.
- **TO CRISP THE CORN SILK NESTS IN THE OVEN:** Preheat the oven to 60°C/140°F or the closest temperature available. Transfer the corn silk nests back to the acetate-lined baking sheet. Transfer the baking sheet to the oven and turn off the heat. Let the corn silk nests crisp and hold in the closed oven until ready to serve.

>>>

Birth, *continued*

PEAR PUREE

INGREDIENTS

5 Bosc pears
12 grams (1 tablespoon) granulated sugar
6 grams (1¼ teaspoons) fine sea salt
0.6 gram xanthan gum

EQUIPMENT

Vacuum bag or resealable plastic
    freezer bag
Vacuum sealer (*optional*)
Immersion circulator or
    cooking thermometer
Blender
Squeeze bottle

At least 90 minutes before serving:

- Peel, quarter, and score the pears.
- **TO COOK THE PEAR SOUS VIDE**: Transfer 600 grams
  (1.3 pounds) of the pear to a vacuum bag, seal the bag, and
  compress at 99%. Cook the pear sous vide in an immersion
  circulator set to 85°C/185°F until tender, about 1 hour.
- **TO COOK THE PEAR ON THE STOVETOP**: Transfer
  600 grams (1.3 pounds) of pear to a resealable plastic freezer bag,
  squeeze out as much air as possible, and seal the bag. Fill a large
  pot three-quarters full with water and attach a cooking thermometer; bring the water to 85°C/185°F over medium-low heat and
  submerge the bag, closely monitoring the heat to maintain a consistent temperature and stirring often, until tender, about 1 hour.
- Open the vacuum bag or resealable plastic freezer bag, transfer
  the pears to a blender, and blend at low speed. Pour the sugar,
  salt, and xanthan gum directly onto the center of the liquid
  without touching the sides of the blender while blending on low
  speed until fully incorporated, 20 seconds.
- Transfer the mixture to a squeeze bottle and refrigerate until
  ready to serve.

VANILLA PUREE

INGREDIENTS

400 grams (1⅔ cups) whole milk
30 grams (2½ tablespoons) granulated
    sugar
4 vanilla beans
4.4 grams agar-agar

EQUIPMENT

Fine-mesh strainer
13 x 18-inch (half-sheet) pan
Parchment paper
Blender
Squeeze bottle

At least 1 hour before serving:

- In a medium pot, combine the milk and sugar and bring to a
  simmer over medium-low heat, then remove from the heat.
- Split the vanilla beans in half. Scrape the vanilla bean seeds into
  the liquid and add the scraped vanilla bean pods to the liquid.
  Cover the pot and allow to steep for 30 minutes.
- Strain the liquid through a fine-mesh strainer.
- In a medium pot, bring the liquid to a simmer over medium-low
  heat. Whisk in the agar-agar for 15 seconds and remove from
  the heat.
- Line a 13 x 18-inch (half-sheet) pan with parchment paper.
  Pour the liquid onto the parchment paper and refrigerate, uncov-
  ered, until the liquid sets to a gel, about 30 minutes.
- Transfer to a blender and puree until smooth, about 2 minutes.
  Refrigerate, covered, until ready to serve.
- Transfer to a squeeze bottle and refrigerate until ready to serve.

COMPRESSED PEAR

INGREDIENTS
200 grams (1 cup) granulated sugar
2 grams (½ teaspoon) ascorbic acid
2 grams (scant ½ teaspoon) fine sea salt
3 Bosc pears

EQUIPMENT
Vacuum bag
Vacuum sealer
Fine-mesh strainer

CHOCOLATE BRANCHES

INGREDIENTS
400 grams (14 ounces) dark chocolate,
    preferably Valrhona Caraïbe,
    66% cocoa
100 grams (3.5 ounces) white chocolate,
    preferably Valrhona Opalys,
    33% cocoa

EQUIPMENT
Double boiler or large metal bowl
Cooking thermometer
Pastry bag
Slotted spoon

At least 40 minutes before serving:

- In a medium pot, combine 200 grams (¾ cup plus 1½ tablespoons) water with the sugar, ascorbic acid, and fine sea salt. Bring to a simmer over low heat and stir until the sugar has dissolved, about 2 minutes. Remove from the heat and let sit, uncovered, until the mixture has cooled to room temperature.
- Peel, halve, and core the pears.
- **TO BRUNOISE THE PEARS:** Lay the pear halves on a cutting board flat-side down and cut lengthwise into ⅛-inch slices. Turn the slices 90 degrees, so that they lie flat against the cutting board, and slice again at ⅛-inch intervals to make matchsticks. Cut against the grain of the matchsticks at ⅛-inch intervals to create ⅛-inch cubes. Discard any imperfect cubes.
- **TO COMPRESS THE PEARS:** In a vacuum bag, combine the pear cubes with the sugar liquid and compress the bag at 99%. Let the pears marinate for 30 minutes.
- Open the bag, strain the contents through a fine-mesh strainer, and discard the liquid.
- Refrigerate, covered, until ready to serve.

- **TO TEMPER THE CHOCOLATE:** Fill a double boiler or small pot halfway with water over low heat and attach a cooking thermometer. When the water begins to steam, place the top of the double boiler or a large bowl over the pot without touching the water. Add the dark chocolate and the white chocolate to the bowl and melt over low heat, stirring often, while raising the temperature to 45°C/113°F to 48°C/118°F.
- Remove from the heat and let cool to 28°C/82°F, stirring often. Return the bowl to the steaming pot and bring the temperature of the chocolate back up to 30°C/86°F.
- Transfer the chocolate to a pastry bag and let sit for 5 minutes at room temperature in the pastry bag.
- Fill a large storage container with very cold water without any ice.
- Working in batches of 2 or 3, squeeze at least twenty 12-inch lengths of chocolate into the water and remove with a slotted spoon to rest on a paper towel. (You may want to create a few extra, in case of breakage.) Allow the chocolate branches to dry thoroughly, then transfer to an airtight container.
- Store at room temperature until ready to serve.

>>>

Birth, *continued*

CORN PEARLS

INGREDIENTS

10 shucked ears corn (reserved from
    corn silk nest component)
35 grams (1.25 ounces) duck fat
2 egg yolks
1 gram fine sea salt

EQUIPMENT

Juicer (*optional*)
Blender
Squeeze bottle
Acetate sheet (*optional*)
Liquid nitrogen (*optional*)
Slotted spoon

If you do not have a juicer or have access to liquid nitrogen:

- Use a sharp knife to slice the corn kernels from the ears of corn. In a medium saucepan, melt the duck fat over very low heat. Add the corn kernels, raise the heat to medium-low, and cook gently, stirring occasionally, for 5 minutes. Keep warm until ready to serve.

If you have a juicer and liquid nitrogen:

- Use a sharp knife to slice the corn kernels from the ears of corn. Juice the corn kernels in a juicer.
- In a small saucepan over very low heat, melt the duck fat.
- In a blender, combine 500 grams (1.1 pounds) of the corn juice with the egg yolks and puree on high speed for 1 minute. Reduce the blender speed to low and slowly pour in the melted duck fat. Turn off the blender and season the mixture with fine sea salt.
- Transfer the corn mixture to a squeeze bottle and allow to cool to room temperature.
- **TO FREEZE THE CORN PEARLS WITH LIQUID NITROGEN:** Line a pan with an acetate sheet. Put on insulated gloves and safety glasses. Working in batches of 20 drops, squeeze small drops of the corn mixture into the liquid nitrogen. Scoop out the frozen corn pearls with a slotted spoon and transfer to the acetate-lined pan. Reserve in the freezer until ready to serve.

PUFFED WILD RICE

INGREDIENTS

160 grams (¾ cup) vegetable oil
20 grams (¼ cup) uncooked wild rice
Fine sea salt

EQUIPMENT

Cooking thermometer
Wire skimmer

- In a small pot with a cooking thermometer attached, heat the vegetable oil over high heat to 190°C/375°F. Add the uncooked wild rice and fry until it puffs and turns golden brown, 30 to 45 seconds. Turn off the heat, remove the wild rice with a wire skimmer, and spread on a paper towel to drain excess oil, about 5 minutes. Season with a generous pinch of fine sea salt.
- Keep in an airtight container at room temperature until ready to serve.

INGREDIENTS

Micro basil

Micro chamomile

- Spoon two 1-tablespoon mounds of wild rice onto each plate. Squeeze 5 dots of the pear puree and 5 dots of the vanilla puree around the plate. Scatter the compressed pear among the other components.
- In the center of each plate, scoop a large quenelle of duck liver pâté and press the corn silk nest into the pâté. Fill the nests with the corn pearls or cooked corn kernels.
- Top each nest with 1 chocolate branch.
- Garnish the entire plate with micro basil and micro chamomile leaves.

This is our version of broccoli beef, though at this point our fermented, cured, emulsified, and dehydrated interpretation hardly resembles the wok-fried dish found at so many American Chinese restaurants. In fact, my favorite part of our version has no counterpart in traditional broccoli beef: the egg sheet that a former chef de cuisine developed in several stages, beginning when he was the pastry chef at another restaurant. The creative process began when he was playing around with egg yolks for a dessert and produced a semi-set clear egg yolk sheet. As he continued to work with it, he found a way to make the egg completely pliable and translucent. We thought about making a flourless egg noodle, but in the end, we decided to play with the tartare by wrapping it in the egg sheet. The final recipe didn't come together until we were working on curing techniques at Atelier Crenn, so it was almost a year between the first egg sheet and its culmination as a translucent wrapper. We cure the beef in ginger, garlic, and scallions, which are central to a lot of Chinese cuisine, and I think that overall, the dish is both playful and respectful in its engagement with another culinary tradition. We are not dogmatic in our adherence to the theme, and we allow ourselves to use sake kasu, which is Japanese, because it helps to firm up our well-marbled Wagyu beef, which is also from Japan. In the end, if there is a conflict between the idea behind a dish and the experience of eating it, we will always choose flavor and texture. | *Serves 10*

NOTE: *This recipe calls for significantly more beef than will be served in the final dish, because the process of curing and fermenting requires a minimum mass to maintain the correct texture. If we were to cure and ferment a small piece of beef, the end product would feel like sausage rather than tartare.*

Broccoli and Beef Tartare

BROCCOLI STEMS AND FLORETS

INGREDIENTS
2 heads broccoli
1,350 grams (5¾ cups) sake kasu

EQUIPMENT
Y-shaped peeler
Cheesecloth
Vacuum bag or resealable plastic
    freezer bag
Vacuum sealer (*optional*)
Slotted spoon
Wire skimmer
Acetate sheet
Dehydrator (*optional*)

At least 2 days before serving:

- Wash the broccoli. Use a sharp knife to cut the florets from the stems and set them aside separately.
- Use a Y-shaped peeler to peel the broccoli stems. In a medium storage container, cover the broccoli in sake kasu, cover the contents of the container with a layer of cheesecloth, and cover with the container's lid, leaving a small crack for ventilation (i.e., do not seal the lid). Let the container sit at room temperature for 2 days.
- Rinse the broccoli stems with cool water. Cut into fine (⅛-inch) dice. Transfer the diced broccoli stems to a vacuum bag or resealable plastic freezer bag and seal. Refrigerate in the sealed bag until ready to serve.

>>>

Broccoli and Beef Tartare, *continued*

At least 1 day before serving:

- Trim the broccoli florets to small (¼-inch) dice.
- Prepare an ice water bath.
- Fill a medium pot three-quarters full with water salted at 2% of the total weight and bring to a boil over medium-high heat. Add the broccoli florets and blanch until soft, about 3 minutes. Remove the broccoli florets with a slotted spoon or wire skimmer and plunge into the ice water bath to cool. Transfer the broccoli florets to paper towels and allow to air-dry at room temperature for 30 minutes.
- **TO DRY THE BROCCOLI FLORETS IN A DEHYDRATOR:** Place an acetate sheet in a dehydrator tray. Evenly spread the broccoli florets across the dehydrator tray. Transfer the tray to a dehydrator set to 95°C/200°F and dry the broccoli until crispy, 24 hours.
- **TO DRY THE BROCCOLI FLORETS IN THE OVEN:** Preheat the oven to 95°C/200°F or the closest temperature available. Place an acetate sheet on a baking sheet. Evenly spread the broccoli florets across the acetate sheet. Transfer the baking sheet to the oven and turn off the heat. Let the broccoli florets dry in the closed oven with the heat off until crispy, 24 hours.
- Season with fine sea salt. Store at room temperature in an airtight container until ready to serve.

EGG YOLK SHEET

INGREDIENTS
24 eggs
Fine sea salt

>>>

NOTE: *This recipe is not recommended if you do not have an immersion circulator and vacuum sealer.*

Six to thirty hours before serving:

- **TO COOK THE EGGS SOUS VIDE:** Submerge the eggs in an immersion circulator set to 64°C/147°F for 2 hours.
- Remove the eggs from the water with a slotted spoon and chill in the refrigerator until cold, about 2 hours.
- Peel the eggs and rinse well in cool water. Use your hands to gently separate the yolks from the whites, and reserve the whites for another use.

Immersion circulator

Pastry scraper

Tamis

Kitchen scale

Pastry bag or squeeze bottle

2 acetate sheets

Nonstick cooking spray

Vacuum bag

Vacuum sealer

- Use paper towels to carefully dry the yolks. If there is any residual water on the yolks, the egg yolk sheet will not be clear.

- Use a pastry scraper to press the yolks through a tamis. Weigh the yolks on a kitchen scale.

- In a large bowl, salt the yolks at 0.8% of the total weight, stirring the yolks gently to avoid incorporating air, until well mixed. At this point, the yolks should have the texture of a thick jam.

- Transfer 300 grams (10.6 ounces) of the mixture to a pastry bag or squeeze bottle for plating and refrigerate until ready to serve.

- **TO PREPARE THE ACETATE SHEETS**: Trim the acetate sheets to fit your vacuum bags. (At Atelier Crenn, we trim them to 8 x 9-inch rectangles to fit our 10 x 12-inch vacuum bags.) Spray the acetate sheets on one side with nonstick cooking spray and wipe down with a paper towel; the residual nonstick coating will suffice. For 8 x 9-inch acetate sheets, place 1 acetate sheet, sprayed-side up, on a kitchen scale, add 55 grams (1.95 ounces) of egg yolk to the acetate sheet, and press down with the coated side of a second acetate sheet. If you are using another size, then add enough egg yolk to press into the thickness of a single sheet of paper. Transfer the acetate sheet to a vacuum bag and compress in a vacuum sealer at 99%. Repeat to create 1 egg sheet per guest.

- Without removing the acetate sheets from the vacuum bag, use a rolling pin to create a smooth and even layer of egg yolk.

- **TO COOK THE SHEETS SOUS VIDE**: Keeping the sheets inside the vacuum bag, submerge in an immersion circulator set to 72°C/162°F to cook for 35 minutes.

- Keeping the sheets inside the vacuum bag, refrigerate for at least 1 hour, but ideally for 24 hours.

- Remove the sheets from the vacuum bags but leave the egg yolk inside the acetate sheets. Trim the acetate sheets into 3½ x 2¼-inch rectangles. There will be some excess egg sheet. Transfer to an airtight container and refrigerate until ready to serve.

>>>

Broccoli and Beef Tartare, *continued*

GINGER-CURED BEEF

INGREDIENTS

80 grams (2.8 ounces) peeled
    fresh ginger
40 grams (1.4 ounces) scallion
15 grams (0.5 ounce) garlic
    (2 to 3 cloves)
300 grams (1½ cups) granulated sugar
280 grams (1 cup plus 2 tablespoons)
    fine sea salt
20 grams (3 tablespoons plus
    1 teaspoon) pink curing salt
1 A1 Wagyu Beef rib cap, untrimmed

EQUIPMENT

Box grater
Kitchen scale

At least 13 hours before serving:

- **TO MAKE THE CURE:** Grate the ginger with a box grater. Wash, trim, and roughly chop the scallion and garlic. In a large bowl, mix together the ginger, scallion, and garlic. Add the sugar, fine sea salt, and pink curing salt and mix well.
- Dip the Wagyu beef in the cure and scoop some on top, making sure the entire surface of the beef is covered. Cover tightly with plastic wrap and refrigerate for 12 hours.

One hour before serving:

- Rinse the beef with cool water and pat dry with paper towels.
- Cut the beef into thirds. Set aside one-third at room temperature, because warmer meat will be easier to scrape. Cut the other two-thirds into ⅛-inch-thick slices and refrigerate, covered, because cold meat is easier to cut. When the beef slices have firmed up, cut each slice into ⅛-inch matchsticks and refrigerate again. When the beef matchsticks have firmed again, cut them into ⅛-inch cubes. Refrigerate, covered, until ready to serve.
- Use a metal spoon to scrape the remaining one-third of the meat, working along the grain to produce a smooth meat paste or puree. As you scrape the meat, transfer it to a kitchen scale, and scrape until you have produced 40 grams (1.4 ounces) of scraped meat.
- Refrigerate, covered, until ready to serve.

MUSHROOM–SOY DRESSING

INGREDIENTS

40 grams (1.4 ounces) scallion

30 grams (1.1 ounces) garlic (5 cloves)

30 grams (1.1 ounces) peeled
   fresh ginger

90 grams (scant ½ cup) granulated sugar

60 grams (¼ cup) sake

30 grams (2 tablespoons) mirin

25 grams (4 teaspoons) high-quality
   soy sauce

450 grams (¾ cup plus 2½ tablespoons)
   Mushroom Broth (page 312)

24 grams Ultra-Tex 3

EQUIPMENT

Stockpot

Fine-mesh strainer

Six hours before serving:

- Prepare the Mushroom Broth (page 312).
- Clean, trim, and roughly cut the scallion, garlic, and ginger.
- **TO MAKE A SOFT CARAMEL:** Heat a large pan over medium-high heat and add the sugar in five increments, swirling the pan as it melts to prevent burning, until it is the color of dark leather, 10 to 15 minutes.
- Add the scallion, ginger, and garlic and cook over medium-high heat, stirring often, until they become aromatic, 2 to 4 minutes.
- Reduce the heat to low and add the sake, mirin, and soy sauce to deglaze, scraping the surface of the pan, until the volume has reduced by half, about 2 minutes.
- Add the mushroom broth and simmer over low heat for 10 minutes.
- Strain through a fine-mesh strainer. Discard the solids and return the liquid to the pan. Reduce the liquid until the flavor is quite concentrated, about 15 minutes.
- Transfer 120 grams (4.25 ounces) of the liquid to a large bowl, cover with plastic wrap, and refrigerate until cold. Whisk in the Ultra-Tex 3.
- Refrigerate, covered, until ready to serve.

GARLIC EMULSION

INGREDIENTS

2 heads garlic

Olive oil

1 large egg

120 grams (½ cup plus 1½ tablespoons)
   beef fat (reserved from ginger-cured
   beef component)

60 grams (4½ tablespoons) neutral
   vegetable oil

5 grams (1 teaspoon) fresh lemon juice

1 gram xanthan gum

1 gram (scant ¼ teaspoon) fine sea salt

0.1 gram cayenne pepper

EQUIPMENT

Blender

Fine-mesh strainer

At least 1 hour before serving:

- **TO ROAST THE GARLIC:** Preheat the oven to 190°C/375°F.
- Cut the tops off the garlic heads, leaving the skins intact. Wrap the garlic heads in aluminum foil and drizzle the exposed tops with olive oil. Roast until soft, 25 to 30 minutes.
- Separate the egg, reserving the white for another use.
- In a small pot, warm the beef fat over low heat until it melts, about 1 minute. Remove the beef fat from the heat and add the vegetable oil. Mix until incorporated.
- **TO MAKE THE GARLIC EMULSION:** In a blender, combine 50 grams (3 tablespoons plus 1 teaspoon) water with 35 grams (1.25 ounces) of the roasted garlic, 15 grams (0.55 ounce) of the egg yolk, the lemon juice, xanthan gum, salt, and cayenne. Puree on high speed until smooth, about 1 minute. Reduce the blender speed to low and slowly pour in the beef fat and vegetable oil until the texture becomes thick and creamy.
- Strain through a fine-mesh strainer.
- Refrigerate, covered, until ready to serve.

   >>>

Broccoli and Beef Tartare, *continued*

FRIED GARLIC

INGREDIENTS
325 grams (2 cups) garlic
Fine sea salt
Vegetable oil

EQUIPMENT
Blender
Fine-mesh strainer
Wire skimmer
Desiccant (*optional*)

- Place the garlic in a blender with enough water to cover. Pulse on medium speed until finely chopped but not pureed, about 1 minute. (If the garlic is blended too finely, it will burn, but if the pieces are too large, it will not be fried through; the water prevents the garlic from becoming a puree by separating the garlic pieces from one another.)
- Strain the garlic through a fine-mesh strainer and run under cold water until the water runs clear.
- **TO BLANCH THE GARLIC:** Transfer the garlic to a medium pot and cover with cold water. Bring to a boil over high heat, then strain through a fine-mesh strainer. Repeat with fresh water. For a third and final blanch, fill the pot with water salted at 1% of the total weight, add the garlic, and bring the water just to a boil. Strain the garlic through a fine-mesh strainer and rinse under cold water until the water runs clear.
- Transfer the garlic to a small pot and cover in cold vegetable oil. Bring to a boil over medium heat and watch closely, because once the water vapor stops rising from the pot, the garlic will begin to brown very quickly, as all of its internal moisture is cooked off, about 20 minutes. When the garlic is golden brown, remove it with a wire skimmer and transfer to a paper towel to cool. Season with fine sea salt.
- Once cooled to room temperature, transfer the garlic to a storage container with a paper towel inside to absorb any residual moisture. Add a desiccant to keep very dry, if desired.

TO SERVE:

INGREDIENTS
5 scallions
5 grams (1⅔ teaspoons) white sesame seeds
Maldon salt
Whole black peppercorns
Egg yolk mixture (reserved from egg yolk sheet component)

At least 2 hours before serving:

- Prepare an ice water bath.
- **TO CUT THE SCALLIONS INTO SKIRTS:** Trim ½ inch from the bottom of the scallions and discard. Trim the green leaves from the scallions and reserve. Cut the central white part of the scallion into ¾-inch lengths. Cut halfway into the scallion lengthwise to butterfly the layers. Use a paring knife to scrape the inside of the scallion until the outer membrane is removed.

EQUIPMENT

Sharp paring knife

Pepper mill

Slotted spoon or wire skimmer

Make a "grass skirt" effect by cutting slits along the grain of the scallion running from ¼ inch away from one end all the way through to the other end. Keep submerged in ice water until the tendrils curl, at least 2 hours.

- **TO MAKE SCALLION CURLS:** Trim the tops and bottoms of the green sections of the scallions and remove any imperfections. Slice through each tube along one side. Slice again on an angle, trying to make the longest, thinnest curl possible. Keep submerged in the ice water bath until they curl, at least 2 hours.

About 30 minutes before serving:

- Dice the fermented broccoli stems.
- **TO MAKE THE VEGETABLE MIXTURE:** In a large bowl, mix together 45 grams (1.6 ounces) of the diced fermented broccoli stems, 15 grams (0.55 ounce) of the fried garlic, 10 grams (0.35 ounce) of the dehydrated broccoli florets, and the white sesame seeds.
- **TO MIX 1 SERVING OF TARTARE:** In a small bowl, mix together 8 grams (0.3 ounce) of the diced beef and 4 grams (0.15 ounce) of the scraped beef. Add 7 grams (0.25 ounce) of the vegetable mixture and stir together with a spoon. Dress with garlic emulsion (about 5 grams per serving). Season with a pinch of Maldon salt and a turn of freshly ground black pepper.
- **TO WRAP THE TARTARE IN THE EGG SHEET:** Remove the egg sheets from the refrigerator; they should be flexible and translucent, like a piece of film. Unwrap one side of 1 acetate sheet from the egg yolk sheet and lay 1 serving of tartare in a stripe down the middle. Peel the egg yolk sheet away from the remaining acetate sheet while rolling the edges over the stripe of tartare. The egg yolk sheet should stick to itself, but can be secured further with a thin film of egg yolk mixture reserved from the egg yolk sheet component.
- Repeat the mixing and wrapping steps for the remaining 9 servings.
- Remove the scallions with a slotted spoon or wire skimmer and let dry on paper towels.
- **TO PLATE:** To secure the beef and egg sheet rolls, squeeze a thin 3-inch stripe of egg yolk jam off center on each plate. Place 1 roll on top of each stripe of egg yolk jam. Next to the roll, squeeze 3 dots of egg yolk jam in an isosceles triangle. Spoon 1 teaspoon of mushroom-soy dressing toward the center of the plate. Place 2 scallion skirts and 3 scallion curls over the egg yolk dots. Sprinkle the scallions with a small pinch of sesame seeds (about 5 seeds per plate).

I always thought of beef carpaccio as a very traditional dish—essentially, the Italian version of steak tartare—but it turns out that carpaccio is a much more recent invention, dating back only to 1950. According to the legend, when Harry's Bar in Venice began covering plates with paper-thin slices of beef, the owner noticed a resemblance to the red-and-white paintings of local painter Vittore Carpaccio, whose work was being shown nearby. I love the way that the history of art and cooking intersect in the story of carpaccio, and so I decided to give the dish yet another twist, by bringing the flat presentation of a classic carpaccio off the "canvas" of the plate into a sculptural dimension. The delicate cylinders of beef in Atelier Crenn's version are shaved from cured and fermented Wagyu beef, which preserves the immediacy and intensity of the meat flavor while accommodating diners who shy away from uncooked beef. The composed dish incorporates classic flavors associated with beef carpaccio, such as capers and red onion, as well as more surprising elements, like curried apple and squid ink brioche. Ultimately, I believe it offers both the pleasure of custom and the thrill of novelty, which is just what our atelier was designed to do. | *Serves 10*

Beef Carpaccio

CURED WAGYU BEEF WITH WHIPPED BEEF FAT

INGREDIENTS

900 grams (2 pounds) Wagyu
    rib-eye roast
1 clove garlic
20 grams (5 teaspoons) granulated sugar
20 grams (4 teaspoons) fine sea salt
2 grams nori powder
0.2 gram pink curing salt
¼ lime
1 beet
1 gram fish sauce, preferably
    Red Boat brand

EQUIPMENT

Juicer

At least 30 hours before serving:

- Use a very sharp knife to trim as much fat and gristle as possible from the beef. Wrap the trimmed fat in plastic wrap and reserve in the refrigerator for use the next day.
- Peel and mince the garlic. In a large bowl, mix together the garlic, sugar, fine sea salt, nori powder, garlic, and pink curing salt.
- Place the trimmed beef in the cure mixture. Use your fingers to rub the cure into the entire surface of the beef. Arrange the contents of the bowl so that the beef is covered with cure. Press plastic wrap into the bowl so that it rests on the beef and limits the amount of air in contact with the meat, then wrap the entire bowl again to ensure an airtight seal. Refrigerate for 24 hours. (At Atelier Crenn, we also ferment the beef in sake kasu for 3 to 4 days after curing it.)

The next day:

- Unwrap the beef and rinse in cool water, then dry thoroughly with paper towels. Tightly wrap each piece in plastic wrap and smooth into a cylindrical shape by rolling against a flat surface. Freeze the beef cylinder until it is frozen solid, at least 5 hours, until ready to serve.

>>>

Beef Carpaccio, *continued*

Up to 2 hours before serving:

- Squeeze the lime, measure out 2 grams (scant ½ teaspoon) of lime juice, and reserve the remainder for another use.
- Use a juicer to juice the beet.
- In a small pot, cook the beet juice over medium heat until it has reduced by half.
- In a double boiler, melt the reserved Wagyu fat over low heat.
- Fill a medium bowl with ice and 40 grams (2¾ tablespoons) water. Place a small metal bowl on top and add 100 grams (1 cup) of the liquid beef fat. Add a pinch of fine sea salt and whisk until the fat starts to harden; continue whisking while gradually adding 2 grams of reduced beet juice together with the fish sauce and lime juice, until fully emulsified, about 5 minutes. Transfer to an airtight container and refrigerate until ready to use.

SQUID INK BRIOCHE SOIL

INGREDIENTS

15 grams (1 tablespoon) unsalted butter
200 grams dry brioche, homemade (page 331) or store-bought
11 grams (0.4 ounce) squid ink powder
2 grams (scant ½ teaspoon) fine sea salt

EQUIPMENT

Food processor
Acetate sheet
Dehydrator (*optional*)

At least 3 hours before serving:

- Let the butter sit at room temperature to soften.
- Cut the brioche into ½-inch pieces.
- In a food processor, combine the softened butter and 1 gram of the squid ink powder and blend on high speed, scraping down the sides with a spatula as needed, until fully incorporated, about 2 minutes.
- Add the brioche pieces and the remaining 10 grams (0.35 ounce) squid ink powder and pulse until the mixture attains a soil-like consistency.
- **TO DRY THE SQUID INK BRIOCHE IN A DEHYDRATOR:** Place an acetate sheet in a dehydrator tray. Evenly spread the brioche soil across the acetate sheet. Transfer the tray to a dehydrator set to 60°C/140°F and dry the brioche for 3 hours.
- **TO DRY THE SQUID INK BRIOCHE IN THE OVEN:** Preheat the oven to 60°C/140°F or the closest temperature available. Place an acetate sheet on a baking sheet. Evenly spread the brioche soil across the acetate sheet. Transfer the baking sheet to the oven and turn off the heat. Let the squid ink brioche dry in the closed oven with the heat off for at least 3 hours.
- Season with fine sea salt.
- Store in an airtight container at room temperature for up to 1 week.

CURRY-APPLE PUREE

INGREDIENTS

3 Granny Smith apples
40 grams (3 tablespoons plus
    1 teaspoon) granulated sugar
4 grams vadouvan (French curry powder)
Fine sea salt

EQUIPMENT

Fine-mesh strainer
Blender

At least 1 hour before serving:

- Preheat the oven to 200°C/390°F.
- Peel, quarter, and core the apples.
- On a baking sheet, spread the apple quarters into a single layer and roast at 200°C/390°F until soft and lightly caramelized, about 25 minutes.
- In a small pot, combine 40 grams (¼ cup) water with the sugar, vadouvan, and a pinch of fine sea salt. Bring to a simmer over high heat, then immediately remove from the heat and steep for 10 minutes.
- Strain the liquid through a fine-mesh strainer into a blender. Add 300 grams (10.6 ounces) of the roasted apple and blend on high speed until the mixture is a very smooth puree, about 30 seconds.
- Refrigerate, covered, for up to 2 days until ready to serve.

HORSERADISH CRÈME FRAÎCHE ÉPAISSE

INGREDIENTS

100 grams (3.5 ounces) peeled
    fresh horseradish
200 grams (7.1 ounces)
    Crème Fraîche Épaisse (page 297)
    or store-bought crème fraîche
0.2 gram guar gum
0.1 gram xanthan gum
Fine sea salt

EQUIPMENT

Juicer or Microplane grater
Fine-mesh strainer (*optional*)
Blender
Squeeze bottle

At least 30 minutes before serving:

- Use a juicer to juice the horseradish; alternatively, grate the horseradish with a Microplane grater and press the pulp through a fine-mesh strainer.
- Transfer 10 grams (0.35 ounce) of the horseradish juice to a blender. Reserve the pulp and any additional horseradish juice for another use. Add the crème fraîche épaisse to the blender and blend on high until fully incorporated, about 10 seconds. Reduce the blender speed to low and pour the guar gum and xanthan gum directly into the liquid without touching the sides of the blender, about 10 seconds.
- Season with fine sea salt.
- Transfer to a squeeze bottle and refrigerate until ready to serve.

>>>

Beef Carpaccio, *continued*

PICKLED MUSTARD SEEDS

INGREDIENTS

150 grams (2¼ cups) yellow mustard
    seeds
50 grams (4 teaspoons) champagne
    vinegar
50 grams (4 teaspoons) sherry vinegar
50 grams (¼ cup) granulated sugar
Fine sea salt

EQUIPMENT

Kitchen scale

- In a small nonreactive pot, combine 200 grams (¾ cup plus 1½ tablespoons) water with the mustard seeds, champagne vinegar, sherry vinegar, and sugar. Simmer over medium-low heat until the mustard seeds are tender and the liquid has thickened to the consistency of a syrup, about 15 minutes.
- Weigh the cooked mustard seeds, add 1% of the total weight in fine sea salt, and mix well.
- Refrigerate in an airtight container for up to 1 week.

INGREDIENTS

30 capers

10 grams whole pink peppercorns

50 grams (1.75 ounces) garlic (8 cloves)

Neutral vegetable oil

Maldon salt

10 micro wasabi leaves (*optional*)

10 micro shiso leaves (*optional*)

10 grams toasted black sesame seeds

EQUIPMENT

Pepper mill

Deli slicer or sharp paring knife

Slotted spoon or wire skimmer

TO SERVE:

- Chill the plates in the refrigerator.
- Drain the capers and let sit on paper towels.
- In a sauté pan, toast the pink peppercorns over medium heat, tossing occasionally to avoid burning, until the peppercorns become fragrant, 30 to 60 seconds. Remove from the heat, let cool to room temperature, and transfer to a pepper mill.
- Mince the garlic. In a medium pan, heat a thin layer of vegetable oil over medium-high heat for 2 minutes. Add the minced garlic and fry until brown and crisp, about 2 minutes.
- Remove the fried garlic from the pan. Add a bit more vegetable oil to the pan and heat over medium-high heat for 1 minute. Add the capers and fry for 1 minute. Transfer the capers to a paper towel to drain excess oil.
- Immediately before serving, remove the cured Wagyu beef from the freezer and unwrap. Use a deli slicer or your sharpest knife to cut the beef lengthwise into very thin slices. Roll each slice into a tight spiral and brush with the whipped beef fat.
- **TO PLATE**: Spread a thin layer of squid ink brioche soil on each plate and place 1 beef spiral on top of it. Sprinkle a few grains of Maldon salt on each beef spiral.
- Use a spoon to drop small dollops of curry-apple gel, red onion gel, and pickled mustard seeds on and around the beef. Squeeze pearls of horseradish crème fraîche épaisse on and around the beef.
- Garnish with the micro wasabi and micro shiso or other seasonal herbs, if desired.
- Garnish the entire plate with the fried garlic, fried capers, toasted black sesame seeds, and ground pink peppercorns. (At Atelier Crenn, we also dust the plate with dehydrated porcini mushroom powder.)

The literal meaning of *foie gras* is "fatty liver," and it is created by force-feeding ducks or geese through *gavage*, a practice that dates back all the way to ancient Egypt. In recent years, some duck and goose farmers have experimented with humane ways to fatten the livers, notably Eduardo Sousa from Spain, who won the Coup de Coeur award at the Salon International d'Alimentation in Paris in 2006. French commentators were upset by this result because it felt like a contradiction in terms; in France, *gavage* is legally required for a product to be labeled as foie gras. On a deeper level, perhaps, it felt like a condemnation of a deeply treasured part of the French experience, which I certainly understand. I was very young when I first ate foie gras, and it was given to me by my aunt, who loved the birds she raised. At the time, it was impossible for me to interpret this rich and creamy delicacy as anything remotely related to cruelty, but these days, I understand foie gras differently, and I have learned to live without it. As an animal lover and a Frenchwoman living in America, though, the whole debate is still quite foreign to me. I can't help thinking that it is strange to see so many people up in arms over a tiny subset of the meat industry, which creates a specialty product served in very small portions, when millions and millions of chickens, pigs, and cattle in this country suffer much worse conditions and scarcely anyone says a word about it. In the end, cruelty is cruelty, and I do not condone foie gras, but I would like to offer my own perspective on the conversation. | *Serves 10*

Foie Gras with Winter Nuances

FOIE GRAS CURLS

INGREDIENTS
I whole lobe grade-A foie gras
1,460 grams (6 cups) whole milk
40 grams (1.4 ounces) kosher salt
19 grams (2⅔ teaspoons) pink
    curing salt

EQUIPMENT
Vacuum bag or resealable plastic
    freezer bag
Vacuum sealer (*optional*)
Immersion circulator or
    cooking thermometer
Sharp flat-bladed knife (slicer)

At least 30 hours before serving:

- Remove the foie gras from the refrigerator and allow to sit at room temperature for I to 2 hours to soften. Rinse the foie gras with cool water and pat dry with paper towels. Gently wipe away any blood spots.
- **TO DEVEIN THE FOIE GRAS:** Gently pull the small and large sections apart without severing the vein between them. Find the main Y-shaped vein and use a butter knife or tweezers to gently scrape the vein from the foie gras, while keeping the vein intact, working alternately on each branch of the Y-shape, until you can use your fingers to tug the entire vein off the foie gras.
- In a storage container, combine the milk, kosher salt, and pink curing salt and whisk for 30 seconds.
- Submerge the foie gras in the milk cure, cover with plastic wrap, and refrigerate for 24 hours.

>>>

Foie Gras with Winter Nuances, *continued*

At least 5 hours before serving:

- **TO COOK THE FOIE GRAS SOUS VIDE:** Remove the foie gras from the milk cure, place the foie gras in a vacuum bag, seal the bag, and compress at 99%. Cook the foie gras sous vide in an immersion circulator set to 30°C/86°F for 2 hours.

- **TO COOK THE FOIE GRAS ON THE STOVETOP:** Remove the foie gras from the milk cure, place the foie gras in a resealable plastic freezer bag, squeeze out as much air as possible, and seal the bag. Fill a large pot three-quarters full with water and attach a cooking thermometer; bring the water to 30°C/86°F over medium heat and submerge the bag, closely monitoring the heat to maintain a consistent temperature and stirring often, for 2 hours.

- Remove the foie gras bag from the water. While it is still warm and soft, use your hands to gently shape the bagged foie gras into a cylinder, then roll the cylinder along a cutting board to further smooth it.

- Transfer the bagged foie gras to the freezer and freeze until solid, at least 2 hours.

- **TO SLICE THE FROZEN FOIE GRAS:** Unwrap the foie gras cylinder and lay it on a cutting board pointing away from you. Using a sharp flat-bladed knife, gently slice as thin as possible and with minimal pressure along the side of the cylinder, following the contour of the cylinder, allowing the foie gras to curl away from the knife blade toward the cutting board. (If you imagine a clock face at the front of the cylinder, you would slice from 2:00 to 5:00 if you are right-handed and from 10:00 to 7:00 if you are left-handed.) One cylinder will yield about 30 curls. Keep the curls in the freezer until ready to serve.

VANILLA PUREE

Four hours before serving, prepare the Vanilla Puree (page 162).

APPLE VINEGAR GEL

At least 90 minutes before serving:

INGREDIENTS

235 grams (¾ cup plus 2¾ tablespoons)
    apple balsamic vinegar, preferably
    Pommes brand
3.2 grams low acyl gellan

EQUIPMENT

Immersion blender
Fine-mesh strainer

- In a small pot, combine the vinegar and low acyl gellan and blend with an immersion blender for 30 seconds. Bring to a boil to activate the low acyl gellan and immediately remove from the heat.
- Strain through a fine-mesh strainer into a small rectangular container. Refrigerate, uncovered, until set, about 1 hour.
- Once the gel is firm, without removing the gel from the container, cut it into 1-centimeter squares. Cover with plastic wrap and refrigerate in the container until ready to serve.

COMPRESSED APPLE

Up to 2 days before serving:

INGREDIENTS

200 grams (1 cup) granulated sugar
5 grams (1 teaspoon) ascorbic acid
4 farm-fresh Granny Smith or
    other tart apples

EQUIPMENT

Vacuum bag
Vacuum sealer

- **TO PREPARE THE SIMPLE SYRUP:** In a small saucepan, combine 235 grams (1 cup) water with the sugar and bring to a boil. Simmer over medium-low heat, stirring, until the sugar has completely dissolved, about 3 minutes. Remove from the heat and allow to cool to room temperature.
- In a medium bowl, dissolve the ascorbic acid in 300 grams (1¼ cups) water.
- Peel and core the apples, then dice them into 1-centimeter cubes, submerging the exposed pieces in the ascorbic acid solution while you work, to keep them from browning.
- In a vacuum bag, combine the diced apples with 100 grams (3.5 ounces) of the simple syrup and compress at 99%.
- Reserve the unused simple syrup for use in the apple puree component.

    >>>

APPLE PUREE

INGREDIENTS

4 farm-fresh Granny Smith or
    other tart apples
140 grams (⅔ cup) extra-virgin olive oil
Fine sea salt
Granulated sugar
50 grams simple syrup (reserved
    from compressed apple component)

EQUIPMENT

Blender
Fine-mesh strainer
Squeeze bottle

INGREDIENTS

Micro Thai basil (*optional*)
Micro chamomile (*optional*)

At least 40 minutes before serving:

- Preheat the oven to 190°C/375°F.
- Quarter and core the apples without peeling them.
- In a large bowl, mix the olive oil together with a pinch of salt and a pinch of sugar. Toss the apple quarters in the olive oil mixture and transfer to a roasting pan.
- Bake the apples until the flesh is extremely soft and the skin has lightly browned, 25 to 30 minutes.
- Use a paring knife to remove the apple peels, which should come off quite easily, and discard the peels.
- In a blender, combine the peeled apple with 50 grams (1.75 ounces) of the simple syrup. Puree on high speed until smooth, about 30 seconds.
- Strain the apple puree through a fine-mesh strainer.
- Season with fine sea salt and transfer to a squeeze bottle.
- Refrigerate until ready to serve.

TO SERVE:

One hour before serving:

- Chill the plates in the freezer.

Immediately before serving:

- Working quickly, place 3 foie curls on each plate, slightly to one side. Squeeze large dots of apple puree and small dots of vanilla gel around the curls and scatter the compressed apple. Sprinkle the apple vinegar gel around the plate and on top of the foie curls.
- Garnish with the micro Thai basil and micro chamomile, if desired.
- Keep the dishes very cold and serve immediately.

Pintade is a domesticated species of bird that you may have encountered as "guinea hen" or perhaps "guinea fowl." It's a large, loud bird with beautiful feathers whose speckled pattern reminds me of a lovely *edo komon*–print kimono. As the English name suggests, pintade is native to Africa, but this dish is about crossing borders, like a pintade strolling through the Japanese countryside. It's not fusion, exactly, but rather an exploration of the flavors of the world from my own personal point of view. I was born with North African blood, spent my youth in Europe, sojourned in Asia, and now I live in North America, so I simply cannot understand why I should limit myself to cooking within a single culinary tradition. At Atelier Crenn, we serve our pintade with preserved lemon, and the citrus accent serves as a kind of hinge between the African and Asian elements in the dish.

The flavor of pintade is often compared to that of pheasant, but it benefits from an extra bit of technique and preparation. At Atelier Crenn, we air-dry pintade breasts on the bones for a few days to allow the fat to surface, so we can remove it easily while we make consommé from the bones, legs, and wings of the previous bird, to be used in the umeboshi glaze, but we have adapted this recipe so that a single bird provides for both the breasts and the consommé, to reduce waste. At Atelier Crenn, we often batter and fry the pintade tenders for our staff meal about once a week, and it is one of my favorite comfort foods. | *Serves 8*

Pintade

PRESERVED LEMON PUREE

INGREDIENTS

10 lemons (plus 2 lemons if not using
    a vacuum sealer)
500 grams (17.6 ounces) kosher salt
5 whole black peppercorns
1 bay leaf
30 grams (2 tablespoons) fresh
    lemon juice
12 grams (1 tablespoon) granulated sugar
0.3 gram xanthan gum

EQUIPMENT

Vacuum sealer or 2 sterile mason jars
Blender
Fine-mesh strainer

NOTE: *At Atelier Crenn, we preserve our own lemons, but one can reduce the advance preparation time by substituting 100 grams of store-bought preserved lemon for the fresh lemons and kosher salt.*

One to two months before serving:

- **TO PRESERVE THE LEMONS WITH A VACUUM SEALER:** Wash the lemons and place them in a vacuum bag along with the kosher salt, peppercorns, and bay leaf. Seal the bag, compress at 99%, and allow to ripen in the refrigerator for 2 months.
- **TO PRESERVE THE LEMONS IN MASON JARS:** Wash and cut an X into the lemons as if you were going to quarter them, but only cut three-quarters of the way through, leaving the base attached. Generously sprinkle kosher salt on the exposed flesh of the lemons. Add 1 tablespoon of kosher salt to the bottom of each jar, and pack the lemon quarters into the jars with the rest of the kosher salt, the peppercorns, and the bay leaf; press down on the lemons to release their juice, adding more fresh lemon juice to cover completely. Allow the lemons to ripen at room temperature, shaking every day to distribute the liquid in the jars, for at least 1 month.

>>>

Pintade, *continued*

At least 1 month later:

- Rinse the preserved lemons in cool water to remove excess salt. Cut the lemons into quarters and remove the pith and flesh, leaving only the peel.
- **TO BLANCH THE PRESERVED LEMON PEEL:** Place 100 grams (3.5 ounces) of the preserved lemon peel in a pot of cold water. To lessen the salinity, bring the contents of the pot to a boil and simmer just below a boil for 5 minutes, then drain, discarding the blanching liquid.
- Repeat the blanching process three times.
- In a blender, combine the blanched preserved lemon peels with 200 grams (¾ cup plus 1½ tablespoons) water, the lemon juice, and the sugar and blend on high speed until smooth, about 2 minutes. Reduce the blender speed to low and pour the xanthan gum directly into the liquid without touching the sides of the blender, about 20 seconds.
- Pass the puree through a fine-mesh strainer and refrigerate, covered, until ready to serve.

CABBAGE CHIPS
WITH NORI POWDER

INGREDIENTS

3 heads napa cabbage

120 grams (4.2 ounces) Pure-Cote

100 grams (¼ cup) powdered glucose

10 grams (2 teaspoons) fine sea salt

20 grams toasted nori (3 or 4 sheets)

EQUIPMENT

Juicer

Wire skimmer

Fine-mesh strainer

Acetate sheet

Nonstick cooking spray

Silicone basting brush

Dehydrator (optional)

Spice grinder

Spice shaker

At least 1 week before serving:

- Remove but do not discard several outer cabbage leaves and set aside 20 medium leaves that are fully intact to turn into cabbage chips.

- Roughly cut all the cabbage except the 20 middle leaves into 1-inch pieces. Use a juicer to juice the cut cabbage and discard the pulp. Remove any foam with a wire skimmer and pass the cabbage juice through a fine-mesh strainer.

- **TO MAKE THE CABBAGE–PURE-COTE SOLUTION:** In a medium pot, combine 1 kilogram (2.2 pounds) of the cabbage juice with the Pure-Cote, powdered glucose, and fine sea salt, bring to a boil, and remove from the heat.

- Strain through a fine-mesh strainer and set aside, uncovered, at room temperature.

- Spray the acetate sheets with nonstick cooking spray and wipe down with a paper towel; the residual nonstick coating will suffice. Brush the 20 reserved cabbage leaves with the cabbage–Pure-Cote solution to cover completely.

- **TO DRY THE CABBAGE CHIPS IN A DEHYDRATOR:** Place an acetate sheet in a dehydrator tray. Arrange the cabbage leaves on the acetate sheet in a single layer without touching one another. Transfer the tray to a dehydrator set to 60°C/140°F and dry the cabbage leaves until completely dry and crispy, about 3 hours.

- **TO DRY THE CABBAGE CHIPS IN THE OVEN:** Preheat the oven to 60°C/ 140°F or the closest temperature available. Place an acetate sheet on a baking sheet. Arrange the cabbage leaves on the acetate sheet in a single layer without touching one another. Transfer the baking sheet to the oven and turn off the heat. Let the cabbage dry in the closed oven with the heat off until completely dry and crispy, about 3 hours.

- Set aside the 20 best-looking cabbage chips for use in the final plating.

- **TO MAKE THE CABBAGE-NORI POWDER:** Use a spice grinder to grind 20 grams of cabbage chips into a powder. Add the nori and grind together into a fine powder. Transfer to a spice shaker.

>>>

Pintade, *continued*

SOUS-VIDE
PINTADE

INGREDIENTS

4 whole pintade (about 1,800 grams/
    4 pounds each)

15 grams (1 tablespoon) fine sea salt

8 cloves garlic

8 sprigs fresh thyme

56 grams (¼ cup) olive oil

20 grams cabbage chips (reserved
    from cabbage chips with nori powder
    component)

EQUIPMENT

Fine-mesh strainer

Cooking thermometer

Vacuum bag or resealable plastic
    freezer bag

Vacuum sealer (*optional*)

Immersion circulator or
    cooking thermometer

Four to six days before serving:

- Use a sharp knife to cut the legs and wings from the pintades
  and reserve. Fillet the breasts from the carcasses. Remove the
  pectoralis minor (tenders) and reserve for another use. Rub each
  breast with 1 to 1½ teaspoons of salt. Let the breasts air-dry on
  a rack in the refrigerator for 4 to 6 days.

- Use a sharp knife to break apart the rib cage and use the bones
  and reserved meat to make Poultry Consommé (page 318) for
  the umeboshi glaze.

At least 1 hour before serving:

- Peel and smash the garlic.

- **TO COOK THE BREASTS SOUS VIDE:** Transfer each pintade
  breast to a vacuum bag and add 1 smashed garlic clove, 1 sprig
  of thyme, and 7 grams (½ tablespoon) of olive oil. Cook the
  breasts sous vide in an immersion circulator set to 60°C/140°F
  for 15 to 20 minutes.

- **TO COOK THE BREASTS ON THE STOVETOP:** Transfer
  the breasts to a resealable plastic freezer bag and add 1 smashed
  garlic clove, 1 sprig of thyme, and 7 grams (½ tablespoon)
  of olive oil. Squeeze out as much air as possible and seal the
  bag. Fill a large pot three-quarters full with water and attach a
  cooking thermometer; bring the water to 60°C/140°F over
  medium-low heat and submerge the bag, closely monitoring the
  heat to maintain a consistent temperature and stirring often,
  until tender, 15 to 20 minutes.

- Keep warm until ready to serve.

FERMENTED LEEKS

INGREDIENTS
16 baby leeks
Fine sea salt
250 grams (1 cup) sake kasu

EQUIPMENT
Vacuum bag
Vacuum sealer (*optional*)

At least 1 day before serving:

- Clean the baby leeks under running water to remove any dirt.
- Prepare an ice water bath.
- Fill a medium pot halfway with generously salted water and bring to a boil. Blanch the baby leeks in the salted water until tender, then plunge into the ice water bath to stop the cooking.
- Dry the baby leeks with a clean kitchen towel.
- Rub the baby leeks in sake kasu, making sure the entire surface is covered in sake kasu. Transfer the baby leeks and sake kasu to a vacuum bag, seal the bag, and compress at 80%; alternatively, transfer the baby leeks and sake kasu to a resealable plastic freezer bag, squeeze out as much air as possible, and seal the bag
- Refrigerate the vacuum bag or resealable plastic freezer bag for 24 hours.

UMEBOSHI GLAZE

INGREDIENTS
1 kilogram (4¼ cups) pintade consommé (reserved from sous-vide pintade component)
80 grams (2.8 ounces) pitted umeboshi (Japanese salted plums)
10 grams (2 teaspoons) fine sea salt
1.5 grams xanthan gum

EQUIPMENT
Fine-mesh strainer
Blender

At least 2½ hours before serving:

- In a medium pot, bring the pintade consommé to a simmer over medium-high heat.
- Remove from the heat and add the umeboshi. Cover and let steep at room temperature for 2 hours.
- Strain the liquid through a fine-mesh strainer and discard the umeboshi or reserve for another use.
- Transfer the liquid to a blender. Blend on low speed while pouring the fine sea salt and xanthan gum directly into the liquid without touching the sides of the blender, about 10 seconds.
- Transfer to a small storage container and refrigerate, covered, until ready to serve.

>>>

Pintade, *continued*

INGREDIENTS

2 cloves garlic
28 grams (2 tablespoons) olive oil
10 grams (2 teaspoons) fresh lemon juice
Fine sea salt
Neutral vegetable oil
15 grams (1 tablespoon) unsalted butter
1 sprig fresh thyme
Basil flowers (*optional*)

EQUIPMENT

Plancha or cast-iron skillet

TO SERVE:

Ten minutes before serving:

- Preheat the oven to 175°C/350°F.
- Heat a plancha or cast-iron skillet over high heat.
- Slice the garlic and set aside.
- Remove the baby leeks and rinse with cool water to remove the sake kasu and pat dry.
- Char the baby leeks on the plancha or grill, until they have blackened sear marks, about 1 minute per side.
- Cut the baby leeks, including the greens, crosswise into 2-inch lengths.
- Dress the leeks with the olive oil and lemon juice to taste. Season with fine sea salt.
- **TO BROWN THE PINTADE:** Coat an oven-safe pan with a thin layer of vegetable oil. Let the oil warm over medium heat for 1 minute. Add the breasts to the pan skin-side down and cook until golden brown, about 1 minute.
- Remove the breasts and oil from the pan. Return the pan to the stove without washing and add the butter, thyme, and garlic and cook over medium-high heat, scraping the bottom of the pan to release residual pintade flavor, until reduced by half, about 2 minutes.
- **TO FINISH THE PINTADE:** Return the breasts to the pan and transfer the pan to the oven to roast for 5 minutes.
- Transfer the breasts to a cutting board and slice off the pointed tip and the sides to remove any overcooked portions. Slice the breasts in half lengthwise.
- Generously brush the sliced middle surface of the breasts with umeboshi glaze.
- Season the pintade breasts with the cabbage-nori powder and fine sea salt.
- Spread a tablespoon of preserved lemon puree in a wide stripe across each plate.
- Place 1 pintade breast sliced-side up on top of the preserved lemon puree. Arrange a few pieces of fermented baby leek around the pintade.
- On each plate, cover the pintade and leeks with 2 cabbage chips, which should lean at an angle over the rest of the food, like parasols. Garnish with basil flowers, if desired.

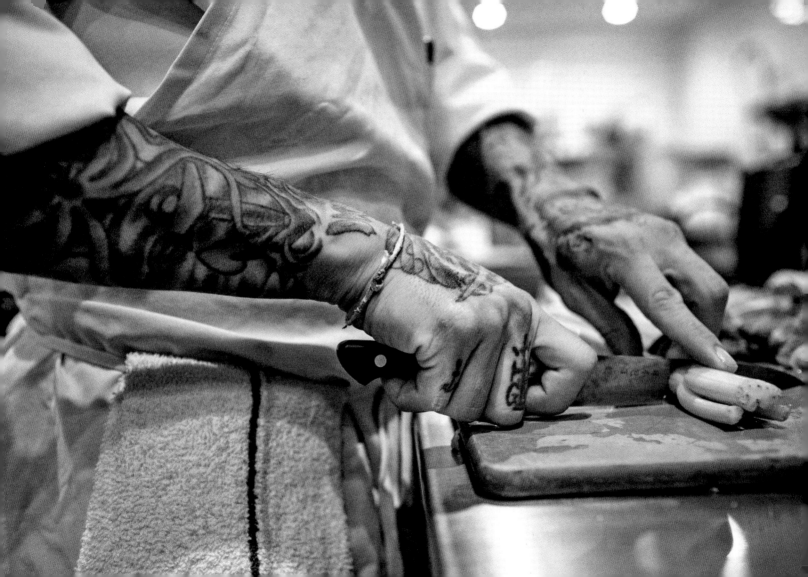

This dish is a representation of winter, when the sun sets early and most of the birds fly off in search of warmer weather. Pigeons, of course, do not migrate, given their strong homing instinct to stay close to their nests, and so they are with us all winter long. We serve this squab (as Americans prefer to call le pigeon in a culinary context) on a dark slate, with dark-colored squid ink chips and parsnip logs coated in squid ink powder, to capture the sense of wintry darkness. The squab breast itself is nice and red, and we slice it down the middle to expose the appealing color of a carefully prepared game bird. As a chef, I love the way that squab strikes a balance between poultry and red meat, not only in its color, but also in our experience of satisfaction. Squab is rich and gratifying, like a steak, but lighter and more refined. It is much less common in the United States than Europe, but I have the feeling that Americans are starting to appreciate le pigeon. | *Serves 8*

Winter Squab

SOUS-VIDE SQUAB

INGREDIENTS

4 whole squab
50 grams (2½ tablespoons) maple syrup
50 grams (2 tablespoons) fish sauce,
    preferably Blis brand

EQUIPMENT

Wire rack
Basting brush
Vacuum bag or resealable plastic
    freezer bag
Vacuum sealer (*optional*)
Immersion circulator or
    cooking thermometer

Four to seven days before serving:

- Use a sharp knife to cut the legs and wings from the squab carcasses and reserve for another use. Place the carcasses on a wire rack set over a baking sheet.
- In an airtight container, mix the maple syrup and fish sauce. Use a basting brush to coat the squab breast; cover and refrigerate the remaining maple syrup–fish sauce mixture. Dry age the squab, uncovered, in your refrigerator for 4 to 7 days, using a basting brush to coat the breasts once every day with the maple syrup–fish sauce mixture.

At least 2 hours before serving:

- Use a sharp knife to cut the breasts from the squab carcasses. Remove the pectoralis minor (tenders) and reserve for another use.
- **TO COOK THE SQUAB BREASTS SOUS VIDE:** Transfer the squab breasts to a vacuum bag, seal the bag, and compress at 99%. Cook the squab breasts sous vide in an immersion circulator set to 55°C/130°F for 20 to 25 minutes.
- **TO COOK THE SQUAB BREASTS ON THE STOVETOP:** Transfer the squab breasts to a resealable plastic freezer bag, squeeze out as much air as possible, and seal the bag. Fill a large pot three-quarters full with water and attach a cooking thermometer; bring the water to 55°C/130°F over medium-low heat and submerge the bag, closely monitoring the heat to maintain a consistent temperature and stirring often, 20 to 25 minutes.

>>>

Winter Squab, *continued*

- Remove the breasts from the bag. Set the breasts on a wire rack to air-dry at room temperature for 45 minutes.

BLACK SESAME POWDER

INGREDIENTS

150 grams (5.3 ounces) tapioca
  maltodextrin
110 grams (½ cup) sesame oil
20 grams (2¼ tablespoons)
  black sesame seeds
5 grams (1 teaspoon) fine sea salt

EQUIPMENT

Robot Coupe or food processor

Up to 1 week before serving:

- Wipe the chamber of the Robot Coupe or food processor with a paper towel to ensure that it is completely dry.
- In a large bowl, whisk the tapioca maltodextrin while slowly drizzling the sesame oil into the mixture until it becomes first a paste and then a powder.
- Transfer the powder to a Robot Coupe. (At Atelier Crenn, we slowly pour up to ½ cup liquid nitrogen into the powder while running the Robot Coupe on high speed, then quickly transfer to cold-safe container before the motor freezes. The liquid nitrogen stabilizes the flavors and creates a remarkably fine powder, but this step is not necessary.) Add the black sesame seeds and fine sea salt and process on high for 1 minute.
- Transfer the black sesame powder to a dry, airtight container and store at room temperature until ready to serve.

SQUID INK CHIPS

INGREDIENTS

325 grams (1½ cups) short-grain
  white rice
5 grams (0.17 ounces) squid ink paste
5 grams (1 teaspoon) fine sea salt

EQUIPMENT

Robot Coupe or food processor
Acetate sheet
Dehydrator (*optional*)

At least 5 hours before serving:

- In a medium pot with a tight lid, combine 650 grams (2¾ cups) of water with the rice and bring to a boil over medium heat. Reduce the heat to medium-low and simmer, covered, until the rice is slightly mushy, about 35 minutes.
- In a Robot Coupe or food processor, combine 500 grams (3 cups plus 1½ tablespoons) of the cooked rice with the squid ink and fine sea salt. Pulse on medium speed until the squid ink is evenly distributed and the texture is a thick paste, about 5 minutes.
- With the food processor running, slowly pour in 100 grams (scant ½ cup) water.
- **TO DRY THE SQUID INK CHIPS IN A DEHYDRATOR:** Place an acetate sheet in a dehydrator tray. Evenly spread the rice mixture in a thin layer across the acetate sheet. Transfer the tray to a dehydrator set to 60°C/140°F and dry the rice mixture for 3 hours; turn the chips over and dehydrate for 1 hour more.

- **TO DRY THE SQUID INK CHIPS IN THE OVEN**: Preheat the oven to 60°C/140°F or the closest temperature available. Place an acetate sheet on a baking sheet. Evenly spread the rice mixture in a thin layer across the acetate sheet. Transfer the baking sheet to the oven and turn off the heat. Let the squid ink chips dry in the closed oven with the heat off until completely dry and crispy, about 3 hours; turn the chips over and dry in the closed oven for 1 hour more. The squid ink chips should be dry and brittle.
- Store in an airtight container at room temperature until ready to serve.

PARSNIP LOGS

INGREDIENTS
4 medium parsnips
10 grams (0.4 ounce) squid ink powder

EQUIPMENT
Vacuum bag or resealable plastic
    freezer bag
Vacuum sealer (*optional*)
Immersion circulator or
    cooking thermometer

One hour before serving:

- Peel the parsnips and shape into cylinders of 2 to 3 inches in length and ½ inch in diameter.
- In a large bowl, whisk the squid ink powder into 100 grams (6¾ cups) cold water to make a slurry, which ensures that the squid ink powder will dissolve evenly.
- **TO COOK THE PARSNIPS SOUS VIDE**: Transfer the slurry to a vacuum bag, coat the parsnip logs in the slurry, seal the bag, and compress at 99%. Cook the parsnips sous vide in an immersion circulator set to 85°C/185°F until tender, about 45 minutes.
- **TO COOK THE PARSNIPS ON THE STOVETOP**: Transfer the slurry to a resealable plastic freezer bag, coat the parsnip logs in the slurry, squeeze out as much air as possible, and seal the bag. Fill a large pot three-quarters full with water and attach a cooking thermometer; bring the water to 85°C/185°F over medium-low heat and submerge the bag, closely monitoring the heat to maintain a consistent temperature and stirring often, until tender, about 45 minutes.

>>>

Winter Squab, *continued*

SHELLFISH BEURRE BLANC

INGREDIENTS
300 grams (10.6 ounces) unsalted butter
20 grams (0.7 ounce) peeled shallot
    (1 to 2 cloves)
10 grams (0.35 ounce) leek
5 grams (0.2 ounce) garlic (1 clove)
10 mussels
5 clams
100 grams (scant ½ cup) heavy cream
0.4 gram xanthan gum
Fine sea salt

EQUIPMENT
Blender
Fine-mesh strainer

- Remove the butter from the refrigerator, cut it into 1-inch cubes, and allow to warm to room temperature.
- Mince the shallot, leek, and garlic.
- In a small pot with a tight lid, melt 20 grams of the butter over medium heat, about 1 minute. Add the minced shallot, leek, and garlic and cook until they are translucent, stirring occasionally to prevent sticking and browning, about 10 minutes.
- Thoroughly clean the mussels and clams and add them to the pot. Cover with a tight lid and cook over medium heat until the shells open, 60 to 90 seconds. Remove the clams and mussels from the pot and add the cream. Bring the liquid to a simmer over medium-high heat and cook for 10 minutes. Reduce the heat to low and whisk in the remainder of the butter, one cube at a time, until fully emulsified.
- Use your fingers to remove the mussels and clams from their shells and transfer the flesh to a blender; discard the shells and any mussels and clams that have not opened. Transfer the cream mixture, including the solids to the blender and blend on high until the shellfish and aromatic vegetables have been pureed, about 30 seconds. Reduce the blender speed to low and pour the xanthan gum directly into the liquid without touching the sides of the blender, about 10 seconds.
- Strain the mixture through a fine-mesh strainer.
- Season with fine sea salt.

INGREDIENTS

4 liters (4.3 quarts) neutral vegetable oil

Fine sea salt

30 grams (2 tablespoons) unsalted butter

2 cloves garlic

1 sprig fresh thyme

EQUIPMENT

Small, deep pot

Cooking thermometer

Wire skimmer

TO SERVE:

Up to 1 day before serving:

- **TO CRISP THE SQUID INK CHIPS:** Break the squid ink chips into irregularly shaped 3 x 3-inch shards. Fill a small, deep pot three-quarters full with vegetable oil and attach a cooking thermometer. Heat over high heat to 215°C/420°F. Working in batches, fry the squid ink chips until they puff up and become very crispy, about 30 seconds, then remove the fried squid ink chips from the oil with a wire skimmer. Allow to cool on paper towels. Season with fine sea salt. Store in an airtight container at room temperature, if frying in advance of serving.

Ten minutes before serving:

- Preheat the oven to 175°C/350°F.
- **TO BROWN THE SQUAB BREASTS:** Coat an oven-safe pan with a thin layer of vegetable oil. Let the oil warm over medium heat for 1 minute. Add the breasts to the pan skin-side down and cook until golden brown, about 1 minute.
- Remove the breasts and oil from the pan. Return the pan to the stove without washing and add the butter, garlic, and thyme. Cook over medium-high heat, scraping the bottom of the pan to release residual squab flavor, until reduced by half, about 2 minutes.
- **TO FINISH THE SQUAB BREASTS:** Return the breasts to the pan. Transfer the pan to the oven to roast for 5 minutes.
- Transfer the breasts to a cutting board and slice off the pointed tip and the sides to remove any overcooked portions. Slice the breasts in half lengthwise.
- **TO PLATE:** Place 2 parsnip logs on each plate. Use a large spoon to drizzle the shellfish beurre blanc across the parsnips with a few additional drops to decorate the plate. Arrange the squab slices so that they rest partly on the plate and partly on the parsnip logs. Lean 1 squid ink chip alongside the parsnip and squab. Dust the entire plate with a generous spoonful of the black sesame powder.

Whereas my Winter Squab (page 197) is dark and maybe even a bit brooding, my Summer Squab is cheerfully bursting with colors and flavors, from the vermilion raspberry veil to the pearly onion soubise spilling out of the orange kumquat peel, in an expression of the bounty of the summer. We showcase the redness of the squab breast by slicing it down the middle, and because squab meat is encircled in a nice layer of fat, it crisps well and each bite provides a perfect finish. There is a satisfying richness to the squab that is perfect for summer because it is not greasy or heavy, but be very careful not to cook squab past medium-rare, because overcooked squab can taste gamy or liverish, which would detract from the dish's summery spirit. | *Serves 8*

Summer Squab

FERMENTED KUMQUAT

INGREDIENTS
900 grams (2 pounds) kumquats
1 kilogram (5¼ cups) granulated sugar
Sake kasu, to cover

EQUIPMENT
Slotted spoon

At least 2 weeks before serving:

- Wash the kumquats and halve them across the middle.
- **TO PREPARE A SIMPLE SYRUP:** In a small saucepan, combine the sugar with 235 grams (1 cup) water and bring to a boil over high heat. Reduce the heat to medium-low and simmer, stirring, until the sugar is completely dissolved, about 3 minutes.
- Prepare an ice water bath.
- Add the sliced kumquats to the simmering simple syrup and blanch until tender, about 1 minute. Scoop out the kumquats with a slotted spoon and immediately plunge into the ice water bath.
- In a storage container, combine the kumquats and enough sake kasu to cover. Seal the container and allow the kumquats to ferment at room temperature for at least 2 weeks.
- Remove the kumquats from the sake kasu and rinse with cool water.
- Use a small spoon to scoop the kumquat flesh from the peels. Discard the flesh or reserve for another use. Transfer the kumquat peels to an airtight container and refrigerate until ready to serve.

SOUS-VIDE SQUAB

Four to seven days before serving, cook the squab sous-vide as on page 197.

>>>

Summer Squab, *continued*

RASPBERRY VEIL

INGREDIENTS
300 grams (2½ cups) raspberries

100 grams (6¾ tablespoons) red wine

60 grams (5 tablespoons) granulated
   sugar

35 grams (2 tablespoons plus
   1 teaspoon) red wine vinegar

EQUIPMENT
Immersion blender or blender

Fine-mesh strainer

Acetate sheet

Nonstick cooking spray

Dehydrator (*optional*)

Parchment paper

At least 7½ hours before serving:

- In a medium pot, combine the raspberries, red wine, sugar, and red wine vinegar. Bring to a simmer over medium heat and simmer for 10 minutes.
- Use an immersion blender or transfer to a blender and puree on high speed until very smooth.
- Pass the raspberry puree through a fine-mesh strainer.
- Spray an acetate sheet with nonstick cooking spray and wipe down with a paper towel; the residual nonstick coating will suffice.
- Spread a thin layer of raspberry puree on the sprayed acetate sheet. Let the raspberry puree air-dry at room temperature until a pliable veil forms, about 1 hour.
- **TO DRY THE RASPBERRY VEIL IN A DEHYDRATOR:** Place the acetate sheet in a dehydrator tray. Transfer the tray to a dehydrator set to 60°C/140°F and dry the raspberry veil until completely dry, about 6 hours.
- **TO DRY THE RASPBERRY VEIL IN THE OVEN:** Preheat the oven to 60°C/140°F or the closest temperature available. Place the acetate sheet on a baking sheet, transfer the baking sheet to the oven, and turn off the heat. Let the raspberry veil dry in the closed oven with the heat off until completely dry, about 6 hours.
- Use kitchen scissors to cut the acetate sheet and raspberry veil into 3 x 3-inch squares. Peel the raspberry veils from the acetate, layer them with parchment paper, and transfer to an airtight container. (At Atelier Crenn, we use a paper cutter to slice the squares.) Store at room temperature until ready to serve.
- (At Atelier Crenn, we also freeze raspberries with liquid nitrogen and gently break the fruit into individual "cells.")

RED QUINOA SOIL

At least 3½ hours before serving, prepare Red Quinoa Soil (page 46)

>>>

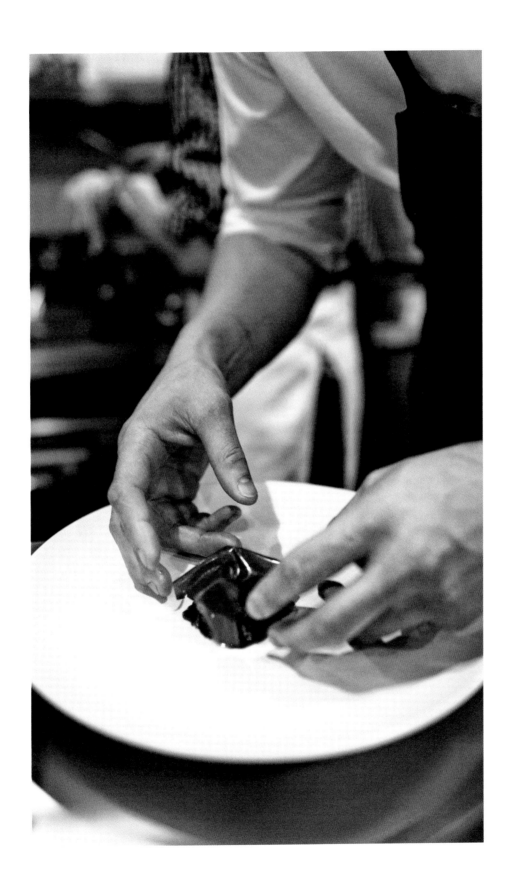

DAIKON AND SAKE KASU PUREE

INGREDIENTS

1.1 grams calcium gluconate

550 grams (1.2 pounds) daikon

4.5 grams low acyl gellan

0.28 grams sodium hexametaphosphate (SHMP)

30 grams (2 tablespoons) sake kasu

3 grams fine sea salt

0.6 grams xanthan gum

EQUIPMENT

Vacuum bag or resealable plastic freezer bag

Vacuum sealer (*optional*)

Cooking thermometer

Fine-mesh strainer

Blender

At least 90 minutes before serving:

- Bloom the calcium gluconate in enough room-temperature water to cover for 5 to 10 minutes.
- **TO COOK THE DAIKON SOUS VIDE**: Chop the daikon into ½-inch pieces. Place the daikon in a vacuum bag, seal the bag, and compress at 99%; alternatively, place the daikon into a resealable plastic freezer bag, squeeze out as much air as possible, and seal the bag.
- Fill a large pot with water and bring to a boil over medium-high heat. Submerge the daikon bag in the water and cook until completely soft, about 20 minutes.
- Open the vacuum bag and transfer the daikon to a medium pot with a cooking thermometer attached. Bring the temperature to 100°C/210°F and stir in the low acyl gellan and SHMP. Remove from the heat, but continue to monitor the temperature as the mixture cools.
- Strain the calcium gluconate.
- When the temperature of the daikon mixture has dropped to 80°C/175°F, add the calcium gluconate. Transfer the contents of the pot to a blender and blend on high for 30 seconds. (At Atelier Crenn, we use a Thermomix to blend the ingredients at the appropriate temperatures.)
- Strain the daikon mixture through a fine-mesh strainer into a shallow container and refrigerate, uncovered, until set to a firm gel, about 1 hour.
- Transfer 600 grams (1.3 pounds) of the daikon gel to a blender. Add the sake kasu and salt and blend on high speed until the texture is thick but smooth, about 30 seconds. Reduce the blender speed to low and pour the xanthan gum directly into the liquid without touching the sides of the blender, about 10 seconds.
- Pass the puree through a fine-mesh strainer.
- Refrigerate, covered, until ready to serve.

  >>>

Summer Squab, *continued*

ONION SOUBISE

INGREDIENTS

1 leek

1 white onion

115 grams (½ cup) unsalted butter

15 grams (scant 2 tablespoons)
   all-purpose flour

300 grams (1¼ cups) buttermilk

3 grams fine sea salt

0.3 gram xanthan gum

EQUIPMENT

Vacuum bag or resealable plastic
   freezer bag

Vacuum sealer (*optional*)

Immersion circulator or
   cooking thermometer

Blender

Sifter

Fine-mesh strainer

One hour before serving:

- Wash and trim the leek, discarding the green leaves. Peel and trim the onion. Dice the leek and onion into ¼-inch cubes.

- **TO COOK THE LEEK AND ONION SOUS VIDE:** In a vacuum bag, combine 75 grams (2.65 ounces) of the diced leek, 75 grams (2.65 ounces) of the diced onion, and 100 grams (7 tablespoons) of the butter and compress at 99%. Cook sous vide in an immersion circulator set to 85°C/185°F until the leek and onion are very soft, about 30 minutes.

- **TO COOK THE LEEK AND ONION ON THE STOVETOP:** In a resealable plastic freezer bag, combine 75 grams (2.65 ounces) of the diced leek, 75 grams (2.65 ounces) of the diced onion, and 100 grams (7 tablespoons) of the butter. Squeeze out as much air as possible and seal the bag. Fill a large pot three-quarters full with water and attach a cooking thermometer; bring the water to 85°C/185°F over medium heat and submerge the bag, closely monitoring the heat to maintain a consistent temperature and stirring often, until the leek and onion are very soft, about 30 minutes.

- Without opening the bag, set aside at room temperature for 10 minutes, then open the vacuum bag or resealable plastic freezer bag and transfer the contents to a blender.

- **TO MAKE A BLONDE ROUX:** In a small saucepan, melt the remaining 15 grams (1 tablespoon) butter over low heat. Sift in the flour while whisking, until the mixture is uniform in texture, then slowly incorporate the buttermilk and cook over low heat for 4 minutes more.

- Transfer the blonde roux to the blender containing the leek-onion mixture. Blend on high until a smooth soubise is formed, about 1 minute.

- Pass the soubise through a fine-mesh strainer and keep warm until ready to serve.

INGREDIENTS

Neutral vegetable oil

15 grams (1 tablespoon) unsalted butter

2 cloves peeled garlic

1 sprig fresh thyme

TO SERVE:

Ten minutes before serving:

- Preheat the oven to 175°C/350°F.
- **TO BROWN THE SQUAB BREASTS:** Coat an oven-safe pan with a thin layer of vegetable oil. Heat the oil over medium heat for 1 minute. Add the breasts to the pan skin-side down and cook until golden brown, about 1 minute.
- Remove the breasts and oil from the pan. Return the pan to the stove without washing and add the butter, garlic, and thyme. Cook over medium-high heat, scraping the bottom of the pan to release residual squab flavor, until reduced by half, about 2 minutes.
- **TO FINISH THE SQUAB BREASTS:** Return the breasts to the pan and transfer the pan to the oven to roast for 5 minutes.
- Transfer the breasts to a cutting board and slice off the pointed tip and the sides to remove any overcooked portions. Slice the breasts in half lengthwise.
- Place 1 squab breast on each plate, sliced-side up, alongside the onion soubise.
- On the other side of the squab breast, spoon a dollop of daikon and sake kasu puree, reserving any remaining puree.
- Lay 1 raspberry veil over the center of each composition.
- Fill the fermented kumquats with daikon and sake kasu puree. Cover with red quinoa soil.
- Place 2 fermented kumquats on each plate, allowing the puree to spill out onto the plate.

DREAM

OUR PASTRY CHEF, Juan Contreras, is my artistic soul mate and a true friend. Before Atelier Crenn opened, Juan and I worked together at Luce, where I was executive chef and he was chef de cuisine. There was a stretch at Luce when we didn't have a pastry chef, and Juan covered that section of the menu, but it was just a few months before Atelier Crenn opened when we decided that Juan would focus on desserts. Now, of course, it seems like he was born to be a chef patissier. His attention to detail, tolerance for hard work, and, above all, his capacity to dream up the most elaborate fantasies make him the greatest partner I could imagine.

Like me, Juan is inspired by nature, and he has an insatiable hunger to learn about the natural world. To develop his honey dessert, for example, Juan threw himself into the local beekeeping culture and absorbed all kinds of information about bees and honey, which ultimately paved the way for the astonishing diversity of the finished dish, which incorporates everything from pollen to honey to beeswax to the honeycombs themselves. For his version of The Sea, Juan went to Monterey on his days off to learn about seaweed, algae, and the California Coast, and he came back brimming with ideas for a radically creative dessert. Honestly, I think there is no project so difficult that Juan wouldn't try and no idea too original for him to consider.

At Atelier Crenn, Juan works extremely long hours, arriving most days at 10:00 a.m., leaving at 2:00 or 3:00 a.m., and spending most of his days off on research, recipe testing, or shopping for obscure ingredients. We can probably thank his family for making Juan so diligent. Though he was born in California, his family moved back to Mexico when he was ten, and he continued to be a star student in San Diego while getting top grades at a night school near his family's home in Tecate, Mexico. (Juan is brilliant.) Juan kept this up for four years, finishing high school in San Diego and going on to the University of California, Riverside, and finally, culinary school. When we met, it was immediately clear that we were a good fit; we just understand each other so intuitively, and our ideas grow and bloom together. Now that he is pastry chef instead of chef de cuisine, our working relationship has shifted a bit, since he has his own separate kitchen across the courtyard from mine, but we are still bouncing ideas off each other all the time. Before I moved, we used to drive to the restaurant together every morning, and it was a real privilege to have Juan's insights and enthusiasm frame my day.

The dessert program that Juan has developed is deeply integrated into the tasting menu and an integral part of our success as a restaurant. At the conclusion of the savory portion of the meal, Juan introduces a few pre-desserts, which arrive in a wave and usher the guest into a new phase of the meal, and then the main dessert, which is a composed dish organized around a theme such as wine (served in custom-made vessels derived from wine bottles) or the sea (see page 249). Juan's creative process is similar to mine in terms of nature, but he will work on a single dish for months, absolutely immersing himself in that topic, and layering many more components into a dish that simply transports the diner and reveals the point of inspiration in an entirely new light.

In terms of flavor and richness, Juan's desserts are a perfect complement to the rest of the tasting menu, so that the meal concludes with a luxurious and even decadent treat that fulfills the ingredient-driven ethos of Atelier Crenn. And while I often find desserts to be overly sweet and heavy, Juan's desserts are actually quite restrained when it comes to sugar and cream, and he is a master of balancing his desserts with floral, fruity, nutty, acidic, spicy, woodsy, and even oceanic notes. Like all of Atelier Crenn, the pastry program is quite accommodating to dietary restrictions, and Juan has taken it as a personal challenge to develop dairy-free and gluten-free recipes that are up to his exacting standards.

Over the last few years, it has been both exciting and satisfying to watch Juan grow as a pastry chef. For as long as I've known Juan, his modernist cooking skills have been impressive, but lately, he has begun to embrace more traditional techniques as well. He said he had a moment of revelation one day when he was attempting to stabilize a tricky foam and had tried practically everything in his hydrocolloid spice rack. All of a sudden, he decided to scale back to the classics, and now Juan says, "I feel consciously guilty if I use two or more hydros. That's just not who I am. Obviously, I'm for artistic manipulation, but I think there has to be a balance with letting the ingredient shine." And that's what I love about Juan: He is always pushing himself to the next stage in his evolution. I cannot wait to see what he comes up with next. Whatever it is, I want to be right there with him.

In the first year of Atelier Crenn, Juan was visiting Peter Jacobson's beautiful farm in Yountville, and he had a moment when he looked down at a Seckel pear that had fallen from a tree into a pile of leaves while catching a whiff of the sage and other herbs growing nearby. That was the seed of inspiration for a dessert centered on the smallest and sweetest pear varietal. Sometimes called a "sugar pear," the bite-size Seckel appears on the plate as a pear-shaped sorbet decorated with green and maroon pigments made from pear skin, chlorophyll oil, and rhubarb oil. This beautiful pear sorbet is served on a bed of sage cake and yogurt snow, and dusted with rhubarb consommé ice for a wintery composition that is warmed up with a tableside infusion of aromatic vegetables, fruits, and spices. In other words, this dish gives us a delightful reminder of the pleasures of winter far beyond the temperate climate of San Francisco. | *Serves 8*

Seckel Pear (Winter)

SAGE CAKE

INGREDIENTS
350 grams (1⅔ cups) extra-virgin
    olive oil
45 grams (1.6 ounces) fresh sage leaves
500 grams (5½ cups) cake flour
24 grams (5½ teaspoons) baking powder
6 grams (0.21 ounce) kosher salt
400 grams (2 cups plus 1½ tablespoons)
    granulated sugar
5 large eggs
500 grams (2 cups) whole milk

EQUIPMENT
Blender
Sifter
Stand mixer with a whisk attachment
Rubber spatula
13 x 18-inch (half-sheet) or two
    9 x 13-inch (quarter-sheet) pans
Parchment paper

At least 1 day before serving:

- In a blender, combine the olive oil and sage leaves and blend on high until a smooth paste forms, about 2 minutes.
- In a large bowl, sift together the cake flour, baking powder, and kosher salt and set aside.
- In the bowl of a stand mixer fitted with the whisk attachment, beat the sugar and eggs on high speed until the mixture is aerated and highly volumized, about 5 minutes; when poured, the mixture should resemble a fluffy yellow ribbon.
- Reduce the speed to medium and slowly add the milk; the batter will loosen and emulsify. Stream in the sage oil to incorporate.
- Turn off the mixer and scrape down the sides with a rubber spatula.
- Turn the mixer speed to low and add the combined dry ingredients in 3 batches to avoid lumps until fully incorporated.
- Transfer the batter to an airtight container and allow to mature in the refrigerator for 12 to 24 hours.

The next day:

- Preheat the oven to 200°C/390°F.
- Line a 13 x 18-inch (half-sheet) pan or two 9 x 13-inch (quarter-sheet) pans with parchment paper.
- Evenly spread 1 kilogram (2.2 pounds) of the batter across the parchment in the half-sheet pan or 500 grams (1.1 pounds) in each quarter-sheet pan.

>>>

Seckel Pear (Winter), *continued*

- Bake for 6 minutes, rotate the pan(s) to ensure even browning, and bake for 6 minutes more.
- Remove the cake(s) from the oven and let cool completely in the pan. Leave the oven on.
- **TO PREPARE THE SAGE CAKE CRISPY CRUMBS:** Remove half the cooled sage cake and break into crumbs. Tightly cover the rest of the sage cake in plastic wrap and set aside at room temperature. Spread the crumbs on a baking sheet and let dry in the oven until crispy, 1½ to 3 hours.
- Transfer the crumbs to an airtight container and store at room temperature for up to 5 days.

SECKEL PEAR SORBET

At least 14 hours before serving:

INGREDIENTS

12 Seckel pears
165 grams (5.8 ounces) Stabilizer Syrup (page 325)
2 grams (½ teaspoon) ascorbic acid
20 grams (4 teaspoons) fresh lemon juice (from 1 lemon)
0.5 gram kosher salt

EQUIPMENT

Steaming basket
Blender
Refractometer (*optional*)
Pacojet or home ice cream maker
Kitchen scale

- Wash, peel, quarter, and core the pears. Reserve the skins and stems for the Seckel pear decoration.
- Fill a medium pot with a few inches of water and insert a steaming basket. Add the pear pieces, cover with a lid, and steam until very tender, about 25 minutes.
- Prepare the Stabilizer Syrup (page 325).
- Transfer 550 grams (1.2 pounds) of the steamed pears to a blender and add 100 grams (scant ½ cup) water. Puree on high speed until smooth, about 2 minutes. Add the ascorbic acid to prevent oxidation and blend on high speed to incorporate, 10 seconds. Add the stabilizer syrup and blend on high for 20 seconds to incorporate. Add the lemon juice and kosher salt and blend to incorporate, about 10 seconds. (The mixture should be around 31 Brix, if you have a refractometer and want to check the sweetness.)
- **TO MAKE THE PEAR SORBET IN A PACOJET:** Transfer the pear mixture to a Pacojet canister and freeze until solid, at least 12 hours, and pacotize to order.
- **TO MAKE THE PEAR SORBET IN A HOME ICE CREAM MAKER:** Transfer the pear mixture to an airtight container and refrigerate until thoroughly chilled. Follow the manufacturer's instructions for your ice cream maker to process to a sorbet.
- When the pear sorbet is processed, place a 10-inch length of plastic wrap on a kitchen scale. Transfer the sorbet to a pastry bag and

pipe 30 grams (1.05 ounces) of the pear sorbet onto the plastic wrap, and working quickly, pick up the plastic wrap and use your cupped hands to sculpt the sorbet through the plastic wrap into the shape of a small Seckel pear. Transfer to a plastic tray, such as the lid of a storage container, and freeze again until very firm; at least 3 hours. (At Atelier Crenn, we have a blast chiller that can tell us when the pears are -15°C/5°F.)

• Peel off the plastic and return the pear-shaped sorbet to the freezer until ready to decorate.

RHUBARB CONSOMMÉ ICE

INGREDIENTS

250 grams (8.8 ounces) rhubarb stalks

10 grams (0.35 ounce) peeled fresh ginger

1 liter (1 quart) mineral water

500 grams (17.6 ounces) strawberry

100 grams (6 tablespoons plus 2 teaspoons) granulated sugar

5 grams (0.18 ounce) dried rose petals

EQUIPMENT

Double boiler or metal mixing bowl

Fine-mesh strainer

Coffee filter

At least 11 hours before serving:

• Trim the ends from the rhubarb and cut crosswise into ½-inch pieces.

• Thinly slice the ginger.

• Fill the bottom of a double boiler or a medium pot halfway with water and bring to a boil over medium heat. In the top of a double boiler or a metal bowl that fits snugly over the pot without touching the water, combine the mineral water, strawberry, rhubarb, sugar, ginger, and rose petals. Wrap the top of the double boiler or metal bowl with plastic film. Set the top of the double boiler or the metal bowl over the pot without touching the boiling water and steep over low heat for 4 hours. Replenish the water as needed.

• Strain the liquid through a fine-mesh strainer and discard the solids.

• Pass the mixture through a coffee filter and discard the solids.

• Transfer 1 liter (1 quart) of the liquid to a shallow storage container and freeze until solid, at least 6 hours. (At Atelier Crenn, we freeze it in a half-sheet pan and then process it in the Robot Coupe with liquid nitrogen, which makes an incredible texture, though it melts quickly.)

• Use a fork to shave into a fine ice and freeze in an airtight container until ready to serve.

Seckel Pear (Winter), *continued*

YOGURT SNOW

INGREDIENTS

500 grams (2 cups plus 2 tablespoons)
    plain yogurt, homemade (page 303)
    or store-bought Greek yogurt
25 grams (1¼ tablespoons) grade-A
    maple syrup

At least 6½ hours before serving:

- In a large bowl, whisk together the Greek yogurt and maple syrup.
- Transfer the mixture to a shallow storage container and freeze until solid, at least 6 hours. (At Atelier Crenn, we transfer the mixture to a pastry bag, pipe it into liquid nitrogen, and then grind it into a snow in our Robot Coupe.)
- Scrape the frozen mixture with a fork to create a snow and freeze in an airtight container until ready to serve.

SECKEL PEAR DECORATION

INGREDIENTS

200 grams (7 ounces) pear skin
    (reserved from Seckel pear sorbet
    component)
100 grams (scant ½ cup) grapeseed oil
    (*optional*)
0.5 grams ascorbic acid (*optional*)
6.25 grams chlorophyll oil (*optional*)
125 grams (4.4 ounces) cocoa butter
125 grams (4.4 ounces) white chocolate,
    preferably Valrhona Ivoire, 35% cocoa
Oil-based green food coloring (*optional*)
12.5 grams (2¾ teaspoons) rhubarb oil
8 Seckel pear stems (reserved from
    Seckel pear sorbet component)

>>>

At least 3 hours before serving:

- **TO CREATE CHLOROPHYLL-BASED DYE WITH AN IMMERSION CIRCULATOR:** In a vacuum bag, combine the pear skins, grapeseed oil, and ascorbic acid, seal the bag, and compress at 99%. Cook sous vide in an immersion circulator set to 65°C/150°F for 1 hour. Refrigerate the dye in the vacuum bag until ready to paint the sorbet pears.
- **TO CREATE CHLOROPHYLL-BASED DYE ON THE STOVETOP:** In a resealable plastic freezer bag, combine the pear skins, grapeseed oil, and ascorbic acid, squeeze out as much air as possible, and seal the bag. Fill a large pot three-quarters full with water and attach a cooking thermometer; bring the water to 65°C/150°F over medium-low heat and submerge the bag, closely monitoring the heat to maintain a consistent temperature and stirring often, for 1 hour. Refrigerate the dye in the freezer bag until ready to paint the sorbet pears.
- Open the bag and strain the liquid through a fine-mesh strainer into a metal bowl, discarding the solids. Add the chlorophyll and mix well.
- **TO MAKE THE COCOA BUTTER BASE:** Fill the bottom of a double boiler or a medium pot halfway with water and bring to a boil over medium heat. In the top of the double boiler or a metal bowl that fits snugly over the pot without touching the

Vacuum bag or resealable plastic
   freezer bag

Vacuum sealer (*optional*)

Immersion circulator (*optional*)

Cooking thermometer

Double boiler or metal mixing bowl

Fine-mesh strainer

Cheesecloth

Paint spray gun

Airbrush

water, mix together the cocoa butter and white chocolate. Set the top of the double boiler or large metal bowl over the pot without touching the boiling water and heat to 45°C/115°F.

- Line a fine-mesh strainer with 1 layer of cheesecloth and strain the cocoa butter base. Discard the solids.

- In a medium bowl with a cooking thermometer attached, let 500 grams (1.1 pounds) of the cocoa butter base cool, uncovered, until the temperature drops to 30°C/85°F.

- Whisk in just enough chlorophyll-based dye or oil-based green food coloring to achieve a light green tone, similar to a pear.

- Use a paint spray gun to coat the sorbet pears with a thin coat of the green cocoa butter spray, making sure not to overcoat. Simultaneously use an airbrush to spray with rhubarb oil to achieve pink/red overtones. Finish with a lighter coat of green cocoa butter spray until the colors are naturally blended. (At Atelier Crenn, we have a designated painting area for this sort of project.)

- Stick 1 pear stem in the top of each sorbet pear. (At Atelier Crenn, we make pear stems from ½-inch pieces of the curved tips of whole vanilla beans, which we dehydrate overnight.)

- Store the sorbet pears in a single layer in an airtight container in the freezer until ready to serve.

> > >

Seckel Pear (Winter), *continued*

GRASS THREADS

INGREDIENTS

200 grams (1 cup plus 1½ tablespoons)
all-purpose flour, plus more for dusting

2 grams kosher salt

40 grams (scant 3 tablespoons) unsalted
butter, plus 15 grams (1 tablespoon)
for brushing

80 grams (⅓ cup) whole milk

1 large egg

4 grams (¼ tablespoon) distilled
white vinegar

EQUIPMENT

Sifter

Cooking thermometer

Silicone mat

At least 90 minutes before serving:

- Lightly flour a work surface.
- Sift the flour and salt onto the surface and form it into a mound. Make a well in the center of the mound.
- In a small pot, melt the butter over low heat. Add the milk, attach a cooking thermometer, and warm the mixture to 50°C/120°F.
- In a large bowl, beat the egg. Add the warm milk-butter mixture and the distilled white vinegar.
- Pour the liquid mixture from the bowl into the well in the flour mound.
- Working quickly with your fingers, combine the dry and wet ingredients, working from the outside of the well until consistently mixed into a dough. If the dough is too sticky to work with, add slightly more flour.
- Knead the dough until pliable and silky, about 10 minutes.
- Brush the surface of the dough with 15 grams (1 tablespoon) melted butter.
- Transfer to a large bowl, cover with a plastic wrap, and let sit in a warm place for 45 minutes.
- Preheat the oven to 150°C/300°F.
- On a lightly floured work surface, roll the dough as thin as possible, working gently from the center toward the edges in order to avoid tearing.
- Use a sharp knife to julienne the dough into long, thin, symmetrical strips about 10 inches long.
- Line a baking sheet with a silicone mat. Transfer the strips to the silicone mat and bake until golden brown, 12 minutes.
- Let the grass threads cool on the silicone mat. Transfer to an airtight container and store at room temperature until ready to serve.

BROWN BUTTER POWDER

INGREDIENTS

300 grams (10.6 ounces) unsalted butter

85 grams tapioca maltodextrin,
    plus more as needed

10 grams (0.35 ounce) 10X
    confectioners' sugar

1 gram kosher salt

EQUIPMENT

Coarse-mesh strainer

Cheesecloth

Robot Coupe or food processor

Up to 5 days before serving:

- **TO PREPARE THE BROWN BUTTER:** Cut the butter into ½-inch slices. Line a strainer with 1 layer of cheesecloth. In a medium saucepan (preferably light colored, so you can assess the color of the butter), melt the butter over medium-low heat, whisking continuously, for 2 to 3 minutes. The butter will begin to foam and brown; as soon as you see brown specks at the bottom, remove from the heat and continue to whisk for 30 seconds. Strain the brown butter through the cheesecloth.
- In a Robot Coupe or food processor, combine 100 grams (3.5 ounces) of the brown butter with the tapioca maltodextrin, 10X sugar, and salt. Pulse the food processor until the texture of the mixture is a powder, stopping before it becomes a paste. You may need to add slightly more tapioca maltodextrin to maintain the texture of a powder.
- Pass the mixture through a coarse-mesh strainer.
- Transfer to an airtight container and store at room temperature for up to 5 days.

SPICED INFUSION

INGREDIENTS

50 grams (1.8 ounces) rhubarb stalk

1 Madagascar vanilla bean

1 orange

3 thin slices peeled ginger

2 grams chamomile stems

2 grams fresh mint leaves

2 rose petals

EQUIPMENT

Japanese siphon

Up to 30 minutes before serving:

- Cut the rhubarb crosswise into ½-inch pieces. Split the vanilla bean lengthwise. Peel the orange, rip the peel into 5 strips, and discard the flesh or reserve for another use.
- In a Japanese siphon, arrange the rhubarb, vanilla bean, orange peel, ginger, chamomile threads, mint, and rose petals. In the lower chamber, add 240 grams (1 cup) water and seal the siphon.

>>>

Seckel Pear (Winter), *continued*

INGREDIENTS

Foraged winter leaves (*optional*)
Honey

TO SERVE:

Seven minutes before serving:

- Temper the pear sorbet at room temperature.
- In a medium bowl, mix together equal amounts of the brown butter powder, grass threads, and crispy sage cake crumbs. Spoon 1 tablespoon of this mixture on one side of each plate.
- Tear the intact half of the sage cake into irregular ½-inch pieces and arrange in a random pattern around the spoonful of cake crumb mixture.
- Spoon ½ tablespoon rhubarb granité in the center of the sage cake circle. Place the frozen pear on top of the rhubarb granité. Dust the frozen yogurt snow over the entire plate.
- Garnish with foraged winter leaves, if desired.
- **TO SERVE THE SPICED INFUSION:** Heat the Japanese siphon tableside for 5 minutes. Extinguish the flame, allow to filter through the siphon, and pour into cups.
- Offer honey for guests to sweeten the spiced infusion.

By the time this dish came onto the menu at Atelier Crenn, Juan had been thinking about making a honey dessert for more than two years. He immersed himself in the local beekeeping community and emerged with enormous respect for apiculture. Rob Keller, an influential bee educator and activist who also founded Napa Valley Bee Co., taught Juan about the meaning of honeycombs and the value of free-form comb building, as opposed to guiding bees with plastic comb frames. Honeycombs truly are a feat of engineering, and the visual design of the dish is a response to that.

All of the honey, beeswax, pollen, and honeycombs in this dish come from Bay Area Bee Company, which is run by husband-and-wife beekeepers, Rokas and Kelli Armonas, who tend hives around San Francisco, each of which produce honey with a different flavor profile. (In Potrero Hill, for example, the honey has a hint of the fennel that flourishes on the hillside.) That relationship between place and taste, even down to a specific neighborhood, made a huge impact on Juan, who says, "What really got me attached and emotional was when I would see the honeycombs, how they looked and tasted different, and could understand where it was coming from." With the floral, fruity, and nutty flavors that appeal to bees, the dish is not just an ode to honey, but a celebration of honeybees and their role in sustaining the entire ecosystem. | *Serves 12*

NOTE: *When coating the caramels, seek out beeswax with floral aromatic qualities that reflect the field or garden where the honey was collected. If you cannot find high-quality beeswax, simply dip in pollen and wrap in cellophane instead.*

Honey (Spring)

BEESWAX SORBET

INGREDIENTS
245 grams (8.65 ounces) Stabilizer
  Syrup (page 325)
170 grams (6 ounces) beeswax
40 grams (1.4 ounces) bee pollen
1 gram kosher salt
0.8 gram xanthan gum
35 grams corn maltodextrin

EQUIPMENT
Vacuum bag
Vacuum sealer
Immersion circulator
Fine-mesh strainer
Blender
12 honeycomb molds (*optional*)
Pacojet or home ice cream maker

NOTE: *In many of the recipes contained in this book, we provide instructions for stovetop alternatives to using an immersion circulator. In this case, however, we do not advise a stovetop method, because we want to warm the beeswax enough to infuse the water without melting. Beeswax has a low melting point (62°C/144°F to 64°C/147°F), and the immersion circulator allows us to keep the water at a constant temperature of 55°C/130°F.*

At least 1 day before serving:

- Prepare the Stabilizer Syrup (page 325).
- **TO COOK THE BEESWAX SOUS VIDE:** In a vacuum bag, combine 800 grams (3⅓ cups) water with the beeswax and bee pollen, seal the bag, and compress at 99%. Warm the beeswax sous vide in an immersion circulator set to 55°C/130°F for 2 hours.
- Prepare an ice water bath.
- Submerge the vacuum bag in the ice water bath to stop the cooking. When the water inside the vacuum bag is cold, about 15 minutes, strain the liquid through a fine-mesh strainer and discard the solids.

  >>>

Honey (Spring), *continued*

- In a blender, combine 700 grams (3 cups) of the infused water with the stabilizer syrup and kosher salt. Blend on high speed until fully mixed, about 1 minute. Reduce the blender speed to low and pour the xanthan gum directly into the liquid without touching the sides of the blender, about 10 seconds. While the blender is running, add the corn maltodextrin and blend for 20 seconds.
- Place the honeycomb molds in the freezer to chill overnight.
- **TO MAKE THE BEESWAX SORBET USING A PACOJET:** Transfer the sorbet mixture to a Pacojet container and freeze overnight or until the temperature reaches -20°C/-4°F. The next day, pacotize the frozen sorbet base until smooth.
- **TO MAKE THE BEESWAX SORBET IN A HOME ICE CREAM MAKER:** Transfer the sorbet base to an airtight container and refrigerate until thoroughly chilled. Follow the manufacturer's instructions for your ice cream maker to process to a sorbet.
- Use an offset spatula to fill the molds with the sorbet and freeze to -20°C/-4°F. (At Atelier Crenn, we use a blast chiller.)
- Keep frozen, in the molds, until ready to serve.

NOTE: *If you do not have access to both a freezer capable of freezing the sorbet to -20°C/-4°F, we do not recommend molding the sorbet, as it will not be possible to remove smoothly.*

HONEY MERINGUE

At least 1 day before serving:

INGREDIENTS

100 grams (3.5 ounces) egg whites
    (from about 3 eggs)
3 grams (8 teaspoons) egg white powder
25 grams (2 tablespoons) granulated
    sugar
60 grams (2¾ tablespoons) filtered
    honey
25 grams corn maltodextrin

EQUIPMENT

Stand mixer with a whisk attachment
Six 14 x 14-inch sheets ⅜-inch
    bubble wrap
Sifter
Dehydrator
Desiccant (*optional*)

- In the bowl of a stand mixer fitted with the whisk attachment, combine the egg whites and egg white powder and mix on medium speed. As the mixture starts to aerate and froth, gradually add the sugar until the mixture becomes airy and eventually forms soft peaks. With the mixer running on medium-high, drizzle in the honey, but do not overwhip to the point of forming hard peaks. With the mixer running on medium-high, sift in the corn maltodextrin until fully incorporated.

- Evenly spread the meringue across 3 sheets of bubble wrap and gently press each covered sheet with 1 other sheet of bubble wrap on top.

- **TO DRY THE MERINGUE IN A DEHYDRATOR**: Transfer each bubble-wrapped meringue to its own dehydrator tray. Transfer the trays to a dehydrator set to 80°C/175°F and dry the meringue until completely dry and crispy, at least 12 hours. **NOTE**: *We do not recommend putting bubble wrap in the oven.*

- Peel off the bubble wrap like a sticker. Hold the meringue in the dehydrator at 50°C/120°F or keep in an airtight container with a desiccant at room temperature until ready to serve.

>>>

ROASTED WHITE CHOCOLATE CRÉMEUX

INGREDIENTS

2 grams (1 sheet) gold strength
    (200 bloom) gelatin
170 grams (6 ounces) white chocolate,
    such as Valrhona Opalys, 33% cocoa
100 grams (scant ½ cup) whole milk
15 grams (1¾ teaspoons) liquid glucose
½ gram kosher salt
200 grams (¾ cup plus 1½ tablespoons)
    heavy cream

EQUIPMENT

18 x 13-inch (half-sheet) pan
Parchment paper
Food processor or blender
Coarse strainer
Pastry bag with a medium
    (804 or ⅜-inch) tip

At least 1 day before serving:

- Preheat the oven to 150°C/300°F.
- **TO BLOOM THE GELATIN:** Submerge the gelatin in enough cold water to cover until it is very pliant, 5 to 10 minutes.
- Line an 18 x 13-inch (half-sheet) pan with parchment paper. Arrange the white chocolate in a single layer on the parchment paper. Roast for 18 minutes.
- **WHILE THE WHITE CHOCOLATE IS ROASTING:** Strain the water out of the gelatin and set aside. When the chocolate has roasted for 14 minutes, in a small pot, combine the whole milk and the liquid glucose and bring to a boil over medium-high heat, whisking to prevent the bottom from scorching. When the milk mixture comes to a boil, add the bloomed gelatin and the kosher salt and whisk to incorporate.
- When the chocolate has roasted for 18 minutes, carefully pick up the sides of the parchment paper, fold the paper into a trough, and pour the melted chocolate into the food processor or blender.
- **TO CREATE AN EMULSION:** Process the white chocolate in the food processor or blend in the blender on low speed, while slowly pouring a steady stream of the milk mixture into the chocolate.
- Continue running the food processor or blender while drizzling in the heavy cream until fully incorporated.
- Pass the white chocolate mixture through a coarse-mesh strainer into a storage container. Refrigerate, covered, for at least 12 hours, to set and crystallize the chocolate mixture.

The next day:

- Transfer the chocolate mixture to a pastry bag fitted with a medium-size (804 or ⅜-inch) round tip.

PISTACHIO PUREE

INGREDIENTS

212 grams (7.5 ounces) shelled
    Sicilian or Iranian pistachios
34 grams (2¼ tablespoons)
    granulated sugar
1.7 grams kosher salt
2.75 grams low acyl gellan

EQUIPMENT

Blender
Cooking thermometer
Fine-mesh strainer
Squeeze bottle

NOTE: *Sicilian and Iranian pistachios are very expensive, but they taste much better than other pistachio varieties. Although we prefer to use local ingredients as a general policy at Atelier Crenn, be advised that this recipe will not work well with regular Californian pistachios.*

At least 1 day before serving:

- Preheat the oven to 150°C/300°F. Arrange the pistachios in a single layer on a sheet pan and roast at 150°C/300°F, removing the pan just when the pistachios start to brown, about 15 minutes.
- In a medium pot, combine 425 grams (1¾ cups plus 2¼ teaspoons) water with the sugar and salt. Bring to a simmer over medium heat, whisking just until the sugar and salt have dissolved. Add half of the pistachios to the pot and stir; reserve the other half for the candied pistachio component. Remove from the heat and let cool to room temperature, then cover and refrigerate overnight.

The next day:

- Bring to a boil over medium heat, then immediately remove from the heat.
- Transfer the contents of the pot to a blender and blend on high until smooth, about 2 minutes.
- **TO INCORPORATE THE LOW ACYL GELLAN:** Turn off the blender and check the temperature of the mixture with a cooking thermometer. If the temperature is at least 80°C/175°F, which is the temperature at which low acyl gellan is activated, run the blender at medium speed, making sure that the contents form a vortex, and add the gellan without touching the sides of the blender, 10 seconds; if the temperature is below 80°C/175°F, transfer the puree to a medium pot and heat to 80°C/175°F before returning to the blender and incorporating the gellan.
- Transfer the mixture to a shallow container and refrigerate, uncovered, until set to a gel, about 1 hour.
- Once set, transfer the gel to a blender and blend on high speed until quite smooth with the texture of pudding, 30 seconds.
- Pass the pudding through a fine-mesh strainer to ensure that there are no residual lumps.
- Transfer to a squeeze bottle and refrigerate until ready to serve.

>>>

Honey (Spring), *continued*

CANDIED PISTACHIOS

INGREDIENTS

300 grams (1½ cups) granulated sugar

30 grams (1¼ tablespoons) liquid glucose

105 grams roasted Sicilian or Iranian pistachios (reserved from pistachio puree component)

At least 1 day before serving:

- In a medium pot, combine 200 grams (¾ cup plus 1½ tablespoons) water with the sugar and liquid glucose and whisk over medium heat until dissolved. Stir in the roasted pistachios reserved from the pistachio puree component and remove from the heat.
- Let sit, uncovered, until cooled to room temperature, then cover and refrigerate overnight. The pistachios may be refrigerated in the liquid for up to 1 week.

ASIAN PEAR CUBES

INGREDIENTS

100 grams (½ cup) granulated sugar

1 Asian pear

25 grams (5 teaspoons) pear vinegar

1 gram ascorbic acid

EQUIPMENT

Vacuum bag or resealable plastic freezer bag

Vacuum sealer (*optional*)

NOTE: *Compressing raw fruit and simple syrup in a vacuum sealer creates a distinctive texture that cannot be replicated without compression, but if you do not have a vacuum sealer, you can still marinate the pears, though you must allow an extra hour of inactive time*

At least 1 day before serving:

- TO PREPARE THE SIMPLE SYRUP: In a small saucepan, combine 115 grams (½ cup) water with the sugar and bring to a boil over high heat. Reduce the heat to medium-low and simmer, stirring, until the sugar is completely dissolved, about 3 minutes. Remove from the heat and allow to cool to room temperature.
- Peel and core the Asian pear. Cut into ½-inch cubes, discarding any imperfect pieces.
- In a small bowl, whisk together 100 grams (3.5 ounces) of the simple syrup and the pear vinegar.
- TO MARINATE AND COMPRESS THE PEAR CUBES WITH A VACUUM SEALER: In a vacuum bag, arrange 48 pear cubes in a tight 6 x 8 rectangle. Add 30 grams (1.05 ounces) of the simple syrup–vinegar mixture and the ascorbic acid. Seal the bag and compress at 99%.
- TO MARINATE THE PEAR CUBES WITHOUT A VACUUM SEALER: In a resealable plastic freezer bag, arrange 48 pear cubes in a tight 6 x 8 rectangle. Add 30 grams (1.05 ounces) of the simple syrup–vinegar mixture and the ascorbic acid.

>>>

Squeeze out as much air as possible, seal the bag, and refrigerate for 1 hour.

- Refrigerate the pears in the vacuum bag or resealable plastic freezer bag until ready to use.

BRAISED PEARS

INGREDIENTS

330 grams (11.6 ounces) skin-on
   sun-dried pears
100 grams (½ cup) granulated sugar
10 grams (0.35 ounces) dry chamomile
   flowers

EQUIPMENT

Vacuum bag or resealable plastic
   freezer bag
Cooking thermometer
Vacuum sealer (*optional*)
Coarse-mesh strainer
Parchment paper
Nonstick cooking spray
18 x 13-inch (half-sheet) pan
Dehydrator (*optional*)
Desiccant (*optional*)

At least 10 hours before serving:

- Place the sun-dried pears, sugar, and chamomile flowers in a vacuum bag or resealable plastic freezer bag.
- Fill a large pot three-quarters full with water, attach a cooking thermometer, and bring to a temperature of 55°C/130°F over low heat.
- Add 600 grams (2½ cups) room-temperature water to the vacuum bag, seal the vacuum bag, and compress at 99%; alternatively, transfer 600 grams (2½ cups) room-temperature water to the resealable plastic freezer bag, squeeze out as much as air possible, and seal the bag. Submerge the bag in the hot water, closely monitoring the heat to maintain a consistent temperature of 55°C/130°F and stirring often, until the pears are soft and plump but not yet mushy, 30 minutes to 2 hours. (At Atelier Crenn, we have used different sources of dried pears and noticed that the amount of time necessary to rehydrate and perfume them varies quite a bit.)
- Strain the contents of the bag, reserving the solids and the liquid separately. Carefully remove the skins from the pears and set aside to cool. Trim each piece of peeled, rehydrated pear in half lengthwise, then cut into thirds in the other direction. Transfer the rehydrated pear and the strained cooking syrup to an airtight container and refrigerate until ready to serve.
- Spray 2 large sheets of parchment paper with nonstick cooking spray and wipe down with a paper towel; the residual nonstick coating will suffice.
- **TO LAMINATE THE PEAR SKINS AND CHAMOMILE FLOWERS:** Arrange the pear skins in a single layer on the sprayed side of 1 sheet of parchment paper. Retrieve some chamomile flowers from the cooking liquid and lay 1 flower on each pear skin, varying the position of the flower on the skin. Cover the pear skins and chamomile flowers with the other sheet

>>>

Honey (Spring), *continued*

of parchment paper, sprayed-side down. Use a rolling pin to smooth and press the pear skins and chamomile flowers between the sheets of parchment paper.

- **TO DRY THE PEAR SKINS IN A DEHYDRATOR**: Place the parchment paper sheets on a dehydrator tray. Transfer the tray to a dehydrator set to 50°C/120°F and dry the pear skins until crispy, at least 8 hours.
- **TO DRY THE PEAR SKINS IN THE OVEN**: Preheat the oven to 50°C/120°F or the closest temperature available. Place the parchment papers on a baking sheet. Transfer the baking sheet to the oven and turn off the heat. Let the pear skins dry in the closed oven with the heat off until completely crispy, at least 8 hours.
- Store the dehydrated pear skins in an airtight container at room temperature until ready to serve. Add a desiccant, if desired.

HONEY CARAMEL WITH CITRUS-BEESWAX COATING

(Makes about 100 caramels)

INGREDIENTS

450 grams (2 cups) unsalted butter

450 grams (2¼ cups) packed brown sugar

395 grams (1 cup plus 2½ tablespoons) honey

160 grams (6¼ tablespoons) liquid glucose

52 grams corn maltodextrin

3 grams (0.1 ounce) kosher salt

1 orange

1 lemon

400 grams (scant 2 cups) grapeseed oil

12 grams (0.4 ounce) dried chamomile flowers

>>>

NOTE: *This is a very loose caramel, designed to melt in the mouth. Much of the structure derives from the beeswax and bee pollen coating. We mix the wax with grapeseed oil because pure beeswax would not be palatable and grapeseed is fairly neutral in flavor. For a simpler method, one could sprinkle the caramel with Maldon salt and bee pollen, then wrap tightly in cellophane. If the caramel is not coated or wrapped, however, it will ooze into a single continuous layer. We strongly recommend making the citrus-beeswax coating sous vide.*

At least 5 hours before serving:

- Cut the butter into ½-inch cubes.
- Cover a 9 x 13-inch (quarter-sheet) pan with parchment paper. Spray the parchment paper with nonstick cooking spray.
- In a medium pot, combine the butter, brown sugar, honey, liquid glucose, corn maltrodextrin, and kosher salt over low heat and whisk. When the contents begin to melt into a syrup, raise the heat to medium while continuing to whisk, until the temperature reaches 118°C/244°F. Immediately pour the mixture into the parchment paper–lined pan.

>>>

96 grams (3.4 ounces) pure beeswax

50 grams (1.8 ounces) cocoa butter

24 grams (0.85 ounces) tangerine oil

30 grams (1.05 ounces) bee pollen

EQUIPMENT

9 x 13-inch (quarter-sheet) pan

Parchment paper

Nonstick cooking spray

Cooking thermometer

Vacuum bag (optional)

Vacuum sealer (optional)

Immersion circulator (optional)

Fine-mesh strainer

Cheesecloth

Dipping fork or small tweezers

Offset spatula

- Let cool, uncovered, at room temperature until set, 3 to 4 hours.
- Meanwhile, zest the orange and lemon.
- **TO MAKE THE CITRUS-BEESWAX COATING SOUS VIDE:** In a vacuum bag, combine the grapeseed oil, chamomile flowers, orange zest, and lemon zest. Seal the bag and compress at 99%. Submerge the vacuum bag in an immersion circulator set to 55°C/130°F and cook sous vide for 2 hours.
- **TO MAKE THE CITRUS-BEESWAX COATING ON THE STOVETOP:** In a medium pot with a cooking thermometer attached, combine the grapeseed oil, chamomile flowers, orange zest, and lemon zest. Bring the liquid to 55°C/130°F over low heat and cook, stirring often to maintain a consistent temperature, for 30 minutes.
- Line a fine-mesh strainer with 1 layer of cheesecloth and position over a medium pot. Strain the coating through the cheesecloth-lined strainer into the pot.
- Add the beeswax, cocoa butter, and tangerine oil and cook over medium heat, without boiling, until the beeswax melts and the temperature of the mixture is in the 70°C/158°F to 80°C/176°F range.
- Allow to cool for 5 minutes.
- Transfer to a small microwave-safe bowl and attach a cooking thermometer, watching for the temperature to dip to 60°C/140°F. Microwave for 5 seconds on high to refresh if/when the coating begins to cool and harden.

  NOTE: *To clean the beeswax out of the pot and bowl, do not add water; use a paper towel to wipe off the wax.*
- Set up a dipping area with a bowl of beeswax, a bowl of pollen, and a dipping fork or small tweezers. Line a tray with clean parchment paper to hold the finished caramels. Spray a cutting board and your hands with nonstick cooking spray.
- **TO COAT THE CARAMELS:** Use a small offset spatula to cut a 6 x ½-inch strip of the caramels and transfer to the sprayed cutting board. Use the spatula to cut the strip into ½-inch cubes. Use your fingers to shape each caramel into a perfect cube. When you have 12 caramels shaped, balance one caramel on the dipping fork or grip with small tweezers and dip fully into the beeswax coating, just once all the way in, scraping the fork along the side of the bowl to prevent dripping, and place the coated caramel on the parchment paper. Immediately sprinkle the top

>>>

Honey (Spring), *continued*

of each caramel with a pinch of bee pollen. After dipping and sprinkling all 12 caramels, dip each again in the beeswax to seal the pollen layer. (Encasing the pollen within 2 layers of beeswax builds both flavor and texture.)

- Repeat the coating process with all the other caramels.
- Store the caramels in a single layer, without stacking, in an airtight container in a cool place. (At Atelier Crenn, we keep the caramels in our wine storage area, but you can refrigerate them as long as you bring the caramels to room temperature about 30 minutes before serving.)

PEAR PUREE

INGREDIENTS

½ whole vanilla bean

3 ripe Bartlett or red Anjou pears

30 grams (2½ tablespoons) granulated sugar

0.25 gram ascorbic acid

2.5 grams low acyl gellan

EQUIPMENT

Cooking thermometer

Vacuum bag or resealable plastic freezer bag

Vacuum sealer (*optional*)

Blender

Fine-mesh strainer

Squeeze bottle

At least 5 hours before serving:

- Fill a large pot three-quarters full with water, attach a cooking thermometer, and bring to a simmer (85°C/185°F) over medium-low heat.
- Split the vanilla bean in half lengthwise and scrape out the seeds, reserving both the pod and seeds.
- Peel, halve, and core the pears.
- Transfer 375 grams (13.25 ounces) of the pears, 95 grams (6½ tablespoons) water, the sugar, ascorbic acid, and vanilla bean seeds and pod to a vacuum bag, seal the vacuum bag, and compress at 99%; alternatively, transfer 375 grams (13.25 ounces) of the pears, 95 grams (6½ tablespoons) water, the sugar, ascorbic acid, and vanilla bean seeds and pod to a resealable plastic freezer bag, squeeze out as much as air possible, and seal the bag. Submerge the bag in the simmering water, closely monitoring the heat and stirring often to maintain a consistent temperature of 85°C/185°F, until the pears are very soft, at least 30 minutes.

>>>

NOTE: *We use a vacuum bag to cook the pears and preserve all of their juices and aromas, but we do not use an immersion circulator, because the temperature is not quite as sensitive for the pears as it might be for chocolate or sugars, which could be considered the "proteins" of the pastry side. The pastry kitchen uses an immersion circulator for the beeswax coating because we want to infuse the aromatics without melting the beeswax, but more often the pastry kitchen relies on Juan's probe thermometer in an ordinary pot of water.*

- While the pears are still hot, open the bag and remove the vanilla bean pod. Transfer the contents of the bag to a blender and blend on high speed until smooth.
- **TO INCORPORATE THE GELLAN**: Check the temperature of the mixture with a cooking thermometer. If the temperature is at least 80°C/175°F, which is the temperature at which gellan is activated, run the blender at medium speed, making sure that the contents form a vortex, and add the gellan without touching the sides of the blender, 15 seconds; if the temperature is below 80°C/175°F, transfer the puree to a medium pot and heat to 80°C/175°F before whisking in the gellan.
- Transfer the mixture to a shallow container and refrigerate, uncovered, until set to a gel, about 1 hour.
- Once set, transfer the gel to a blender and blend on high speed until quite smooth, with the texture of pudding, about 30 seconds.
- Pass the puree through a fine-mesh strainer to ensure that there are no residual lumps.
- Transfer to a squeeze bottle and refrigerate until ready to serve.

>>>

Honey (Spring), *continued*

HONEY CHAMOMILE CAKE

INGREDIENTS

23 grams (0.85 ounce) dried
   chamomile flowers
220 grams (1¾ cups) Cup4Cup
   gluten-free flour or all-purpose flour
7 grams (1⅔ teaspoons) baking powder
3 grams (½ teaspoon) kosher salt
2.5 grams (scant ⅔ teaspoon) baking
   soda
170 grams (½ cup) honey
115 grams (½ cup) grapeseed oil
110 grams (½ cup plus 3½ teaspoons)
   granulated sugar
40 grams (3¼ tablespoons) brown sugar
2 large eggs

EQUIPMENT

Fine-mesh strainer
Spice grinder
9 x 13-inch (quarter-sheet) baking pan
Kitchen scale
Cake tester (*optional*)
2-inch-diameter cookie cutter
   preferably hexagonal)

NOTE: *The original version of this recipe used all-purpose flour, but we experimented with Cup4Cup flour to accommodate our gluten-free diners, and found that we preferred the texture of Cup4Cup in this recipe. Now the whole dish is gluten-free without any extra prep work. This recipe also works very well with all-purpose flour, substituted at a 1:1 ratio.*

At least 1 hour before serving:

- Preheat the oven to 175°C/350°F.
- **TO BREW THE CHAMOMILE TEA**: Combine 180 grams (scant 1 cup) water to a boil with 4 grams (0.15 ounce) of the chamomile and steep for 5 minutes. Strain through a fine-mesh strainer and refrigerate, uncovered, for at least 30 minutes.
- In a spice grinder, grind the remaining 19 grams (0.7 ounce) chamomile flowers into a fine powder.
- In a medium bowl, sift together the flour, chamomile powder, baking powder, kosher salt, and baking soda.
- In a large bowl, whisk together the honey, oil, granulated sugar, brown sugar, and eggs. Whisk in the dry ingredients in batches. Last, stir in the chamomile tea until fully incorporated.
- Set a 9 x 13-inch (quarter-sheet) pan on a kitchen scale and tare to zero. Add 315 grams (11.1 ounces) of the cake batter and spread it evenly across the pan. (Cup4Cup is very sticky because it contains rice flour, so we weigh the amount in every pan to make sure we produce a consistent product.)
- Bake until the cake pulls away from the sides of the pan or until a cake tester inserted into the center comes out clean, about 11 minutes.
- Let the cake cool, uncovered, to room temperature.
- Use a 2-inch-diameter cookie cutter (preferably hexagonal), to cut the cake into individual portions.
- Cover the cake pieces tightly with plastic wrap and set aside at room temperature until ready to serve.

>>>

Honey (Spring), *continued*

PISTACHIO POWDER

INGREDIENTS

100 grams (¾ cup plus 2½ teaspoons) shelled Sicilian or Iranian pistachios

EQUIPMENT

Insulated gloves (*optional*)
Safety glasses (*optional*)
Liquid nitrogen (*optional*)
Spice grinder (*optional*)

INGREDIENTS

Bee pollen
Fresh chamomile threads
Micro red lemon balm
Fresh elderflower

EQUIPMENT

Pen torch (*optional*)

- **TO MAKE PISTACHIO POWDER WITH LIQUID NITROGEN AND A SPICE GRINDER:** Put on insulated gloves and safety glasses. Freeze the pistachios with liquid nitrogen, which will make the nuts brittle without leaching out the oils. Immediately transfer the frozen pistachios to a spice grinder and grind to a textured powder, but do not grind all the way to dust.
- **TO MAKE PISTACHIO POWDER WITH A KNIFE:** Use a sharp knife to chop the pistachios as fine as possible. Do not use a grinder because it will turn into pistachio butter rather than powder.

TO SERVE:

NOTE: *At Atelier Crenn, we serve our honey dessert on a custom-made hexagonal plate, in which a honeycomb is encased in a wooden box covered with glass. The entire composition is organized around a hexagonal pattern.*

- Set the honey caramels out to come to room temperature, if refrigerated.
- In the center of each plate, squeeze 1 dot of pistachio puree, which will prevent the chamomile cake from slipping. Place 1 piece of chamomile cake on top of the pistachio puree.
- Leaving a ½-inch margin of space around the chamomile cake, pipe a circular ring of white chocolate crémeux around the cake. Use a pen torch to quickly glaze the crémeux, if desired. (Slightly melting the crémeux helps to anchor the other components that will be placed on it, but one must be careful not to melt the crémeux entirely or to singe the chamomile cake.)
- Imagine the ring of crémeux as a clockface. Squeeze dollops of pistachio puree at 11:00 outside the ring, 5:00 on the inside the ring, 7:00 outside the ring, and 1:00 inside the ring. Squeeze dollops of pear puree across the ring from the pistachio puree: 11:00 inside the ring, 5:00 outside the ring, 7:00 inside the ring, and 1:00 outside the ring.

- Carefully strain the candied pistachios and braised pears and let the pieces sit on a clean kitchen towel; you will need 4 candied pistachios per plate and 3 pieces of braised pear per plate. (At Atelier Crenn, we use a perforated spoon to remove the pieces we need for a single table and drain the excess moisture on a surgical tray lined with a C-fold towel.)
- Sprinkle a pinch of bee pollen on the ring of crémeux, as though encrusting it. Sprinkle pistachio powder along the ring.
- Place 1 piece of candied pistachio on top of each dollop of pistachio puree. Place 1 Asian pear cube on top of each dollop of pear puree. Top each candied pistachio with chamomile threads. Top each Asian pear cube with micro red lemon balm, with the colored side facing upward.
- Place 3 pieces of braised pear on top of the crémeux: 1 piece at 12:00, 1 piece at 3:00, and 1 piece at 9:00.
- Break the dehydrated pear skins into 3 shards (i.e., one-third of a skin per shard). Top each braised pear with 1 shard of dehydrated pear skin.
- Remove the honey meringue from the dehydrator and break off 1- to 2-inch pieces.
- Use the crémeux to anchor 3 pieces of honey meringue in a vertical orientation, with the browned side facing toward the guest: 1 piece between 10:00 and 11:00, 1 piece between 1:00 and 2:00, and 1 piece at 6:00.
- Remove the beeswax sorbet from the mold and place gently on top of the chamomile cake; alternatively, scoop 1 small quenelle of beeswax sorbet on top of the chamomile cake and top with 1 additional piece of honey meringue. (At Atelier Crenn, we garnish each plate with 1 additional serving of beeswax sorbet, which we freeze in a custom-made beeswax-patterned column-shaped mold.)
- Serve the honey caramels with citrus-beeswax coating on the side, as an accompaniment to the rest of the dish. (At Atelier Crenn, we serve the caramels perched in the empty spaces of a drone comb, which has been mounted vertically and placed at the center of the table.)

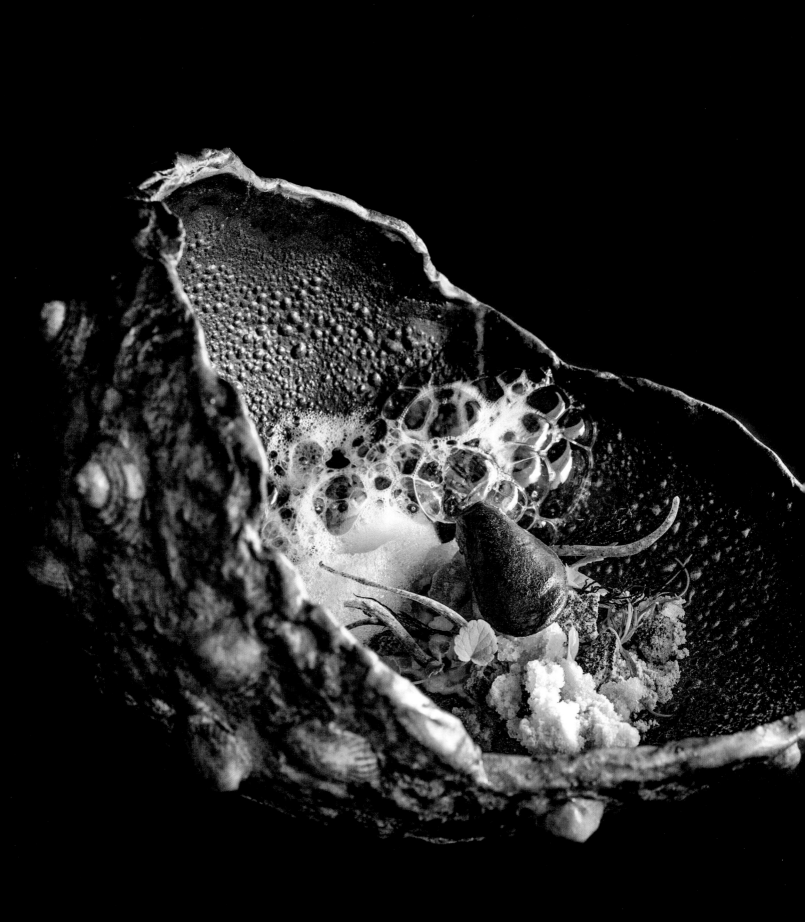

Juan is always pushing the boundaries of the pastry chef's domain, but this dish inspired by the sea—and by The Sea (page 123), a dish from the savory side of the kitchen—might be his most thought-provoking, groundbreaking dish. I love the way he transforms the textures, colors, and flavors of the ocean into such a surprisingly intuitive dessert.

This version of The Sea begins with three pre-desserts that introduce some of the themes that will be carried through the main dessert. First to arrive is a palate cleanser of pineapple water with blue-green algae floating upward through it. Next, our guests receive a small dish of compressed aloe flavored with sea lettuce and shiso. Last, a thin matcha-nori wafer, which Juan has ingeniously created using oblaat, an edible wrapper used in Japan to wrap candies or as a vehicle for administering medicine to children. (Made from potato starch, oblaat dissolves instantly when it comes in contact with water, so it must wrap something dry or moistened with fat rather than water. Ferran Adrià used it to wrap caramels that could be eaten whole, whereas Juan melts sugars onto oblaat to make a glass-like wafer.)

For the main dish, Juan made seaworthy vessels and molds by melting acetate onto mussel, clam, and oyster shells from the savory side of the kitchen and from other shells he found himself on the beach. The main dessert is served in a vessel inspired by a reflective moment Juan had while watching the crescent moon reflected in the waves. He poured silicone to make prototypes and then sent those to be replicated by a woman he knows (who always asks, "What do you do with these things, anyway?"). The final dish looks like a tide pool washed with foam and brimming with life, like an intricate ecosystem that unites complex components into something wondrous. | *Serves 12*

The Sea (Summer)

SAKE KASU SORBET

INGREDIENTS

400 grams (2 cups plus 2½ tablespoons) uncooked koshihikari rice

125 grams (4.4 ounces) Stabilizer Syrup (page 323)

42 grams (2½ tablespoons) sake kasu (sake lees)

25 grams corn maltodextrin

1 gram kosher salt

0.5 gram xanthan gum

EQUIPMENT

Blender

Fine-mesh strainer

Pacojet or home ice cream maker

At least 2 days before serving:

• Preheat the oven to 175°C/350°F.

• **TO MAKE TOASTED RICE WATER:** Spread the rice in a single layer on a baking sheet. Toast the rice in the oven until golden brown, 25 minutes. Let cool, uncovered, until room temperature.

• Transfer the toasted rice to a storage container and add 2 liters (2¼ quarts) cold water. Cover and let sit at room temperature overnight.

• Meanwhile, prepare the Stabilizer Syrup (page 325).

The next day:

• Transfer the rice and water to the blender and blend on low speed to break up the rice and release some rice flavor but not long enough to puree, about 20 seconds. Transfer the rice water back to the container and let sit at room temperature until the rice sediment settles to the bottom, 30 to 40 minutes.

>>>

The Sea (Summer), *continued*

- Strain the rice water through a fine-mesh strainer and discard the solids.
- In a blender, combine 500 grams (2 cups plus 2 tablespoons) of the rice water with the stabilizer syrup, sake kasu, corn malto-dextrin, kosher salt, and xanthan gum. Reserve the remaining toasted rice water for use in the coconut-kasu mousse and the coconut ash gel.
- **TO MAKE THE SAKE KASU SORBET IN A PACOJET**: Transfer the rice water–sake kasu mixture to a Pacojet and freeze until solid, at least 12 hours or overnight, and pacotize the next day.
- **TO MAKE THE SAKE KASU SORBET IN A HOME ICE CREAM MAKER**: Transfer the rice water–sake kasu mixture to an airtight container and freeze until solid, at least 12 hours or overnight. Follow the manufacturer's instructions for your ice cream maker to process into a sorbet.

PINEAPPLE WATER WITH BLUE-GREEN ALGAE

INGREDIENTS

500 grams (2 cups) fresh cold-pressed pineapple juice

425 grams (1¾ cups plus ¾ tablespoon) mineral water

37 grams (3 tablespoons plus ¼ teaspoon) granulated sugar

1.8 grams agar-agar

100 grams (½ cup) granulated sugar

15 grams (0.53 ounce) fennel fronds

10 grams (0.35 ounce) lemongrass

3 grams (0.1 ounce) peeled sliced fresh ginger

240 grams (8.47 ounces) liquid blue-green algae

>>>

At least 29 hours before serving:

- In a medium pot, combine the pineapple juice, mineral water, sugar, and agar-agar. Bring to a simmer over medium heat, whisking continuously, and simmer for 1 minute. Remove from the heat, transfer to a 2-liter (2¼-quart) container, and refrigerate until completely set to a gel, about 4 hours.
- Place a perforated hotel pan in a deep hotel pan. Line the perforated hotel pan with 3 large layers of cheesecloth overhanging the edges on both sides.
- Use a whisk to break up the pineapple gel until it resembles a lumpy liquid, then pour the broken pineapple gel into the cheesecloth-lined perforated hotel pan. Carefully cover the broken pineapple gel with the overhanging layers of cheesecloth so that it is fully wrapped. Position a standard hotel pan on top of the pineapple gel. Add weights to the top pan so that the liquid drips out slowly. Refrigerate overnight.
- **TO PREPARE THE SIMPLE SYRUP**: In a small saucepan, combine 230 grams (1 cup) water with the sugar and bring to a boil. Simmer over medium-low heat, stirring, until the sugar has

>>>

0.2 gram xanthan gum

25 grams (0.88 ounce) basil seeds

12 bronze fennel fronds

1 gram fresh fennel pollen

EQUIPMENT

Perforated hotel pan

2 standard hotel pans

Cheesecloth

Weights (such as canned tomatoes)

Fine-mesh strainer

Blender

Fine kitchen scissors

completely dissolved, about 3 minutes. Remove from the heat and allow to cool to room temperature. Refrigerate overnight.

The next day:

- Use both hands to gently squeeze any remaining liquid from the cheesecloth and discard the solids remaining in the cheesecloth.
- Transfer the pineapple water to a small pot and bring to a simmer over medium heat. Add the fennel fronds, lemongrass, and ginger and remove from the heat. Cover the pot with plastic wrap and allow to infuse for 30 minutes. Pass the liquid through a fine-mesh strainer and refrigerate until thoroughly chilled, about 1 hour.

At least 2 hours before serving:

- **TO MAKE THE BLUE-GREEN ALGAE GEL:** In a blender, combine 200 grams (7.05 ounces) of the blue-green algae and the xanthan gum. Blend on high speed until fully incorporated. Let the mixture sit for 2 hours to release bubbles. Strain through a fine-mesh strainer. Skim off any bubbles and refrigerate, covered, until ready to serve.

At least 30 minutes before serving:

- **TO PREPARE THE BASIL SEEDS:** In a small container, mix together 230 grams (1 cup) water and the basil seeds. Let sit at room temperature, whisking occasionally to prevent clumps from forming, until the basil seeds are fully hydrated, about 15 minutes. Add the remaining 40 grams (1.41 ounces) liquid blue-green algae and 30 grams (1½ tablespoons) of the simple syrup and whisk to incorporate. Reserve the remaining simple syrup for use in the seaweed croquant and algae slush component. Refrigerate, covered, until ready to serve.
- Use fine kitchen scissors to cut the bronze fennel fronds into very small pieces.
- In a large storage container, mix together 500 grams (2 cups plus 2 tablespoons) of the pineapple water with the bronze fennel fronds. Stir in 50 grams (1.8 ounces) of the hydrated basil seeds and the fennel pollen. Refrigerate until ready to serve.

>>>

The Sea (Summer), *continued*

COCONUT-KASU MOUSSE

INGREDIENTS

225 grams (scant 1 cup) fresh
coconut milk

40 grams (2 tablespoons plus
1 teaspoon) sake kasu

300 grams (1¼ cups) toasted rice water
(reserved from sake kasu sorbet
component)

50 grams (¼ cup) granulated sugar

6 grams agar-agar

2.5 grams matcha powder

1.2 grams (0.04 ounce) kosher salt

EQUIPMENT

Blender

Whipped cream charger

One day before serving:

- In a blender, combine the coconut milk and sake kasu and blend on medium speed until smooth, about 1 minute.
- Transfer the coconut–sake kasu mixture to a medium pot and bring to a simmer over medium-low heat. Remove from the heat and let cool, uncovered, to room temperature. Transfer to an airtight container and refrigerate overnight to allow the flavors to mature.

The next day:

- In a medium pot, mix the cooled coconut–sake kasu mixture with the toasted rice water, sugar, agar-agar, matcha powder, and kosher salt and bring to a boil over medium heat. Remove from the heat and pour into a shallow container. Refrigerate until set to a gel, about 1 hour.
- In a blender, blend the mixture on high speed until smooth, about 3 minutes.
- Transfer to a whipped cream charger and charge twice. (At Atelier Crenn, we use iSi cream chargers.)
- Refrigerate the charged mousse until ready to serve.

SPIRULINA SEAWEED TUILE

INGREDIENTS

100 grams (⅓ cup plus 1½ tablespoons) fresh coconut milk

17 grams (2 tablespoons) kuzu (kudzu) starch

16 grams (4 teaspoons) granulated sugar

1 gram kosher salt

2.5 grams spirulina powder

1 gram phytoplankton powder

EQUIPMENT

Blender

Cooking thermometer

Pastry bag

Acetate sheet

Nonstick cooking spray

Cheesecloth

Dehydrator (*optional*)

One day before serving:

- In a blender, combine 100 grams (6¾ tablespoons) water with the coconut milk, kuzu, sugar, and kosher salt. Blend on high speed until the kuzu crystals break down and are incorporated into the liquid, about 30 seconds.
- Transfer to a small pot with a cooking thermometer attached and cook over medium-high heat, whisking continuously. The liquid will start to swell at about 70°C/158°F, when the thickening properties of the kuzu starch are activated. Continue whisking until the mixture comes to a boil, then remove from the heat and whisk in the spirulina powder.
- Allow to cool, uncovered, until the temperature reaches 60°C/140°F, then transfer the mixture to a pastry bag.
- Spray 1 acetate sheet with nonstick cooking spray and wipe down with a paper towel; the residual nonstick coating will suffice.
- **TO SHAPE THE TUILES:** Cut a very small opening in the pastry bag and pipe the mixture onto the acetate sheet in squiggly shapes reminiscent of seaweed, 1½ inches long.
- Place 1 gram of phytoplankton powder on a double layer of cheesecloth and gather it into a small sachet. Tap the sachet over the tuiles to sprinkle with a light dusting of phytoplankton powder.
- Let the tuiles sit at room temperature for 30 minutes to allow the kuzu to set. Do not wait too long before drying, because the color will darken from green to black.
- **TO DRY THE TUILES IN A DEHYDRATOR:** Place the acetate sheet in a dehydrator tray. Transfer the tray to a dehydrator set to 80°C/175°F until completely dry and crispy, about 12 hours.
- **TO DRY THE SEAWEED IN THE OVEN:** Preheat the oven to 80°C/175°F or the closest temperature available. Place the acetate sheet in a baking sheet. Transfer the baking sheet to the oven and turn off the heat. Let the tuiles dry in the closed oven until completely dry and crispy, about 12 hours.
- Hold the tuiles in the dehydrator or in an airtight container at room temperature until ready to serve.

>>>

SEAWEED CROQUANT

INGREDIENTS

2 cups fresh chain bladder seaweed
Simple syrup (reserved from Pineapple
    Water component)

EQUIPMENT

Acetate sheet
Nonstick cooking spray
Dehydrator (*optional*)

At least 1 day before serving:

- Rinse the chain bladder seaweed, changing the water until the water runs clear. In a quart container, cover the seaweed with fresh cool water and refrigerate overnight to leach out some of the salinity.

The next day:

- Drain the liquid from the seaweed and rinse with fresh cool water.
- In a medium bowl, dress the seaweed with a light coating of the simple syrup. Reserve any unused simple syrup for use in the algae slush component. Transfer the seaweed to a paper towel to allow some of the excess liquid to drain off.
- Spray 1 acetate sheet with nonstick cooking spray and wipe down with a paper towel; the residual nonstick coating will suffice.
- **TO DRY THE SEAWEED IN A DEHYDRATOR:** Place the acetate sheet in a dehydrator tray. Evenly spread the seaweed across the acetate sheet. Transfer the tray to a dehydrator set to 80°C/175°F and dry the seaweed until it has shrunk considerably and is completely dry and crispy, about 7 hours.
- **TO DRY THE SEAWEED IN THE OVEN:** Preheat the oven to 80°C/175°F or the closest temperature available. Place the acetate sheet in a baking sheet. Evenly spread the seaweed across the acetate sheet. Transfer the baking sheet to the oven and turn off the heat. Let the seaweed dry in the closed oven with the heat off until it has shrunk considerably and is completely dry and crispy, about 7 hours.
- Hold the seaweed croquants in the dehydrator or in an airtight container at room temperature until ready to serve.

>>>

The Sea (Summer), *continued*

COCONUT ASH GEL

INGREDIENTS

6 young coconuts

200 grams (¾ cup plus 1½ tablespoons) toasted rice water (reserved from sake kasu sorbet component)

200 grams (¾ cup plus 1¼ tablespoons) fresh coconut milk

65 grams (⅓ cup) granulated sugar

1.5 grams (0.05 ounce) kosher salt

2.5 grams low acyl gellan

1 gram xanthan gum

EQUIPMENT

2 x 2-inch sorbet molds (at least 12 divots, preferably seashell shaped)

Parchment paper

Propane torch

Spice grinder

Cooking thermometer

Pastry bag

Offset spatula

At least 5 hours before serving:

- Place the sorbet molds in the freezer to chill.
- Preheat the oven to 190°C/375°F.
- Cut the peel off the young coconuts. Line a baking sheet with parchment paper. Arrange the coconut peels in an even layer on the parchment paper and bake until completely dry, about 1 hour.
- Char the coconut peels evenly with a propane torch. Lower the oven temperature to 190°C/375°F and return the baking sheet to the oven for 2 hours, to remove residual moisture.
- Grind the dried coconut peels in a spice grinder to make coconut ash.
- In a medium pot with a cooking thermometer attached, combine the reserved rice water, coconut milk, and 300 grams (1¼ cups) water. In a small container, whisk together the sugar, 6 grams (0.2 ounce) of the coconut ash, the kosher salt, gellan, and xanthan gum. Reserve the remaining coconut ash for use in the sand component.
- Without heating, whisk the dry ingredients into the wet ingredients in the pot, then bring the mixture up to 80°C/175°F. Remove from the heat and let sit in the pot at room temperature, whisking every 2 minutes to prevent a skin from forming, until the mixture cools to between 60°C/140°F and 62°C/144°F. (If the liquid is too hot, it won't stick to the molds and form a gel.) Transfer 1 cup of the liquid to a container with a spout.
- Remove the sorbet molds from the freezer. As quickly as possible, pour the liquid into the mold divots, filling them completely, and immediately invert the molds to let the excess drain off. There should be a thin skin of gel in each divot. If there are spots where it is not covered, repeat the process by chilling the molds in the freezer and adding the gel at 60°C/140°F to 62°C/144°F.
- After the gel has stuck to the molds, scrape the top and return the coated molds to the freezer until firm, about 30 minutes.
- Transfer the sake kasu sorbet to a pastry bag.
- Pipe enough sorbet to fill the cavity in each mold. Use an offset spatula to scrape away excess sorbet and frozen ash skin on the top.
- Freeze the filled sorbet molds until ready to serve.

ALGAE SLUSH

INGREDIENTS

300 grams (1 cup plus 3¼ tablespoons)
    fresh orange juice
75 grams (2.65 ounces) liquid blue-green
    algae
55 grams (1.95 ounces) simple syrup
    (reserved from seaweed croquant
    component), plus more as needed
50 grams (3¼ tablespoons) fresh
    grapefruit juice

EQUIPMENT

Robot Coupe or food processor

COMPRESSED ALOE

INGREDIENTS

300 grams (1½ cups) granulated sugar
100 grams (4¾ tablespoons) honey
1.6 grams citric acid
80 grams (2.8 ounces) fresh sea lettuce,
    rinsed
10 shiso leaves
1 whole aloe leaf
10 grams (0.35 ounce) kosher salt

EQUIPMENT

Vacuum bags
Vacuum sealer

At least 4 hours before serving:

- In a medium bowl, whisk together the orange juice, 120 grams (½ cup) water, the algae, simple syrup, and grapefruit juice. Taste the mixture—if it is too acidic, add water and simple syrup to taste.
- Freeze in a shallow pan in the freezer until completely frozen solid, about 4 hours.
- Grind in a Robot Coupe or food processor until slushy, about 2 minutes.
- Wrap and freeze in an airtight container until ready to serve.

At least 90 minutes before serving:

- **TO MAKE THE HERB-HONEY SYRUP:** In a large pot, combine 300 grams (1¼ cups) water, 200 grams (1 cup) of the sugar, the honey, and the citric acid. Cook over medium heat until the sugar has completely dissolved, about 5 minutes. Remove from the heat and immediately add the sea lettuce and shiso leaves. Cover and let steep at room temperature for 20 minutes. Uncover and transfer to the refrigerator to cool.
- Use a sharp knife to remove and discard the thorns from the aloe. Very carefully slice under the aloe skin to remove it, bracing the aloe against a cutting board because the flesh is very slippery. Discard the skin. Use the back of the knife to scrape off and discard some of the gelatinous material in the aloe. Rinse the aloe under cool water. Cut the aloe into 1-inch cubes.
- **TO BLANCH THE ALOE:** In a large pot, combine the aloe cubes with enough cold water to cover. Add 20 grams (1 table-spoon plus 2 teaspoons) of the sugar and 2 grams (0.7 ounce) of the kosher salt. Over medium heat, bring the liquid to a low boil and immediately remove from the heat. Strain the aloe through a fine-mesh strainer and discard the liquid. Rinse the aloe in cold water to stop the cooking.

>>>

The Sea (Summer), *continued*

- Repeat the blanching process 4 additional times with 20 grams (1 tablespoon plus 2 teaspoons) of sugar and 2 grams (0.7 ounce) of kosher salt each time, to leach out the bitterness of the aloe without overcooking and affecting the natural texture. Prepare an ice water bath. After the final blanch, rinse the aloe and plunge it into the ice water bath. Let chill for 15 minutes, and drain the ice water.
- In a vacuum bag, combine the blanched aloe with enough of the cooled herb-honey syrup to cover (about 50 grams) and compress at 99%.
- Refrigerate the aloe in the vacuum bag until ready to use.

MATCHA DACQUOISE

Ninety minutes before serving:

INGREDIENTS

160 grams (1⅔ cups) almond flour

135 grams (1 cup plus 2 tablespoons) confectioners' sugar

15 grams matcha powder

200 grams (7.1 ounces) egg whites (from about 6 eggs)

50 grams (¼ cup) granulated sugar

2 grams nori powder

EQUIPMENT

Sifter

Stand mixer with whisk attachment

Pastry bag with plain tip

2 silicone mats

- In a medium bowl, sift together the almond flour, confectioners' sugar, and matcha powder.
- In the bowl of a stand mixer fitted with the whisk attachment, whip the egg whites on medium-high speed until foamy, about 1 minute. With the mixer running on medium-high speed, incorporate the granulated sugar in 3 increments. Raise the speed to high and whip into a stiff, glossy meringue, about 2 minutes.
- In 3 increments, fold the meringue into the almond flour mixture. With each increment, fold a bit more gently.
- Transfer the dacquoise mixture to a pastry bag fitted with a plain tip.
- Line 2 baking sheets with silicone mats. On the silicone mats, pipe 4- to 5-inch-diameter pinwheels. Sprinkle each pinwheel with a light dusting of nori powder.
- Bake until the dacquoise is dry, about 15 minutes. Reduce the oven temperature to 95°C/200°F and bake for 30 minutes more to crisp.
- Let the dacquoises cool to room temperature before removing them from the silicone mats. Store in an airtight container at room temperature until ready to use or serve. (Do not worry about breaking the dacquoises, as they will be broken into ¼-inch pieces before being served.)

MATCHA-NORI WAFER

INGREDIENTS

50 grams (4¼ tablespoons) isomalt sugar
50 grams (¼ cup) fondant
50 grams (2 tablespoons) liquid glucose
3 grams matcha powder
2 sheets high-quality nori
12 (2-inch-diameter) oblaat sheets
Maldon salt

EQUIPMENT

9 x 13-inch (quarter-sheet) pan
Silicone mat
Cooking thermometer
Spice grinder
Sheet pan or toaster oven tray
Fine-mesh strainer or tea strainer
Salamander or toaster oven
Parchment paper
Desiccant (*optional*)

NOTE: *We make this caramel using the same technique as ordinary caramels or brittles but because we use fondant and isomalt, which can withstand higher temperatures before browning, the resulting caramel is white and translucent, or "neutral."*

At least 1 hour before serving:

- **TO MAKE A NEUTRAL CARAMEL:** Line a 9 x 13-inch (quarter-sheet) pan with a silicone mat. In a small pot with a cooking thermometer attached, combine the isomalt sugar, fondant, and liquid glucose and cook over medium-high heat until the temperature reaches 160°C/320°F. Remove from the heat and pour the mixture in an even layer onto the silicone mat. Let cool, uncovered, at room temperature until completely set, about 15 minutes.

- **TO GRIND THE POWDERS:** Make sure that the spice grinder is completely dry. Break the neutral caramel into pieces small enough to fit the spice grinder and grind into a fine powder. Transfer the ground caramel powder to a dry storage container. Add the matcha powder and stir to mix thoroughly. Clean and dry the spice grinder thoroughly. Grind the nori to a fine powder and set aside separately.

- **TO COAT THE OBLAAT SHEETS:** Set a silicone mat on a sheet pan or toaster oven tray and arrange the oblaat sheets in a single layer on the silicone mat; you may need to work in batches. Transfer a small amount of the caramel and matcha powder to the fine-mesh strainer or tea strainer and tap over the oblaat sheets to cover in a very thin, even layer.

- Use your fingers to sprinkle a fine, even layer of nori powder on top of the caramel-and-matcha powder. Drop 2 crystals of Maldon salt on each oblaat sheet, one on the middle of each side. (Ideally, 1 crystal will be consumed per bite.)

- **TO MELT THE OBLAAT SHEETS IN A SALAMANDER:** Transfer the sheet tray to the salamander and heat until melted, about 20 seconds.

- **TO MELT THE OBLAAT SHEETS IN A TOASTER OVEN:** Set the toaster oven to the broiler setting at the highest temperature, and place the tray in the toaster oven to heat until melted, about 30 seconds.

>>>

The Sea (Summer), *continued*

- The sugars will become glossy before browning; do not allow them to brown or burn.
- Allow the wafers to cool to room temperature. Transfer to an airtight container, separated by sheets of parchment paper. Add a desiccant, if desired.
- Store at room temperature until ready to serve.

RICE PORRIDGE

INGREDIENTS

400 grams (1⅔ cups) fresh coconut milk

80 grams (6 tablespoons plus 2 teaspoons) granulated sugar

3 grams (0.1 ounce) kosher salt

10 grams (0.35 ounce) dried lemon verbena

120 grams (⅔ cup) uncooked koshihikari rice

EQUIPMENT

Fine-mesh strainer

At least 1 hour before serving:

- In a medium pot, mix together 600 grams (2½ cups) water with the coconut milk, sugar, and kosher salt. Bring to a boil and remove from the heat. Add the lemon verbena, cover, and let steep at room temperature for 3 to 4 minutes. Do not steep for too long or the cooking liquid will become bitter rather than pleasantly citrusy.
- Strain the liquid through a fine-mesh strainer into a clean medium pot, discarding the solids.
- Rinse the rice until the water runs moderately clear but not completely clear.

NOTE: *For a thicker porridge, rinse less.*

- Add the rice to the pot and bring to a low boil over medium heat. Reduce the heat to low and simmer, uncovered, until the rice is tender but not mushy, 18 to 20 minutes. The rice will appear rather runny when warm, but will thicken to a porridge consistency as it cools. Remove from the heat and transfer to a cool container.
- Refrigerate, uncovered, until completely cool, then cover and refrigerate until ready to serve.

SAND

INGREDIENTS

60 grams (scant ⅓ cup) tangerine oil
28 grams (3¾ tablespoons)
    confectioners' sugar
8 grams (0.3 ounce) matcha powder
2 grams coconut ash (reserved from
    coconut ash gel component)
1.5 grams nori powder
0.5 grams kosher salt
150 grams (5.3 ounces) tapioca
    maltodextrin
250 grams (8.8 ounces) matcha
    dacquoise (reserved from matcha
    dacquoise component)

EQUIPMENT

Robot Coupe or food processor
Spice grinder

PAMPLEMOUSSE BUBBLES

INGREDIENTS

12 grams Sucro
750 grams (1 bottle) moscato,
    preferably La Caudrina
125 grams (4.4 ounces) grapefruit
    liqueur, preferably Combier
    Pamplemousse Rose

EQUIPMENT

Blender

Up to 5 days before serving:

- In a medium bowl, mix together the tangerine oil, confectioners' sugar, matcha powder, coconut ash, nori powder, and kosher salt and stir until the mixture forms a black paste. Transfer to a Robot Coupe or food processor, add the tapioca maltodextrin, and process until combined and the color turns dark green, about 2 minutes. Scrape down the sides of the canister to ensure that all the ingredients are fully incorporated.
- Break up the matcha dacquoise and pulse in a spice grinder until a medium-fine powder, not a very fine powder. Add the dacquoise powder to the sand and mix well.
- Store the sand in an airtight container at room temperature.

- In a blender, combine 500 grams (2 cups plus 2 tablespoons) water with the Sucro and blend on medium speed until incorporated, about 30 seconds. Reduce the blender speed to low and drizzle in the moscato and grapefruit liqueur until fully incorporated.

    >>>

The Sea (Summer), *continued*

INGREDIENTS

24 sea grape stems
I grapefruit
36 bronze fennel tips (*optional*)
12 agretti leaves (if in season)

EQUIPMENT

12 (9-inch) clear glass test tubes or
   champagne flutes
Eye dropper or fine-tipped squeeze bottle
Aquarium pump

TO SERVE:

- **TO PREPARE THE PINEAPPLE WATER PALATE CLEANSER:**
  Chill the test tubes or champagne flutes in the refrigerator.
  Fill each test tube or champagne flute one-third full with the
  pineapple water mixture. Add I sea grape stem per test tube or
  champagne flute. Transfer the blue-green algae mixture to an
  eye dropper or fine-tipped squeeze bottle and add 10 grams of
  blue-green algae to each test tube or champagne flute. Fill each
  test tube or champagne flute with the remaining pineapple water
  mixture and top with a final garnish of sea grape. The algae
  will streak upward through the pineapple water like a lava lamp.
  Serve immediately.
- Serve the compressed aloe.
- Serve the matcha-nori wafer.
- **TO CUT THE GRAPEFRUIT INTO SUPREMES:** Use a sharp
  knife to slice the stem and flower ends from the grapefruit.
  Stand the grapefruit on its end and slice downward, following the curvature of the fruit, to remove all the peel and pith,
  rotating to remove the entire peel. Slice along each membrane to
  free each segment without any pith. Remove any seeds. Cut each
  grapefruit supreme into 3 equal-size pieces. (At Atelier Crenn,
  we freeze the grapefruit with liquid nitrogen and gently break
  the fruit into individual "cells" instead.)
- **TO PLATE:** Spoon I tablespoon of rice porridge onto the center of each plate. Imagining the porridge as a clockface, place
  2 pieces of grapefruit on the porridge at 3:00 and 9:00. Place
  ½ teaspoon of basil seeds in the center of the rice porridge.
- Place I thread of bronze fennel on top of each grapefruit piece
  and another at 12:00, if desired.
- Use a miniature spoon to lay I teaspoon of sand in a thin line
  along the edge of the plate in the area closest to the diner,
  slightly off center. Lay I agretti leaf, if in season, on top of the
  sand. Place 2 spirulina seaweed tuiles at 4:00 and 8:00 on the
  rice porridge. Place 2 seaweed croquants right below the tuiles
  (i.e., 4:30 and 7:30 on the rice porridge).

- Transfer the grapefruit-moscato mixture to a large, deep container and aerate with an aquarium pump. Adjust the settings to create tiny bubbles. You may continue plating while the bubbles accumulate.
- Break the matcha-nori dacquoise into ¼-inch pieces. Arrange 7 pieces around the perimeter of the porridge.
- Dispense ½ tablespoon of coconut-kasu mousse over the center of the porridge. Spoon ½ tablespoon of algae slush on top of the mousse.
- For each plate, remove 1 sake kasu sorbet from its mold and place on top of the algae slush.
- Use a large spoon to scoop 1 tablespoon of grapefruit bubbles onto the edge of the plate behind the sake kasu sorbet.
- Serve immediately.

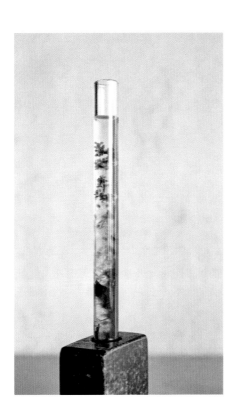

Juan loves walking among the redwoods growing outside the city, in the counties north of San Francisco, and in the early days of Atelier Crenn, he had been in the habit of collecting some of the acorns he found on his rambles. At the time, he hadn't been thinking about the acorns as part of a dessert recipe, but just admired them as small objects of beauty. As the second autumn of Atelier Crenn approached, however, we wanted to capture the experience of walking through a forest covered in acorns and fallen leaves, and all the smells of fall, so Juan decided to cast the acorns as candy molds and create hard candies with Nocino, an aromatic walnut liqueur originally from Emilia-Romagna, but also produced locally in Napa Valley. Oak leaves collected from Napa Valley became the models for thin molds that are filled with a thin butternut squash gel and dehydrated to make crisp fallen leaves. As the dish evolved, the acorns and leaves came to rest on a slice of brioche seasoned with fall spices and topped with apple, butternut squash, and celery root accompaniments. The dish is served on a hollowed log filled with foliage and decorated with a bonsai-like oak branch. I love the way all the components of the dish seem to fall into place, like acorns and leaves in autumn. | *Serves 12*

Spiced Brioche (Autumn)

SWEET ACORN

INGREDIENTS
750 grams (1 bottle) Nocino, preferably
    Napa Valley Nocino
38.4 grams (1.35 ounces) mannitol

EQUIPMENT
Dehydrator
Sifter
Cooking thermometer
½ x ½-inch silicone candy mold
Dremel rotary tool
Desiccant

At least 2 days before serving:

- Evenly divide the Nocino among 3 shallow containers. Transfer the containers to a dehydrator set to 50°C/120°F and dry until all the liquid has evaporated, leaving only liqueur solids, about 2 days. Sift the liqueur solids into an airtight container and store at room temperature until ready to use.
- **TO COAT THE CANDY MOLD:** In a very small pot (Juan uses a 1-pint pot) with a cooking thermometer attached, place 3.2 grams (0.11 ounce) of the mannitol and swirl over high heat, without stirring, while the mannitol liquefies and the temperature rises to 150°C/300°F. Immediately remove from the heat, add a pinch of Nocino powder, swirl the pot again once, pour the contents of the pot into one half of a silicone candy mold, close the mold, and shake vigorously for 30 seconds to evenly distribute across the internal surface of the candy mold. (At Atelier Crenn, we use custom-cast candy molds shaped like acorns.) Let the candy mold sit at room temperature until completely cooled, about 5 minutes. Remove the candy shell and repeat the coating process to create 1 candy shell per person.
- Use a Dremel rotary tool to poke a small hole in each candy shell for inserting the liqueur.
- Keep the candy shells in a dry, airtight container with a desiccant until ready to serve.

>>>

Spiced Brioche (Autumn), *continued*

NOCINO CANDY FILLING

INGREDIENTS
750 grams (1 bottle) Nocino,
    preferably Napa Valley Nocino
24 grams Ultra-Tex 3

EQUIPMENT
Sifter
Fine-mesh strainer
Pastry bag

One hour to one week before serving:

- In a medium pot, cook the Nocino over medium heat until all the alcohol has evaporated, about 20 minutes.
- Measure 300 grams (10.6 ounces) of the cooked Nocino into a large bowl. Place the Ultra-Tex 3 in a sifter and sift it onto the liquid with one hand while whisking well with the other to avoid clumping. (Ultra-Tex 3 activates instantly and works well in the presence of alcohol without being heated.)
- Strain the mixture through a fine-mesh strainer to ensure a silky consistency.
- Transfer the mixture to a pastry bag and refrigerate until ready to serve, up to 1 week.

SPICED BRIOCHE

Makes 2 loaves

INGREDIENTS
340 grams (12 ounces) unsalted butter
10 large eggs
1,135 grams (8¼ cups) bread flour,
    plus more for dusting
295 grams (1¼ cups) whole milk
140 grams (15 tablespoons) fresh yeast
115 grams (½ cup plus 1½ tablespoons)
    granulated sugar
37 grams (scant ⅓ cup) ground
    cinnamon
37 grams (scant ⅓ cup) ground aniseed
37 grams (scant ½ cup) unsweetened
    cocoa powder
17 grams (0.6 ounces) kosher salt
7 grams (1 tablespoon) freshly grated
    nutmeg
7 grams (1 tablespoon plus 1 teaspoon)
    ground ginger
3 grams (1 tablespoon) ground cloves

>>>

One day before serving:

- Cut the butter into ½-inch pieces and let sit at room temperature to soften.
- In a medium bowl, beat 9 to 10 eggs and measure out 450 grams (1 pound), reserving any unused egg as an egg wash to brush on the loaves.
- In the bowl of a stand mixer fitted with the dough hook attachment, combine the beaten eggs with the bread flour, whole milk, fresh yeast, sugar, cinnamon, aniseed, cocoa powder, kosher salt, nutmeg, ginger, and cloves. Mix on medium speed until a dough forms, about 3 minutes. Reduce the mixer speed to low and mix for 20 minutes more.
- Raise the mixer speed to medium and gradually add the softened butter, one piece at a time, until fully incorporated. Continue to mix on medium speed until the dough begins to pull away from the edges, 5 to 6 minutes.
- Lightly flour a work surface. Transfer the dough, which will be quite sticky, to the lightly floured work surface, using a silicone spatula or dough scraper to remove all of the dough from the bowl. Without kneading or rolling, pat and stretch the dough a few times to remove the air and work the gluten.

Stand mixer with dough hook attachment
Nonstick cooking spray
Silicone scraper or spatula
Two 8.5 x 4.5-inch loaf pans
Basting brush
Cake tester
Wire rack
1-inch ring mold
Parchment paper
Spice grinder

- Coat a large bowl with nonstick cooking spray. Transfer the dough to the bowl, cover with plastic wrap, and let rise at a warm room temperature (21°C/70°F to 24°C/75°F) until the dough has almost doubled in volume, about 1 hour.
- Lift the dough around the edges, allowing it to deflate in the bowl. Cover the bowl with plastic wrap and refrigerate overnight. (Refrigeration will slow the process of fermentation, which makes the dough rise, while chilling the butter, which makes the dough easier to shape.)

The next day:

- Lightly flour a work surface. Using a silicone scraper or spatula, release the dough from the bowl onto the floured surface. Pat the dough, divide into 2 equal portions, and transfer each to a loaf pan, pressing gently to make sure the dough is evenly distributed in each pan.
- Use a basting brush to coat the dough with the unused beaten egg, or beat another egg to make an egg wash. Let the dough proof in the loaf pans at room temperature, uncovered, for 2½ to 3 hours. (At Atelier Crenn, we put a clean box over the uncovered loaf pans to allow some air to circulate while protecting the dough.)
- Preheat the oven to 175°C/350°F.
- Place the loaf pans on a middle rack and bake until golden brown and a cake tester inserted into the center comes out clean, about 25 minutes.
- Remove the brioche loaves from the loaf pans and let cool on a wire rack until room temperature.
- Trim the ends off the brioche loaves and cut into ¼-inch slices, reserving any crumbs. Trim each slice into a 2½-inch square, reserving any crumbs. Use the ring mold to punch a 1-inch hole from the center of each slice, reserving any crumbs.
- Transfer the brioche slices to an airtight container and store at room temperature until ready to serve.
- Preheat the oven to 95°C/200°F.
- Line a baking sheet with parchment paper and arrange the brioche crumbs on the baking sheet in an even layer. Dry the crumbs in the oven until crispy and dry, about 1 hour.
- Grind the crumbs in a spice grinder.
- Transfer the crumbs to an airtight container and store at room temperature until ready to serve.

>>>

Spiced Brioche (Autumn), *continued*

CELERY ROOT ICE CREAM

INGREDIENTS

1 large celery root
1,200 grams (scant 5 cups) whole milk
3.5 grams (0.12 ounce) kosher salt
280 grams (9.9 ounces) Stabilizer Syrup
 (page 325)
1 gram guar gum
1 gram xanthan gum

EQUIPMENT

Fine-mesh strainer
Blender
Pacojet or home ice cream maker

At least 1 day before serving:

- Peel the celery root and slice it against the grain as thin as possible (about ⅛ inch wide).
- In a small pot, combine 200 grams (7.05 ounces) of the sliced celery root with the milk and salt. Simmer until tender, about 20 minutes. Remove from the heat and let cool, uncovered, until room temperature, then refrigerate, covered, overnight.

The next day:

- Strain the infused milk through a fine-mesh strainer. Discard the solids.
- In a blender, combine 1 kilogram (4¼ cups) of the infused milk with the stabilizer syrup, guar gum, and xanthan gum. Blend to incorporate, about 20 seconds.
- **TO MAKE THE CELERY ROOT ICE CREAM IN A PACOJET:** Transfer the celery mixture to a Pacojet canister and freeze until solid, at least 12 hours, and pacotize to order.
- **TO MAKE THE CELERY ROOT ICE CREAM IN A HOME ICE CREAM MAKER:** Transfer the celery root mixture to an airtight container and refrigerate overnight. Follow the manufacturer's instructions for your ice cream maker to process to an ice cream. Keep frozen in an airtight container until ready to serve.

SQUASH OAK LEAVES

INGREDIENTS

1 medium butternut squash
20 grams Pure-Cote
10 grams (2½ teaspoons) granulated
 sugar
1 gram low acyl gellan

>>>

At least 22 hours before serving:

- Peel and quarter the squash. Scrape out and discard the seeds.
- Use a juicer to make squash juice.
- Strain the squash juice through a fine-mesh strainer.
- In a blender, combine 500 grams (1.1 pounds) of the squash juice with the Pure-Cote, sugar, and low acyl gellan and blend on high for 30 seconds.
- Transfer the squash mixture to a medium pot with a cooking thermometer attached. Warm over medium-low heat to 90°C/195°F and remove from the heat. (At Atelier Crenn, we use a Thermomix to hydrate the Pure-Cote and low acyl gellan at 90°C/195°F.)

EQUIPMENT

Juicer

Fine-mesh strainer

Blender

Cooking thermometer

9 x 13-inch (quarter-sheet) pan

Vacuum sealer (*optional*)

Squeeze bottle

12 leaf-imprint silicone molds
    (1 x ½ inch)

Small brush

Acetate sheet

Dehydrator (*optional*)

- Pour the squash mixture into a 9 x 13-inch (quarter-sheet) pan and refrigerate, uncovered, until set to a loose gel, about 30 minutes.
- Transfer the squash gel to a blender and puree on medium speed for 30 seconds.
- Transfer the squash gel to a shallow container small enough to fit in a vacuum chamber, and vacuum the entire container to remove air bubbles; alternatively, transfer the squash gel to a shallow container and refrigerate, uncovered, overnight while the bubbles float to the surface.
- Transfer the squash gel to a squeeze bottle.
- **TO COAT THE LEAF IMPRINTS:** Squeeze a small drop of the squash gel into 1 leaf imprint mold and use a small brush to cover the leaf imprint with a very thin layer of squash pudding. (Juan actually uses the back of a tiny tweezer to scrape the gel around to create an extraordinarily thin layer of gel that might be so small that the brush itself would absorb it.) Repeat for each of the molds.
- Allow to air-dry until the gel becomes a thin film with a texture similar to fruit leather, about 12 hours.
- Gently peel the films from the molds and transfer to an acetate sheet in a single layer.
- **TO DRY THE SQUASH OAK LEAVES IN A DEHYDRATOR:** Place the acetate sheet in a dehydrator tray. Transfer to a dehydrator set to 85°C/185°F and dry the leaves until they are hard and crisp, about 7 hours.
- **TO DRY THE SQUASH OAK LEAVES IN THE OVEN:** Preheat the oven to 85°C/185°F. Place the acetate sheet on a baking sheet, transfer the baking sheet to the oven, and turn off the heat. Let the squash oak leaves dry in the closed oven with the heat off until they are hard and crisp, about 7 hours.
- Hold in the dehydrator or in an airtight container at room temperature until ready to serve.

>>>

Spiced Brioche (Autumn), *continued*

CARAMELIZED PEPITAS

INGREDIENTS

300 grams (2½ cups plus
    1½ tablespoons) pepitas
    (pumpkin seeds)
95 grams (½ cup) granulated sugar
15 grams (scant 2 teaspoons)
    liquid glucose
Kosher salt

EQUIPMENT

Silicone mat
Fine-mesh strainer
Desiccant (*optional*)

At least 90 minutes before serving:

- Preheat the oven to 150°C/300°F.
- Line a baking sheet with a silicone mat. Spread the pepitas in a single layer on the silicone mat and roast until fragrant and slightly caramelized, about 15 minutes. Leave the oven on.
- **TO MAKE A STRONG SIMPLE SYRUP:** In a small pot, combine the sugar with 67 grams (4½ tablespoons) water and the liquid glucose over medium heat. Simmer until completely dissolved into a syrup, about 5 minutes.
- Add the roasted pepitas to the pot and simmer over low heat for 5 minutes.
- Strain the pepitas through a fine-mesh strainer and discard the syrup.
- Line a baking sheet with a silicone mat. Spread the candied pepitas in a thin layer without touching one another on the silicone and season with a light sprinkling of kosher salt.
- Bake for 15 minutes.
- Reduce the oven temperature to 95°C/205°F and let the pepitas bake for 35 minutes more to dry them. Remove the baking sheet and allow the pepitas to cool, uncovered, to room temperature.
- Store the pepitas in an airtight container at room temperature until ready to serve. Add a desiccant, if desired.

COMPRESSED FUJI APPLE

INGREDIENTS

60 grams (⅓ cup) granulated sugar
1 Fuji apple
0.5 grams ascorbic acid

EQUIPMENT

Ball cutter (3-centimeter diameter)
Vacuum bag (*optional*)
Vacuum sealer (*optional*)

At least 1 hour before serving:

- **TO PREPARE A SIMPLE SYRUP:** In a small saucepan, combine the sugar with 60 grams (¼ cup) water and simmer over medium-low heat, stirring, until the sugar has completely dissolved, about 3 minutes. Allow to cool, uncovered, to room temperature.
- Peel, halve, and core the apple. Use a ball cutter to create 3-centimeter spheres. (In French culinary technique, large spheres are called parisiennes, while smaller spheres are called noisettes.)
- **TO MARINATE THE APPLE PARISIENNES IN A VACUUM SEALER:** Transfer the apple parisiennes to a vacuum bag, cover with 30 grams (1.05 ounces) of the simple syrup and the ascorbic acid, and compress at 99%. Refrigerate in the vacuum bag until ready to serve.

>>>

- **TO MARINATE THE APPLE PARISIENNES WITHOUT A VACUUM SEALER**: Transfer the apple parisiennes to a medium bowl and add the ascorbic acid. Add enough simple syrup to cover and refrigerate, covered, for at least 1 hour or until ready to serve.

ROASTED FUJI APPLE PUDDING

INGREDIENTS

5 Fuji apples
Granulated sugar
0.25 gram ascorbic acid
Low acyl gellan

EQUIPMENT

Silicone mat
Blender
Kitchen scale
9 x 13-inch (quarter-sheet) pan
Fine-mesh strainer
Fine-tipped squeeze bottle

At least 1 hour before serving:

- Preheat the oven to 160°C/320°F.
- Halve and core the apples; do not peel them.
- Line a baking sheet with a silicone mat. Lay the apples, skin-side up, on the silicone mat. Roast the apples until the flesh is tender, about 35 minutes.
- Remove the apples from the oven, reserving any cooking liquid, and allow to cool on the baking sheet for 10 minutes.
- Set the blender canister on a kitchen scale and tare to zero.
- Use a large spoon to scoop the apple flesh out of the skins. Transfer the flesh to the blender canister along with any residual cooking liquid and weigh again. Calculate 8% of the total weight and add that amount in sugar. Blend on high speed for 1 minute. Add the ascorbic acid and blend for 10 seconds to incorporate. Blend on high speed until very smooth. Weigh the blender canister again to find the new total weight. Transfer the apple puree to a medium pot with a cooking thermometer attached. Calculate 0.4% of the new total weight and whisk in that amount in low acyl gellan. Over medium-high heat, bring the mixture up to a temperature of 80°C/175°F to 90°C/195°F and remove from the heat. (At Atelier Crenn, we use a Thermomix machine to weigh, blend, and cook food in a single device. For the apple puree, we blend the mixture at 80°C/175°F.)
- Pour the apple puree into a 9 x 13-inch (quarter-sheet) pan and refrigerate, uncovered, until firm, about 15 minutes.
- When the apple gel has set, transfer to a blender and puree on high speed until the consistency of pudding, about 2 minutes.
- Strain the apple pudding through a fine-mesh strainer.
- Transfer the apple pudding to a fine-tipped squeeze bottle and refrigerate until ready to serve, up to 5 days.

>>>

Spiced Brioche (Autumn), *continued*

SQUASH PUDDING

INGREDIENTS

1 small butternut squash
50 grams (2½ tablespoons) grade-A
    maple syrup
30 grams (2¼ tablespoons) olive oil
3 grams kosher salt
Low acyl gellan

EQUIPMENT

Vacuum bag or resealable plastic
    freezer bag
Vacuum sealer (*optional*)
Immersion circulator (*optional*)
Blender
Kitchen scale
9 x 13-inch (quarter sheet) pan
Fine-mesh strainer
Fine-tipped squeeze bottle

At least 1 hour before serving:

- Peel, seed, and cut the butternut squash into 1-inch cubes.
- **TO COOK THE SQUASH SOUS VIDE:** In a vacuum bag, combine 500 grams (1.1 pounds) of the cubed butternut squash with the maple syrup, olive oil, and kosher salt and seal without compressing. Cook the bag in an immersion circulator set to 90°C/195°F for 45 minutes.
- **TO COOK THE SQUASH ON THE STOVETOP:** In a resealable plastic freezer bag, combine 500 grams (1.1 pounds) of cubed butternut squash with the maple syrup, olive oil, and kosher salt, squeeze out as much air as possible, and seal the bag. Fill a large pot three-quarters full with water and attach a cooking thermometer; bring the water to 90°C/195°F over low heat and submerge the bag, closely monitoring the heat to maintain a consistent temperature and stirring often, for 45 minutes.
- While the squash is still hot, set the blender canister on a kitchen scale, tare to zero, transfer the contents of the vacuum bag or resealable plastic freezer bag to the canister, and weigh. Calculate 0.5% of the total weight of the squash mixture, add that amount in low acyl gellan to the blender, and blend on high for 1 minute. (At Atelier Crenn, we use a Thermomix to blend the mixture at 90°C/195°F.)
- Pour the squash puree into a 9 x 13-inch (quarter-sheet) pan and refrigerate, uncovered, until firm, about 5 minutes.
- In a blender, puree the squash gel on medium-high until smooth, about 1 minute.
- Strain through a fine-mesh strainer.
- Transfer the squash pudding to a fine-tipped squeeze bottle and refrigerate until ready to serve, up to 4 days.

INGREDIENTS

84 grams (6 tablespoons) unsalted butter

Micro anise leaves

Grade-A maple syrup, preferably
     Blis brand, aged in oak barrels

EQUIPMENT

Pacojet (*optional*)

Pastry bag with fine tip

Fine-tipped squeeze bottle

6-inch pan

TO SERVE:

NOTE: *At Atelier Crenn, we serve this dish on a hollowed log filled with an autumnal scene and fitted with a piece of glass, which we can remove and wash. We inject cinnamon vapor under the glass and mount a decorative dried oak branch on top to complete the autumnal scene.*

- If using a Pacojet, pacotize the celery root ice cream.
- Transfer the celery root ice cream to a fine-tipped pastry bag and keep in the freezer.
- Use the fine-tipped squeeze bottle to fill the acorn candy shells three-quarters full with Nocino syrup and set aside.
- **TO TOAST THE BREAD:** In a 6-inch pan, melt 7 grams (½ tablespoon) of the butter over low heat. Toast 1 brioche square slowly to achieve an amber-colored caramelized crust, about 2 minutes, then flip the brioche square over to toast the other side for 2 minutes. Drizzle the top of each slice with maple syrup and transfer to a paper towel to absorb excess oil while assembling the rest of the dish. Repeat for the remaining bread slices.
- **TO PLATE:** Spoon 1 teaspoon of spiced brioche crumbs on one side of the plate. Place 1 slice of toasted brioche on top of the crumbs. Squeeze 5 dots of the apple pudding and 5 dots of butternut squash pudding in a random pattern on and around the brioche square. Place 1 apple parisienne on top of each of the apple puree dots.
- Pipe celery root ice cream into the center cavity of the toasted brioche.
- Sprinkle the caramelized pepitas around the perimeter of the toast.
- Garnish each plate with micro anise leaves.
- Garnish each plate with 3 squash oak leaves per plate in a random pattern, reminiscent of leaves falling in autumn.
- Top with 1 acorn candy per plate.

After the main dessert, the meal concludes with a series of small, sweet bites called mignardises, which constitute the time-honored final course in a grand tasting menu. There are many varieties of mignardises, and we like to close with a bountiful selection that pays homage to the classics, with our own special twists. We present our mignardises in three custom boxes: The first holds fruit-flavored treats, including passion fruit marshmallows; nougat flavored with goji berries, mango, or pineapple; and various pâtes de fruits. The second box is a hollow cedar log, filled with polished stones, fresh leaves, and cedar macarons. The third box is full of house-made chocolates. In the final moments of the meal, guests pluck these small morsels from their boxes as they reflect on the tasting menu they have just enjoyed.

Juan hesitated to include his recipe for pâtes de fruits in this book because they are more traditional than the rest of his creations. Yet that is exactly what interests me about pâtes de fruits in this context, as an opportunity to show the full range of his talents, which are equally comfortable with the classic and the cutting edge. As a pastry chef, Juan tends to steer away from easy crowd-pleasers, but when he wants to make something sweet and simple, like pâtes de fruits, he does so with flair. | *Makes 100 (½ x ½-inch) pieces*

Mango-Douglas Fir Pâtes de Fruits

INGREDIENTS

500 grams (2⅓ cups plus ¼ cup) granulated sugar

14 grams (0.5 ounce) pectin

25 grams (5 teaspoons) fresh lemon juice

7 grams (0.25 ounce) citric acid

10 drops Douglas fir sap resin

740 grams (26.1 ounces) mango puree, preferably Cap Fruit brand

160 grams (6½ tablespoons) liquid glucose

Sanding sugar or organic granulated sugar

EQUIPMENT

Cooking thermometer

9 x 13-inch (quarter-sheet) pan

Latex gloves

Parchment paper

At least 6 hours before serving:

- In a small container, mix together 50 grams (¼ cup) of the granulated sugar and the pectin.
- In another small container, combine the lemon juice, citric acid, and Douglas fir sap resin.
- In a large pot, with a cooking thermometer attached, combine the mango puree with the remaining 450 grams (2⅓ cups) granulated sugar over medium heat. When the mixture comes to a simmer, add the sugar-pectin mixture and whisk continuously until fully incorporated, about 1 minute. Raise the heat to medium-high and bring to a boil. Add the liquid glucose, continuing to whisk until the temperature reaches 105°C/221°F to 106°C/223°F. Add the lemon juice–citric acid mixture, whisk vigorously to incorporate, and remove from the heat.
- Pour the liquid into a 9 x 13-inch (quarter-sheet) pan and let sit at room temperature, uncovered, until set to a firm gel, about 5 hours.
- Use a sharp knife to slice the gel into ½-inch squares.
- **TO COAT THE PÂTES DE FRUITS WITH SUGAR:** Fill a pint container halfway with large-crystal sugar. Put on latex gloves and transfer a few pâtes de fruits onto the sugar. Shake the container gently to cover the pâtes de fruits with sugar, then use gloved hands to gently transfer to an airtight container, separating levels of pâtes de fruits with parchment paper.

>>>

Mango-Douglas Fir Pâte de Fruits, *continued*

(At Atelier Crenn, we use organic granulated sugar, which has a larger crystal than conventional granulated sugar, making it good for coating the pâtes de fruits, but traditional pâtes de fruits recipes call for sanding sugar, which also has large crystals.)

• Store at room temperature in an airtight container until ready to serve.

NOTE: *To make flavors of pâtes de fruits other than mango, decrease the amount of fruit puree to 730 grams. For tart fruits, like raspberry, decrease the citric acid to 4 grams. Pectin levels may vary for fruits with high levels of pectin.*

Many people don't realize that most of the flavor in macarons originates with the filling component, rather than the cookie shell. If you were to taste the shells right out of the oven, they might seem overbaked and underflavored, but because we press the shells together with the ganache and allow them to mature in the refrigerator, they soften and acquire the flavor of the filling. The amount of time needed to mature will depend, in part, on the fat content of the filling: We need forty-eight hours to mature the ganache-filled macarons in this recipe, but when we make our raspberry-rose or blackberry-jasmine macarons, they are ready in just six hours, because the moisture of fruit fillings acts more rapidly to soften and infuse the shells with flavor. | *Makes 100*

Cedar Macarons

INGREDIENTS

225 grams (2⅓ cups) almond flour

225 grams (1¾ cups) confectioners'
    sugar

1½ whole vanilla beans

6 large eggs

225 grams (1 cup plus 2¾ tablespoons)
    granulated sugar

7 drops green food coloring

135 grams (4.75 ounces) unsweetened
    white chocolate

110 grams (½ cup) heavy cream

7 drops cedar essence

Kosher salt

3 (6-inch) fresh green cedar branches

EQUIPMENT

Sifter

Stand mixer with whisk attachment

Cooking thermometer

Rubber spatula

2 pastry bags

Teflon or silicone mat

Immersion blender

Pestle

At least 2 days before serving:

- In a large bowl, sift together the almond flour and confectioners' sugar. Split the vanilla beans lengthwise and scrape the seeds into the almond-sugar mixture. Discard the scraped pods or reserve for another use.

- Separate the eggs, reserving the yolks for another use. (At Atelier Crenn, we freeze our egg whites for 3 days to break down the albumen, then thaw and skim the egg whites so that they are completely liquid and easier to work with.)

- Add 80 grams (2.8 ounces) of the egg whites to the almond-sugar mixture and mix together with a spoon. Transfer to the bowl of a stand mixer fitted with the whisk attachment.

- In a medium pot with a cooking thermometer attached, combine the granulated sugar with 55 grams (scant ¼ cup) water. Over low heat, slowly raise the temperature to 118°C/245°F. While the sugar water is heating, add the food coloring to the almond-sugar mixture and mix together until thoroughly combined. When the sugar water reaches 115°C/239°F, whip the egg whites in the stand mixer on the highest speed until the meringue holds soft peaks. Once the temperature of the sugar water reaches 118°C/245°F, add the sugar water to the egg white mixture, while continuing to whip for 2 to 3 minutes.

>>>

Cedar Macarons, *continued*

- Turn off the mixer and check the temperature with the cooking thermometer. When the temperature drops to 40°C/105°F, pour the meringue into the almond mixture in three batches, using a rubber spatula to fold just until the batter slowly drips off the spatula and back into the mass like lava, about 5 turns for the first and second batches and 15 gentler turns for the third batch. Do not overmix. Transfer the mixture to a pastry bag.
- Preheat the oven to 165°C/325°F.
- Line a baking sheet or sheet tray with a Teflon or silicone mat.
- Pipe 1-inch rounds of the almond flour mixture onto the Teflon or silicone and let sit, uncovered, at room temperature until a soft skin forms, 25 to 30 minutes. (To test the skin, gently touch the surface with your finger to see if it leaves an impression. The skin will take longer to form in humid or rainy weather.)
- Bake for 12 minutes. Allow to cool completely before removing from the Teflon or silicone mat.
- WHILE THE MACARONS ARE BAKING, MAKE THE GANACHE: Fill a small pot halfway with water and heat over low heat. When the water begins to steam, fit a large bowl on top, such that the bowl does not touch the water. Add the white chocolate to the bowl and melt over low heat. In another small pot, scald the cream over medium-high heat. Remove both from the heat and pour the cream into the bowl of melted white chocolate. Use an immersion blender to emulsify until you see a light sheen, about 2 minutes. Season with the cedar essence and a pinch of kosher salt and mix well. Press a piece of plastic wrap onto the surface of the ganache and let the bowl sit at room temperature until the mixture changes from the consistency of pudding to the consistency of frosting, 45 minutes to 2 hours. (Test the ganache periodically with a spoon; the process will take longer in humid or rainy weather.)

- Transfer the ganache to a pastry bag.
- Match pairs of macarons by size and pipe 1 teaspoon of ganache onto the flat side of 1 macaron and press with the flat side of its match.
- Bruise the cedar branches with a pestle to release their oils. Line a sheet pan or baking sheet with parchment paper and lay the cedar branches on it. Arrange the macarons between the branches so that they don't touch anything other than parchment paper. Tightly wrap the sheet pan or baking sheet with plastic wrap across the top of the branches, without touching the macarons, and refrigerate to mature for at least 48 hours.

The third and final phase of our mignardises presentation is a box full of chocolates, one of each type for each diner, including layered ganaches encrusted with chocolate caviar; milk chocolate shards with sesame seeds, quinoa, and vanilla sea salt; almond dragées; chocolate-covered brittles; and, of course, bonbons. Here are our bonbons with two different fillings: our mocha bonbons—made with cream from Sightglass Coffee in San Francisco—and smoked praline bourbon bonbons. But really, the possibilities are nearly infinite. Since we opened Atelier Crenn, Juan has spiced bonbons with cardamom, star anise, cinnamon, black pepper, allspice, clove, and orange, among other flavors. (In most cases, one can add a few grams of a spice to the warm cream, before mixing it with the chocolate.) Regardless of the filling flavor, the real technical challenge when making bonbons is tempering the chocolate, which requires some time and attention to detail, but once you learn to temper, you can make practically anything with chocolate.

The tempering process is composed of three steps designed to manipulate the complex crystal structure of chocolate, which is composed of unstable "alpha" crystals, which melt at a relatively low temperature (15°C/59°F to 28°C/82°F) and stable "beta" crystals, which melt at a higher temperature (32°C/89°F to 34°C/93°F). We want to encourage beta crystals at the expense of alpha crystals, so that the chocolate will be glossy and have an appealing "snap." To temper chocolate, we first raise the temperature of the chocolate high enough to melt both the alpha and the beta crystals. Second, we allow the chocolate to cool to the point that beta crystals will begin to form again, while the alpha crystals remain melted, and we add a small amount of solid chocolate to "seed" the melted chocolate with starter beta crystals. The addition of unmelted chocolate lowers the temperature of the whole, so the third and final step is warming the chocolate to keep it in the temperature range where beta crystals form and alpha crystals do not. (There is an alternate method of tempering chocolate called "tabling," but it requires a large marble work surface, which we do not have at Atelier Crenn.) At this point, the chocolate may be poured into any shape. Take care to cool the molded chocolate slowly, at a warm room temperature, so that alpha crystals do not form suddenly. The ideal room temperature for tempering chocolate is 22°C/71°F, and we do not advise attempting this recipe in a room any warmer than 24°C/75°F or cooler than 18°C/65°F. | *Makes 40*

Bonbons
(with Mocha Filling or Praline Bourbon Filling)

BONBON SHELL

At least 2 days before serving:

INGREDIENTS

Edible 24-carat gold flakes (*optional*)

570 grams (1.25 pounds) dark chocolate,
    preferably Valrhona Caraïbe,
        66% cocoa

50 grams (1.75 ounces) cocoa butter

>>>

- Use a kitchen towel to clean the chocolate mold thoroughly. There should be no blemishes or scratches.

- If desired, use a clean paintbrush to decorate the bottom of each mold with a few gold flakes, leaving some space between flakes for the chocolate to show through.

- In a small microwave-safe container, combine 50 grams (1.75 ounces) of the dark chocolate with the cocoa butter and

>>>

Bonbons, *continued*

Kitchen towel

1-inch demisphere polycarbonate
chocolate molds (40 divots)

Clean paintbrush

Cooking thermometer

Airbrush gun (*optional*)

Stainless-steel bowl

High heat–resistant silicone spatula

Small ladle

Parchment paper

Offset spatula

Cotton or latex gloves

microwave on high, stirring and checking often with a cooking thermometer, until the contents melt and reach a temperature of 45°C/115°F. Let the melted chocolate and cocoa butter sit at room temperature, uncovered, until the mixture cools to 30°C/85°F. If using gold flakes, transfer the melted dark chocolate and cocoa butter to an airbrush gun and spray the molds with a thin, even layer over the gold flakes. If not using gold flakes, use a clean paintbrush to cover the molds with a thin, even layer of chocolate and cocoa butter. Set aside, uncovered, at room temperature.

- **TO TEMPER THE CHOCOLATE FOR THE SHELL:** Fill a medium pot with 1 inch of water and bring to a low simmer over medium heat. Cover the pot with a stainless-steel bowl and add 200 grams (7.05 ounces) of the dark chocolate to the bowl, stirring the chocolate with a silicone spatula as it melts. Use a cooking thermometer to monitor the temperature of the chocolate; when it reaches 55°C/131°F to 58°C/136°F, add 60 grams (2.1 ounces) of unmelted dark chocolate as a seed, remove the bowl from the heat, and stir until the seed has melted thoroughly and the temperature drops to 28°C/82°F.

NOTE: *When working with chocolate, it is very important to know the cocoa content. Dark chocolate requires a higher temperature than milk chocolate or white chocolate to temper and different brands will temper differently, depending on their specific contents. (We generally use Valrhona chocolate and our temperatures are based on our experience working with their chocolates; see chart for the temperatures we use at Atelier Crenn.) Dark and light chocolate also react differently when heated; whereas the added sugars in milk chocolate will dissolve into a fluid syrup, cocoa particles will dry and solidify. It is best not to substitute milk chocolate and dark chocolate for each other in recipes.*

	DARK CHOCOLATE	MILK AND WHITE CHOCOLATE
MELTING	55°C/131°F to 58°C/136°F	45°C/113°F to 48°C/118°F
SEEDING	28°C/82°F	28°C/82°F
REHEATING	31°C/88°F	30°C/86°F

Transfer the stainless-steel bowl back to the pot and monitor the temperature as it rises to 31°C/88°F, then immediately remove from the heat.

- **TO FORM THE CHOCOLATE SHELL:** Use a small ladle to fill each divot in the chocolate molds. Use a spatula to scrape off any chocolate above the rim. Firmly tap the sides of the chocolate mold several times to release air bubbles. Set a piece of parchment paper on a plate or work surface. Invert the molds over the stainless-steel bowl and let the melted chocolate drain out, leaving a delicate chocolate shell. While the mold is facing downward, use the spatula to scrape along the edge of the mold to remove excess chocolate. Set the chocolate mold face-down on another piece of parchment paper and allow to drain for 1 minute. Turn the chocolate mold right-side up and use the spatula to scrape off any excess chocolate again. Set the chocolate mold aside, uncovered, at warm room temperature to allow the chocolate to crystallize. Reserve any remaining chocolate for the final stage of forming the chocolate shell. (At Atelier Crenn, we keep tempered chocolate in a warmer so that we always have some soft and ready to use.)
- Follow instructions for Mocha Bonbon Filling (page 290) or Praline Bourbon Bonbon Filling (page 291).

The next day:

- Fill a medium pot with 1 inch of water and bring to a low simmer over medium heat. Cover the pot with a stainless-steel bowl and add 200 grams (7.05 ounces) of the dark chocolate to the bowl, stirring the chocolate with a silicone spatula as it melts. Use a cooking thermometer to monitor the temperature of the chocolate; when it reaches 55°C/131°F to 58°C/136°F, add the remaining 60 grams (2.1 ounces) unmelted dark chocolate as a seed, remove the bowl from the heat, and stir until the seed has melted thoroughly and the temperature drops to 28°C/82°F. Transfer the stainless-steel bowl back to the pot and monitor the temperature as it rises to 31°C/88°F, then immediately remove from the heat.

>>>

- Use a ladle to cover each divot in the chocolate mold. Use an offset spatula to scrape off any excess chocolate. Let the mold sit, uncovered, at warm room temperature until the chocolate sets, about 10 minutes.

- **TO REMOVE THE CHOCOLATES FROM THE MOLDS:** Put on cotton or latex gloves to prevent fingerprinting the bonbons. Transfer the mold to the refrigerator, which will help the bonbons to contract and loosen from the chocolate mold, for 10 minutes. Do not leave the bonbons in the refrigerator for more than 10 minutes, however, as the humid environment will soften them. Set out a piece of parchment paper and invert the mold onto it. Flex the corners of the mold gently to ease the bonbons out. Transfer the chocolates to an airtight container and store at cool room temperature, ideally around 15°C/60°F, for up to 1 week. (At Atelier Crenn, the sommelier has offered us a little real estate in the wine cellar where we store our chocolates.) Do not refrigerate the chocolate.

>>>

Bonbons, *continued*

MOCHA BONBON FILLING

INGREDIENTS

20 grams (4 teaspoons) unsalted butter

25 grams (0.9 ounce) espresso beans

200 grams (¾ cup plus 1½ tablespoons) heavy cream

150 grams (6 tablespoons) trimoline inverted sugar

140 grams dark chocolate, preferably Valrhona Caraïbe, 66% cocoa

128 grams milk chocolate, preferably Valrhona Jivara, 40% cocoa

EQUIPMENT

Mortar and pestle

Fine-mesh strainer

Cheesecloth

Cooking thermometer

Deli-style quart container or similar

Immersion blender

Pastry bag

NOTE: *This may be the most cream in any dessert at Atelier Crenn.*

- Cut the butter into ½-inch cubes and let sit at room temperature to soften.
- Crush the espresso beans with a mortar and pestle.
- In a medium pot, bring the cream to a low boil over medium heat. Add the crushed espresso beans. Remove the pot from the heat, cover with plastic wrap, and steep at room temperature for 1 hour.
- Line a fine-mesh strainer with 1 layer of cheesecloth. Strain the liquid through the cheesecloth-lined strainer into a medium pot, discarding the solids. Add the trimoline inverted sugar to the pot and bring the liquid just to a boil over medium heat. Immediately remove the pot from the heat and set aside.
- Fill another medium pot with 1 inch of water and bring to a low simmer over medium heat. Cover the pot with a stainless-steel bowl and add the dark chocolate and milk chocolate to the bowl, stirring the chocolate with a rubber spatula as it melts. Use a cooking thermometer to monitor the temperature of the chocolate; when it reaches 45°C/113°F, transfer the melted chocolate to a deli-style quart container, or a similarly narrow but deep container.

NOTE: *To make a perfect emulsion, both the cream and the chocolate should be 45°C/113°F when they are mixed. It may be necessary to rewarm the chocolate or the cream over the boiling water.*

- **TO MAKE THE FILLING:** Pour the cream into the container with the chocolate. Use an immersion blender to emulsify the mixture until it becomes shiny and reaches the consistency of pudding, about 3 minutes. Add the cubed butter and continue to blend with the immersion blender until fully incorporated, about 1 minute.
- Cover the top of the container with plastic wrap to prevent a skin from forming. Set aside at room temperature and allow to cool to 30°C/86°F.
- Transfer the filling to a pastry bag. Pipe into the chocolate shells, leaving 2 millimeters of unfilled space below the edge of the mold, which will be filled in later as a final layer of chocolate shell. Let the mold sit, uncovered, at room temperature, overnight or until a fine skin forms, 8 to 10 hours.

PRALINE-BOURBON BONBON FILLING

INGREDIENTS

225 grams (1 cup plus 2 tablespoons)
  granulated sugar
85 grams (3½ tablespoons) liquid
  glucose
125 grams (4.4 ounces) blanched
  almonds, toasted
125 games (4.4 ounces) whole skinned
  hazelnuts, toasted
75 grams (5 tablespoons) heavy cream
60 grams (2.1 ounces) cocoa butter
30 grams (1.05 ounces) bourbon

EQUIPMENT

13 x 18-inch (half-sheet) pan
Silicone mat
Cooking thermometer
Silicone spatula
Food processor
Stainless-steel bowl
40 grams (1.4 ounces) oak wood chips
Butane torch
Food processor
Pastry bag

- Line a 13 x 18-inch (half-sheet) pan with a silicone mat.
- In a medium saucepan with a cooking thermometer attached, mix together the sugar, 75 grams (5 tablespoons) water, and 25 grams (1 tablespoon) of the liquid glucose. Cook over medium heat as the mixture becomes a light caramel and reaches a temperature of 160°C/320°F.
- Remove from the heat and stir in the almonds and hazelnuts and mix well with a silicone spatula. Pour the mixture onto the silicone-lined pan and let cool at room temperature for 1 hour.
- When the caramel has cooled and hardened, break it into small (1 x 1-inch) pieces.
- **TO MAKE THE PRALINE PASTE:** Working in batches, if necessary, transfer the praline to a food processor and grind until the mixture has a smooth, runny consistency, about 5 minutes.
- **TO SMOKE THE PRALINE PASTE:** Transfer the praline paste to a medium stainless-steel bowl and place the bowl in a deep roasting pan or hotel pan. Place the oak wood chips in the pan surrounding the stainless-steel bowl. Use a butane torch to ignite the oak wood chips. Confirm that the wood is smoking and cover with aluminum foil. Smoke the praline paste until it has a well-rounded smoky accent, 20 to 30 minutes.
- Meanwhile, in a small saucepan, mix together the heavy cream and the remaining 60 grams (2½ tablespoons) liquid glucose. Bring to a boil to ensure the glucose dissolves, then remove from the heat and let cool to 30°C/86°F.
- In another small saucepan, melt the cocoa butter to 45°C/113°F.
- Transfer 250 grams (8.8 ounces) of the praline paste to a food processor. Run the food processor while drizzling the cocoa butter into the praline paste until well incorporated. Drizzle in the cream-glucose mixture. Drizzle in the bourbon to stabilize the emulsion.
- Allow the mixture to cool at room temperature to 30°C/86°F and transfer to a pastry bag. Pipe into the chocolate shells, leaving 2 millimeters of unfilled space below the edge of the mold, which will be filled in later as a final layer of chocolate shell. Let the mold sit, uncovered, at room temperature, overnight or until a fine skin forms, 8 to 10 hours.

CRAFT

FROM STAFFING TO EQUIPMENT to storage space, there are plenty of differences between a home kitchen and Atelier Crenn's kitchen, but I believe that one of the biggest disparities is the building-block ingredients that are rarely, if ever, in the spotlight at the restaurant, but represent a crucially important foundation that allows us to construct layers and layers of flavor.

This chapter contains recipes for the stocks, dairy products, and artisanal breads that are the "secret ingredients" in our composed dishes. When it comes to craft items like these, however, every cook should exercise enormous freedom to improvise, experiment, and craft new recipes in her or his own style. Ultimately, this chapter is about the day-to-day work of maintaining the kind of pantry that will support creativity, and it is not glamorous, but I find that it helps to remember that many of the world's noblest culinary traditions originated with a farmwife's refusal to waste food. In other words, I encourage you to throw leftover bones and shells into a stockpot with a few vegetable scraps and unfinished bottles of wine, simmer for a few hours, and see what happens. Turn buttermilk into crème fraîche, crème fraîche into cultured butter, cultured butter into buttermilk, and begin the cycle again. Save a bit of dough from one baking project as a starter for the next. And so on.

Many of the broth recipes that follow were improved and streamlined by our former sous chef Daniel Beal. With regard to the bread, I want to extend my deepest and warmest thanks to Mehdi Boudiab, who is a great friend and an even better baker; it is an honor to have your recipes in my restaurant and my book.

In France, *crème fraîche* refers to fresh liquid cream, while *crème fraîche épaisse* is a deliciously thick, fermented dairy product that is like a creamier, less sour version of American sour cream. Here in the United States, "crème fraîche épaisse" is abbreviated to "crème fraîche," which was confusing to me at first, but c'est la vie, right? Crème fraîche épaisse can be used in any recipe that calls for sour cream, but it is much more flexible than its American cousin. At 30 percent fat minimum, crème fraîche épaisse will not curdle when heated, as sour cream does with its relatively lean 18 percent fat content, so a dollop of crème fraîche épaisse can elevate vegetable preparations like sautéed corn, peas, or potatoes with absolutely minimal effort. In cold presentations, the subtly sweet tang of crème fraîche épaisse makes an excellent companion to fruit and fruit-based desserts. It's equally appropriate in savory applications, like my horseradish crème fraîche épaisse (see page 179), and to dessert, where it is very good drizzled with Armagnac. In France, we often spread crème fraîche épaisse on open-faced sandwiches topped with tomatoes, figs, or whatever is handy. In some ways, crème fraîche épaisse can be thought of as a kind of super-charged butter, and in fact, it is the secret ingredient in our Cultured Butter (page 299).

Plus, this is the easiest recipe in this book, guaranteed. | *Makes 500 grams (2 cups)*

Crème Fraîche Épaisse

INGREDIENTS

500 grams (2 cups) heavy cream
56 grams (3½ tablespoons) buttermilk
   with live active cultures

EQUIPMENT

Large (1-liter/1-quart) glass jar with lid
Cheesecloth

- In the large glass jar, combine the heavy cream and buttermilk. Cover with cheesecloth and let sit at warm room temperature until thick, 24 to 48 hours.
- Refrigerate, covered, for up to 1 week.

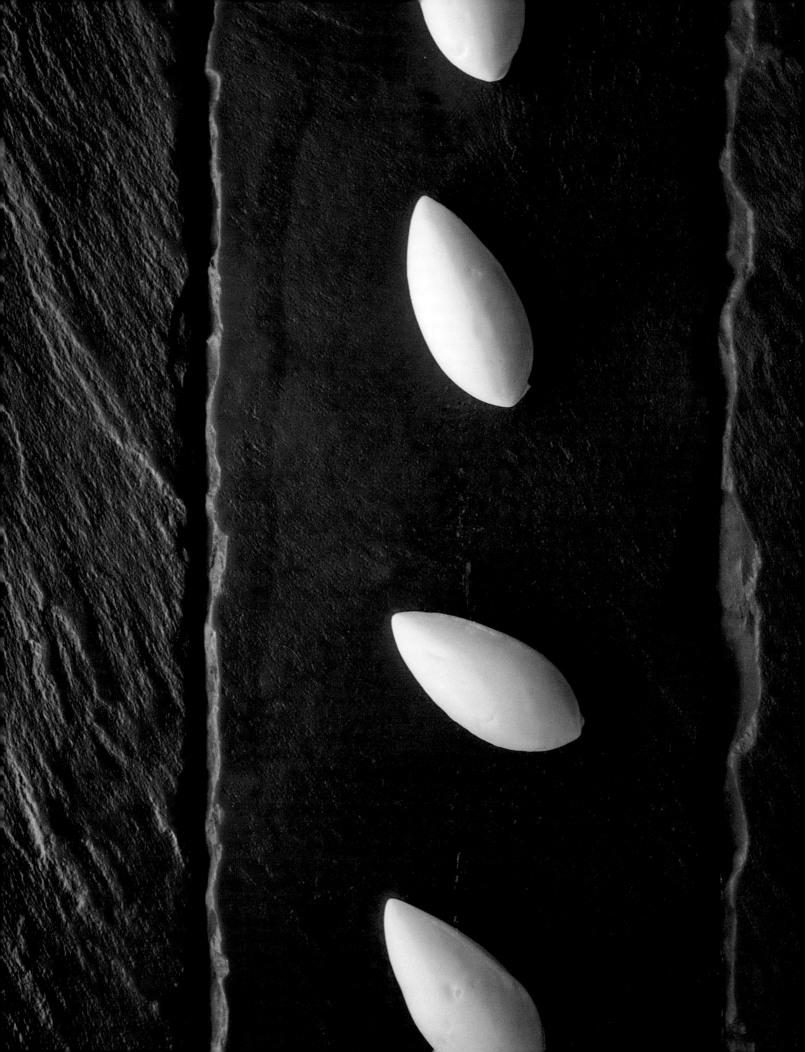

I love butter. I love, love, love it. When I was growing up, my favorite after-school snack was baguette with butter and chocolate, and I still breakfast on chocolate croissants several times a week, even though American croissants lack the true buttery luxury of the French version, which absolutely bleed butter. Perhaps the depth of my butter love comes as a surprise, given the way my recipes often update traditional French cuisine by steering away from the rich, creamy flavors of the past. Yet I must admit that I am still a true child of Brittany, where we say *"Au bon beurre salé!"* ("Here's to good salted butter!") when we sit down to eat. Brittany has been famous for its butter for centuries, and as food writer Harold McGee explains, Breton butter was traditionally "made on small farms using cream that was pooled from several milkings, and was therefore a day or two old and somewhat soured by lactic acid bacteria. Continental Europe still prefers the flavor of this lightly fermented 'cultured' butter to the 'sweet cream' butter made common in the 19th century by the use of ice, the development of refrigeration, and the mechanical cream separator."[2] In the United States, almost all butter is "sweet cream" and 2 to 6 percent lower in butterfat than its European counterpart.

Fortunately, it is easy enough to make your own delicious cultured butter.

Start with the best cream you can find. A cow pastured on nice fresh grass will produce richer milk with more orange carotene pigmentation in the fats, meaning butter produced from that milk will not only taste better but also appear a deeper yellow. If you have access to unpasteurized milk, just let it sit at room temperature for a day or so, the way the Bretons used to; otherwise, you can culture the butter by mixing it with crème fraîche épaisse (page 297), as we do in this recipe, or any form of dairy containing active cultures, such as buttermilk or yogurt (page 303). Fresh buttermilk is a delicious by-product of the butter-making process, which you can reserve to make more butter, or drink as a treat that is totally unlike commercial buttermilk. Once you have separated the butter from the buttermilk, though, it is worthwhile to remove the residual buttermilk, because it hastens spoilage. I recommend mixing in some good sea salt, which functions as a preservative at a concentration of 2 percent of the total volume of butter, though that may feel excessively salty. For me, the capstone of the butter-making process is sprinkling in some fleur de sel to taste. And taste. And taste. In other words: *Au bon beurre salé!* | *Makes 340 grams (¾ pound)*

Cultured Butter

INGREDIENTS

500 grams (1 quart) heavy cream
   (not ultra-pasteurized)
40 grams (2 tablespoons plus
   2 teaspoons) crème fraîche épaisse,
   homemade (page 297) or
   store-bought
Fleur de sel

>>>

At least 1 day before serving:

- In a medium bowl, mix together the cream and crème fraîche épaisse. Cover tightly with plastic wrap and set aside in a warm place (21°C/70°F to 24°C/75°F) to culture for 24 hours.
- Refrigerate the cultured cream until its temperature is 15°C/60°F, 1 to 2 hours.
- Transfer the cultured cream to the bowl of a stand mixer fitted with the whisk attachment and attach a splatter guard or wrap the top of the bowl in plastic wrap. Mix on low for 1 minute,

>>>

----

2. Harold McGee, On Food and Cooking, *revised edition (Scribner, 2004), page 33.*

Cultured Butter, *continued*

Cooking thermometer

Stand mixer with whisk attachment

Fine-mesh strainer

Silicone spatula

Waxed paper

then gradually increase the speed to high and whip until the fat solids (i.e., butter) separate from the liquid (i.e., buttermilk), 5 to 10 minutes.

- Place a fine-mesh strainer over a storage container and strain the buttermilk out of the butter. Reserve the buttermilk in the bowl for another use, such as making Crème Fraîche Épaisse (page 297).

- **TO WASH THE BUTTER:** Rinse out the bowl of the stand mixer and return the butter to the bowl. Add 1 cup very cold water, attach a splatter guard or wrap the top of the bowl in plastic wrap, and mix on low for 1 minute, then gradually increase the speed to high and mix for 3 minutes.

- Strain the butter through a fine-mesh strainer, discarding the liquid.

- **TO CHURN THE BUTTER:** Working in batches, use a silicone spatula to press the butter against the side of a bowl to release residual buttermilk. Periodically rinse off the buttermilk that drips to the bottom.

- When a batch has expressed all its residual buttermilk, sprinkle in a generous pinch of fleur de sel and use the spatula to work the salt through the softened butter.

- **TO STORE THE BUTTER:** Place the butter on waxed paper and roll it into a tightly wrapped log. Store the wrapped butter in an airtight, opaque container in the refrigerator or freezer. Butter should be protected from light, air, and strong odors. Do not wrap in aluminum foil as direct contact with metal will oxidize the fats and hasten spoilage. Properly stored butter will keep for 2 to 3 weeks in the refrigerator.

I once read that yogurt is one of the foundations of civilization, because it helped ancient people to preserve milk and therefore encouraged them to become herders rather than simple hunter-gatherers. That theory feels right to me because the process of making yogurt is so beautifully elemental: We add a bit of yogurt to warm milk and the active cultures do the rest. In the United States, yogurt is often thickened with additives and sweetened with all manner of flavors, but in France, plain yogurt is much more common. Some say that yogurt is the reason French women (supposedly) don't get fat, but the truth is, we certainly like to dress up our plain yogurt with jam and ground nuts. Here are some recipes demonstrating how we like to eat yogurt in France, but they are just suggestions, with plenty of room for substitution. The truth is, I love to start my day with blackberries because I grew up picking *les mûres* with my father, tramping through the forests of Brittany. This simple breakfast connects me with my father, so that I carry a bit of him into my day, the way one generation of yogurt gives rise to the next. | *Makes 900 grams (3⅔ pounds)*

Yogurt with Ground Nuts

INGREDIENTS

900 grams (3⅔ cups) whole milk

38 grams (2½ tablespoons) plain
    whole-milk yogurt with live and
    active cultures

EQUIPMENT

Cooking thermometer

Heatproof spatula

Large (1-liter/1-quart) glass jar with
    tight-fitting lid

- In a medium pot with a cooking thermometer attached, heat the milk over medium heat, stirring all the way to the bottom with a heatproof spatula every 2 minutes, until the temperature reaches 82°C/180°F. Stop stirring and reduce the heat to low, keeping the temperature steady at 82°C/180°F for 20 to 25 minutes.

NOTE: *The longer the milk is cooked, the thicker the yogurt will be.*

- While the milk is cooking, sterilize a large glass jar: Bring 1.25 liters (5 cups) water to a boil. Set the large glass jar in a shallow bowl, pour the boiling water into and over it, and let stand for 5 minutes. Carefully drain the water and allow the glass jar to air-dry.

- When the milk has thickened, fill a large bowl with ice water. Remove the pot from the stove and rest it in the ice water to cool. Stir the milk while watching the cooking thermometer closely; when the temperature reaches 43°C/110°F to 45°C/115°F, remove the pot from the ice water bath and stir in the yogurt until fully incorporated.

>>>

Yogurt with Ground Nuts, *continued*

- Transfer the yogurt mixture to the sterilized glass jar and secure the lid. Wrap the jar in a kitchen towel and set it aside in a warm spot, such as a closed oven with the heat off. Let sit for 10 to 12 hours.
- Taste the yogurt; if you would prefer a tarter flavor, let the yogurt sit in a warm spot for up to 8 hours more.
- Refrigerate, covered, for at least 3 hours. The yogurt will thicken as it cools.
- Store the yogurt in an airtight container in the refrigerator for up to 3 weeks.

GROUND NUTS

INGREDIENTS

80 grams (½ cup) oats
35 grams (¼ cup) almonds
30 grams (¼ cup) walnuts
8 grams (1 tablespoon) flaxseeds
40 grams (¼ cup) golden raisins

EQUIPMENT

Coffee grinder
Medium (½-liter/1-pint) glass jar

- Working in batches, grind the oats in a coffee grinder until oat powder is formed. Transfer the oat powder to a medium glass jar.
- Roughly chop the almonds and walnuts. Working in batches, transfer the nuts to the coffee grinder and pulse several times, checking the texture after each pulse, until a medium-textured meal forms. Do not overgrind to a paste. Add the nut powder to the jar and stir until evenly mixed with the oat powder.
- Add the flaxseeds and golden raisins to the jar, seal the jar, and shake well. Refrigerate until ready to serve.

RAW BLACKBERRY-CHAMOMILE JAM

Makes 575 grams (20 ounces)

INGREDIENTS

1 lemon

5 grams (1 teaspoon) dried chamomile
  flowers

425 grams (3 cups) fresh ripe
  blackberries

1.25 grams (¼ teaspoon) fine sea salt

190 grams (1 cup) granulated sugar

22 grams (2½ tablespoons) instant pectin

EQUIPMENT

Fine-mesh strainer

Spice grinder

Three 8-ounce mason jars

NOTE: *This style of raw fruit jam is also called "refrigerator jam," because we don't go through the whole canning process to make the jam shelf-stable. This process is much less work and allows for a much more seasonal approach, because the jam will only keep for a few weeks. I make small batches of whatever is in season, keep some, and give the rest to friends. I prefer to use Pomona's Universal Pectin because, unlike many other commercial pectin brands, it contains no preservatives.*

- Squeeze 17 grams (2 tablespoons) of lemon juice, reserving any remaining lemon for another use. Pass the lemon juice through a fine-mesh strainer into a large bowl.
- In a spice grinder, grind the chamomile to a powder and add to the bowl with the lemon juice.
- Add the blackberries and fine sea salt. Use a fork to break up the blackberries and release some juice, but do not pulverize.
- In a medium bowl, mix together the sugar and pectin, stirring until thoroughly blended. Pour the sugar mixture into the blackberry mixture and stir until the sugar has dissolved, about 2 minutes.
- Transfer the mixture to clean mason jars, leaving ½ inch of room at the top of each jar. Close the jars and let sit at room temperature until set to the consistency of jam, about 24 hours.
- Refrigerate for up to 3 weeks or freeze for up to 1 year. Once opened, keep frozen jam in the refrigerator.

TO SERVE:

- Fill a medium bowl with homemade yogurt, top with equal amounts of ground nuts and blackberry-chamomile (or other) jam, and stir roughly. Do not overmix.

With the smooth texture of yogurt and the rich flavor of cheese, fromage blanc is an incredibly useful ingredient to keep on hand, delicious with everything from the lightest fruit to the richest stew, so when I moved here, I was surprised to see that it's practically unknown in the United States. Recently, I've noticed a few specialty stores selling fromage blanc, but I still think of it as something to make for myself because the stuff sold here is much too dry. Instead of melting in your mouth, with all the silky fat spreading across your tongue, even expensive American fromage blanc crumbles like a misguided diet food. Perhaps it's a trick of memory, but I was raised on Gervais brand fromage blanc, which is certainly not fancy or expensive at all, and I remember that even a single spoonful gave me such a luxurious feeling.

Americans tend to believe that cleaner is always better (and in a professional kitchen, we certainly scrub and sanitize very thoroughly), but the truth is that we can never kill all the bacteria in our environment, and if we did, we would only be killing ourselves. Making fromage blanc from scratch requires a starter culture of "good bacteria," which forces us to really acknowledge all the tiny organisms that keep us healthy and create amazing flavor. | *Makes 2 cups*

Fromage Blanc with Honeycomb

INGREDIENTS

3.75 liters (1 gallon) whole milk
    (pasteurized, but not ultra-
    pasteurized)
1 packet fromage blanc starter culture
Honeycomb or high-quality honey
Seasonal fresh fruit (*optional*)

EQUIPMENT

Cooking thermometer
Cheesecloth
Strainer
Long-handled mixing spoon

Twelve to twenty-four hours before serving:

- Pour the milk into a medium pot with a cooking thermometer attached. Bring the milk to 29°C/85°F over medium-high heat, stirring all the way to the bottom to avoid scorching. Once the milk reaches the desired temperature, transfer to a large, nonreactive (plastic, glass, or stainless-steel) container and immediately sprinkle in the starter culture. Wait for 1 minute, then stir for 1 minute. Cover with cheesecloth and set aside in a warm place, about 22°C/72°F, for 12 to 24 hours. The cheese will thicken to a yogurt-like consistency and separate from the mostly clear whey along the edges of the container.
- Line a strainer with a generous double layer of cheesecloth and place it in a large bowl. Gently spoon the cheese into the strainer, tie the ends of the cloth around a long mixing spoon balanced across the top, and allow to drain at room temperature for 6 to 8 hours. The longer you strain the cheese, the thicker it will be.
- Serve with the honeycomb as a beautifully simple dessert unto itself, or garnish with seasonal fresh fruit, particularly berries and stone fruit, if desired.
- Store in an airtight container in the refrigerator for up to 1 week.

We call this onion broth, but in fact, it is a celebration of the whole genus *Allium*, which includes not only onions but also garlic, leek, chives, scallions and many other edible plants. Once you tune into alliums as a category, you discover them everywhere, not only in cuisine, but also in nature. I've heard that there are people in India who won't eat alliums, because they are strict vegetarians and alliums seem alive to them; I relate to this belief, in the sense that alliums vibrate with life, though I eat them very happily. In this broth, we combine three kinds of onion with leeks and shallots to celebrate alliums as a source of deep, rich, vegetable flavor; we serve this broth in our Onion Soup (page 71) and we use it as a cooking liquid for heartier vegetarian staff meals. | *Makes 6 liters (6.3 quarts)*

Onion Broth

INGREDIENTS

150 grams (¾ cup) dried chickpeas

6 yellow onions

40 grams (3 tablespoons) neutral
    vegetable oil

6 red onions

3 leeks

4 shallot cloves

800 grams (1.75 pounds) cipollini onions

250 grams (1 cup) balsamic vinegar

150 grams (5.3 ounces) hard cheese rind,
    such as Comté

100 grams (⅓ cup plus 2 tablespoons)
    apple cider vinegar

100 grams (5.5 tablespoons) tamari

40 grams (3 tablespoons plus
    1 teaspoon) granulated sugar

10 grams (0.35 ounce) kombu

Fine sea salt

EQUIPMENT

Plancha or cast-iron skillet

Sheet tray or baking sheet

Fine-mesh strainer

At least 17 hours before using:

• Soak the dried chickpeas in enough water to cover and leave at room temperature for at least 12 hours.

At least 5 hours before using:

• Trim, peel, and roughly dice the yellow onions.
• In a stockpot, heat the vegetable oil over medium-low heat. Add 1,500 grams (3.3 pounds) of the diced yellow onions and sweat until soft and translucent, but not browned, about 20 minutes.
• While the yellow onions are cooking, preheat the oven to 190°C/375°F.
• Preheat the plancha or cast-iron skillet over high heat.
• Trim and peel the red onions, leeks, and shallots, keeping each variety separate. Cut each variety crosswise into ½-inch rings, keeping the rings together as discs and keeping each variety separate. Grill the red onions, leeks, and shallots in separate areas of the plancha or cast-iron skillet until the exteriors are blackened, about 20 minutes.
• Trim, peel, and halve the cipollini onions and transfer to a sheet tray or baking sheet. Roast the cipollini onions until browned, about 20 minutes.

>>>

Onion Broth, *continued*

- Transfer 1,100 grams (2.4 pounds) of the charred red onion, 500 grams (1.1 pounds) of the roasted cipollini onion, 150 grams (5.3 ounces) of the charred leek, and 130 grams (4.6 ounces) of the charred shallot to the stockpot with the yellow onions, reserving any remaining alliums for another use.
- Add the balsamic vinegar to the stockpot and scrape along the surface of the stockpot to deglaze. Cook over medium-low heat until the volume has decreased by half, about 5 minutes.
- Drain the chickpeas and discard the soaking liquid. Add 315 grams (11.1 ounces) of the soaked chickpeas to the stockpot.
- Add 7 liters (7.4 quarts) water and bring to a boil over medium heat, then reduce the heat to maintain a simmer and cook, uncovered, for 4 hours.
- Add the cheese rind, apple cider vinegar, tamari, sugar, and kombu and simmer for 30 minutes.
- Strain the liquid through a fine-mesh strainer.
- Season with fine sea salt.
- Use immediately or refrigerate, covered, until ready to use. Onion broth may be frozen for later use.

If you want to boost umami, or the feeling of meaty richness, in a vegetarian dish, mushroom broth is a huge asset. While all mushrooms contain umami, darker varieties like shiitake will offer more umami. Seaweed is another excellent vegetarian source of umami, and kombu is a very convenient form of seaweed, with an incredibly long shelf life. Together, mushrooms and kombu make a powerfully savory broth, perfect for vegetarians and omnivores alike. We use this broth as a cooking liquid for the mushrooms in A Walk in the Forest (page 79) and as a soup broth for staff meals. This mushroom broth is excellent with Japanese vegetables and noodles, such as udon, ramen, or soba noodles, particularly in foggy San Francisco weather. | *Makes 3 to 4 liters (3.2 to 4.2 quarts)*

Mushroom Broth

INGREDIENTS

900 grams (2 pounds) shiitake or
    button mushrooms
3 cloves peeled garlic
30 grams (2¼ tablespoons) neutral
    vegetable oil
65 grams (2.3 ounces) kombu
Fine sea salt

EQUIPMENT

Fine-mesh strainer

At least 4½ hours before using:

- Clean and trim the stems of the mushrooms.
- Roughly chop the garlic.
- Coat the bottom of a stockpot with the vegetable oil and heat over medium-high heat. When the oil begins to smoke, add the mushrooms and sear, tossing occasionally, until the mushrooms are browned, about 15 minutes. Add the garlic and continue cooking for 1 minute.
- Add 5 liters (5¼ quarts) water and the kombu and bring the water to a low simmer over low heat. Simmer for 4 hours.
- Strain the liquid through a fine-mesh strainer, discarding the solids.
- Season with fine sea salt.
- Use immediately or refrigerate, covered, until ready to use. Mushroom broth may be frozen for later use.

We ate a lot of rutabagas when I was growing up, and I still love them, but if rutabagas aren't to your taste, feel free to substitute other root vegetables like turnip or parsnip, or even substitute carrot for half. I do think the subtle spiciness of rutabagas is what give this broth such a fascinatingly complex flavor, but I understand that they can be hard to find in American markets. We serve this broth warm as part of our Crab with Sunchoke dish (page 139) and serve it cold as part of the Carrot and Aloe dish (page 45). I've also been known to sip on a cup of rutabaga-grapefruit broth as an alternative to tea. | *Makes ⅔ liter (⅔ quart)*

Rutabaga-Grapefruit Broth

INGREDIENTS

1 gram (½ teaspoon) fennel seed

1 gram (scant ½ teaspoon) whole allspice

1 gram (scant ½ teaspoon) whole cloves

1 gram (scant ½ teaspoon) whole coriander seed

1 gram (scant ½ teaspoon) crushed whole nutmeg

1 cinnamon stick

4 large rutabaga

4 red grapefruit

1 gram (2 teaspoons) whole saffron threads

EQUIPMENT

Juicer

Fine-mesh strainer

At least 1 hour before using:

- In a sauté pan, combine the fennel seed, allspice, cloves, coriander, nutmeg, and cinnamon stick. Toast over medium heat, tossing occasionally to avoid burning, until the spices become deeply fragrant, 30 to 60 seconds. Remove from the heat and transfer to a medium pot.
- Peel the rutabaga and cut into 1-inch pieces. Juice the rutabaga and discard the pulp.
- Halve the grapefruits and squeeze out the juice. Pass the grapefruit juice through a fine-mesh strainer and discard the pulp and seeds.
- Add the rutabaga juice, grapefruit juice, and saffron to the pot with the spices and bring to a simmer, uncovered, over medium-low heat. Simmer until the volume has reduced by half, about 20 minutes.
- Use immediately or refrigerate, covered, until ready to use. Rutabaga-grapefruit broth should not be frozen.

Tomato consommé is as versatile as tomatoes themselves. We use tomato consommé to make lobster brain-tomato gel for our Lobster Bisque (page 145) and in three different ways in our Tomato dish (page 63): as a poaching liquid, fortifying liquid, and very light broth poured tableside. I also like to keep tomato consommé on hand during the summer, to poach and dress light seafood dishes or to mix into vinaigrettes or cold drinks. | *Makes about 1 liter (1 quart)*

Tomato Consommé

INGREDIENTS

700 grams (1.5 pounds) Roma tomatoes

1 gram (¼ teaspoon) sherry vinegar

Fine sea salt

EQUIPMENT

Juicer

Wire skimmer

Paper coffee filter

Thirty minutes before using:

- Juice the tomatoes in a juicer, discarding the pulp and skins.
- In a medium pot, bring the tomato juice to a simmer over medium heat. Cook until the solids separate from the liquid and float to the surface, about 15 minutes, then remove from the heat.
- Use a wire skimmer to skim off and discard the tomato solids.
- Add the sherry vinegar.
- Strain the liquid through a paper coffee filter.
- Season with fine sea salt.
- Use immediately or refrigerate, covered, until ready to use. Tomato consommé should not be frozen.

Dashi is to Japanese cooking what bouillon is to French cooking: Both are vegetarian cooking liquids that provide a strong foundation for a final dish. As a Frenchwoman, I love bouillon, but at Atelier Crenn, I actually prefer to use dashi as a basis for vegetarian dishes because the ginger and daikon add a sharpness that helps to balance flavors. For pescatarian dashi, we will add dried bonito and katsuoboshi (smoked bonito shavings) for umami and smokiness. We often use bonito dashi to cook rice or deglaze vegetables for staff meal, because it is a healthy way to boost flavor. | *Makes 6 liters (6.3 quarts)*

Dashi

INGREDIENTS

600 grams (1.3 pounds) daikon

100 grams (3.5 ounces) peeled fresh
    ginger

90 grams (3.2 ounces) kombu

30 grams (1.05 ounces) bonito flakes
    (*optional*)

10 grams (0.35 ounce) katsuobushi
    (*optional*)

48 grams (3 tablespoons plus
    ½ teaspoon) fine sea salt

48 grams (3¼ tablespoons) organic mirin

EQUIPMENT

Fine-mesh strainer

At least 2½ hours before serving:

- Peel the daikon and cut it into ¼-inch cubes.
- Rinse and julienne the ginger.
- In a large stockpot, bring 6 liters (6.3 quarts) water to a boil over high heat. Add the daikon and ginger. Cover, remove from the heat, and let steep for 1 hour.
- Add the kombu and bring the liquid up to a boil over medium-high heat, then remove from the heat and let steep for 1 hour.
- **FOR PESCATARIAN DASHI**: Add the bonito and katsuobushi and let steep until the shavings sink to the bottom, about 30 minutes.
- Strain the liquid through a fine-mesh strainer and discard the solids.
- Stir in the fine sea salt and mirin.
- Use immediately or refrigerate, covered, until ready to use. Dashi may be frozen for later use.

At Atelier Crenn, we make lobster stock in large batches for use in our lobster bisque and many seafood-oriented staff meals. To turn lobster stock into lobster bisque broth, reduce the lobster stock, and blend it with milk, salt, sugar, and guar gum (see page 147). For best results, double this recipe, as the liquid will cover the lobster bodies better and lobster stock may be frozen and used again at a later date. | *Makes 3 to 3.5 liters (3.2 to 3.7 quarts)*

Lobster Stock

INGREDIENTS

5 whole lobster shells or fresh
     live lobsters
Neutral vegetable oil
2 carrots
2 leeks
1 large fennel bulb
4 stalks celery
5 whole black peppercorns
1 bay leaf
2 tomatoes
250 grams (1 cup plus 1 tablespoon)
     dry vermouth
¼ bunch fresh thyme
¼ bunch fresh tarragon

EQUIPMENT

Rondeau or wide heavy-bottomed pan
Fine-mesh strainer

At least 5 hours before using:

- If you are starting with live lobsters, plunge a sharp knife directly behind each lobster head. Cut the heads from the bodies. Remove the gills from the bodies and discard. Remove the antennae from the heads and discard. Rinse with cool water.
- Cook the lobsters according to your recipe or steam in court bouillon (see page 147).
- Separate the meat from the shells and set the meat aside.
- In a rondeau or wide heavy-bottomed pot, heat a thin film of vegetable oil over medium-high heat. Add the lobster shells and pan roast, turning occasionally, until browned, 10 to 15 minutes.
- Wash and peel the carrots and cut them into ½-inch pieces. Add 175 grams (6.2 ounces) of the carrots to the pot, reduce the heat to medium-low, and cook for 5 minutes.
- Wash the leeks, fennel, and celery stalks and cut them into ½-inch pieces. Add 175 grams (6.2 ounces) of the leek, 175 grams (6.2 ounces) of the fennel, and 75 grams (2.65 ounces) of the celery to the pot and cook over medium-low heat. Add the peppercorns and bay leaf to the pot and cook until the vegetables are very fragrant, about 10 minutes.
- Cut the tomatoes into ½-inch pieces and add 150 grams to the pot. Cook, stirring occasionally to prevent scorching, for 10 minutes.
- Pour the vermouth into the pot to deglaze, scraping along the bottom of the pot to release flavor, until dry, 5 to 10 minutes
- Add 4 liters (4.25 quarts) water to the pot. Simmer over medium-low heat for 2 hours.
- Add the thyme and tarragon, cover, remove the pot from the heat, and allow to steep for 1 hour.
- Strain the liquid through a fine-mesh strainer and discard the solids.
- Use immediately or refrigerate, covered, until ready to use. Lobster stock may be frozen for later use.

At Atelier Crenn, we tend to showcase the breast meat in our poultry dishes, but we make good use of the rest of the birds by turning the bones and reserved meat into consommé. A classic French technique, clarifying consommé is a perennial task on our kitchen to-do list, and part of what links us to generations of cooks who preceded us, stretching all the way back to the Middle Ages. Yet we make consommé in our own modern way, with a clarifying raft made of egg white powder rather than plain egg whites, because it is quicker and produces a more consistent result. (We experimented with another modernist consommé technique, in which the broth is filtered through agar-agar, but it was more time-consuming and resulted in a different mouthfeel.) The clean, rich taste of consommé makes it an important building block in our sauces, which tend to be very light and refined, but consommé can also be served on its own, in a cup or bowl. (When I'm feeling sick, I want nothing more than a warm cup of consommé to clear my head—especially if someone else has cooked it for me.) | *Makes 3 to 4 liters (3.2 to 4.2 quarts)*

Poultry Consommé

INGREDIENTS

4 whole (excluding breast meat) game
    bird carcasses, such as duck,
    pintade, or squab

4 carrots

4 stalks celery

2 white onions

1 sprig fresh thyme

60 grams (3⅓ cups) egg white powder

Fine sea salt

EQUIPMENT

Large roasting pan

Stockpot

Fine-mesh strainer

Ladle

Blender

Paper coffee filter or double layer
    of cheesecloth

At least 1 day before using:

- Preheat the oven to 190°C/375°F.
- Use a sharp knife to break apart the rib cages of the game bird carcasses. Place the meat and bones in a large roasting pan and roast until browned, about 40 minutes.
- While the meat and bones are roasting, peel and dice the carrots, celery, and onions, keeping them separated.
- Transfer the poultry meat and bones to a stockpot and deglaze the pan with 500 grams (2 cups plus 2 tablespoons) water, scraping to dislodge any flavorful caramelized bits from the bottom of the pan. Transfer the deglazing liquid to the stockpot.
- Add 5.5 liters (5.8 quarts) water, 200 grams (7.05 ounces) of the carrot, 200 grams (7.05 ounces) of the celery, 200 grams (7.05 ounces) of the white onion, and the thyme to the stockpot. Bring to a gentle simmer over medium-low heat and simmer, uncovered, for 3 hours.
- Strain the liquid through a fine-mesh strainer. Discard the bones and vegetables; reserve the meat for another use.
- Allow the liquid to cool, uncovered, then refrigerate, covered, overnight.

The next day:

- **TO CLARIFY THE CONSOMMÉ**: Scrape off and discard the solid layer of fat and impurities that have risen to the surface. Ladle 4 liters (4.25 quarts) of the stock into a stockpot, discarding the sediment at the bottom of the congealed stock. Warm the stock to room temperature and, working in batches, use a ladle to transfer 4 liters (4.25 quarts) of the poultry stock to a blender. Add the egg white powder and blend on high speed for 15 seconds.
- Transfer the mixture to a stockpot and bring to a simmer over medium-low heat, stirring occasionally to prevent scorching, until the egg white powder begins to congeal. A raft will gradually form and float to the top. Continue to simmer without stirring for 15 minutes to allow any remaining impurities to cling to the raft.
- Use a spoon to gently remove part of the raft to make room for a ladle to dip into the liquid.
- Ladle out the consommé and strain through a coffee filter or a double layer of cheesecloth set in a fine-mesh strainer. Discard the solids.
- Season with fine sea salt.
- Use immediately or refrigerate, covered, until ready to use. Poultry consommé should not be frozen.

This recipe actually contains three types of ham-infused liquid: stock, consommé, and broth. If you want, you can make ham stock and stop right there, since it tastes great on its own even as a hot beverage for a cold day, or you can proceed to clarify it into consommé as a more refined base for simple soups, or continue further and thicken and season ham consommé to make the ham broth used in our Squid with Lardo dish (page 133).

This ham broth was inspired by El Viejo León in Madrid, one of the oldest restaurants in Spain. Their ham broth has definitely stood the test of time, so I asked them how they made it. Of course, one key is starting with Ibérico ham, which already has incredible flavor, and the other key is to fortify it with chickpeas. It was a revelation for me. When I returned to San Francisco, I made a dish called *memoires d'enfance*, in which we cooked potatoes in their own dirt and topped them with ham broth and melted Comté cheese. It's not as refined as what we are doing at Atelier Crenn these days, but it was delicious and people loved it. | *Makes 3 to 3.5 liters (3.2 to 3.7 quarts)*

Ham Broth

INGREDIENTS

45 grams (¼ cup) dried chickpeas
1 white onion
2 kilograms (4.4 pounds) ham hock
60 grams (3⅓ cup) egg white powder
30 grams (2 tablespoons) fine sea salt
4.5 grams xanthan gum

EQUIPMENT

Fine-mesh strainer
Stockpot
Cheesecloth
Blender
Ladle
Paper coffee filter or double layer
   of cheesecloth

At least 1 day before using:

- Soak the chickpeas in enough water to cover and set aside at room temperature for 12 hours.
- Drain the chickpeas in a fine-mesh strainer and transfer to a stockpot.
- Trim, peel, and coarsely dice the white onion. Add 150 grams (5.3 ounces) of the white onion to the stockpot.
- **TO MAKE THE HAM STOCK:** Cover the chickpeas and white onion with 5 liters (5¼ quarts) water and add the ham hock. Bring the liquid to a boil over medium heat, then reduce the heat to low and simmer, uncovered, for 5 hours.
- Line a fine-mesh strainer with a double layer of cheesecloth. Strain the liquid and discard the solids. Allow the liquid to cool, uncovered, then refrigerate, covered, overnight. The next day scrape off any fat and impurities floating on top of the stock.
- **TO MAKE THE HAM CONSOMMÉ:** Warm the stock to room temperature and, working in batches, transfer 4 liters (4.2 quarts) of the ham stock to a blender, leaving the sediment at the bottom undisturbed. Discard the sediment. Add the egg white powder to the blender canister and blend on high speed for 15 seconds.

- Transfer the mixture to a stockpot and bring to a simmer over medium-low heat, stirring occasionally to prevent scorching, until the egg white powder begins to congeal. A raft will gradually form and float to the top. Continue to simmer without stirring for 15 minutes to allow any remaining impurities to cling to the raft.
- Use a spoon to gently remove part of the raft to make room for a ladle and gradually ladle the consommé into a coffee filter or a double layer of cheesecloth set in a fine-mesh strainer. Discard the solids.
- **TO MAKE THE HAM BROTH**: Working in batches, in a blender, combine 3 liters (3.2 quarts) of the ham consommé with the fine sea salt and xanthan gum. Blend on high speed until the broth is thick, about 20 seconds. Let the broth settle at room temperature until all the bubbles rise to the top, 30 minutes.
- Use immediately or refrigerate, covered, until ready to use. Ham broth may be frozen for later use.

One of the biggest challenges in making ice cream and sorbet is creating the perfect texture, and homemade ice creams and sorbets are particularly prone to getting icy because they are generally frozen relatively slowly, resulting in larger ice crystals. One way to ensure a smooth texture is to use a stabilizer like Sevarome or Cremodan, which create a smoother mouthfeel, in part by preventing the ice cream or sorbet from subtly melting and refreezing inside a home freezer as the machine cycles on and off. The stabilizers are activated with heat, and though many pastry chefs will activate the stabilizer as part of each sorbet or ice cream recipe, Juan prefers to mix a big batch of stabilizer syrup and keep it on hand, because it is a more efficient use of time, as suggested by Francisco Migoya, former pastry chef of The French Laundry. This is a pretty minimal recipe, which leaves room to tailor each sorbet or ice cream recipe to the particular flavor, but it will ensure a reliably smooth texture every time. | *Makes 1,665 grams (5¼ cups)*

Stabilizer Syrup

INGREDIENTS

335 grams (1¾ cup) granulated sugar

12 grams (0.45 ounce) Sevarome 64/G stabilizer

300 grams (¾ cup) powdered glucose

150 grams (6 tablespoons) liquid glucose

150 grams (6 tablespoons) trimoline inverted sugar

EQUIPMENT

Cooking thermometer

- In a small bowl, mix together 100 grams (3.5 ounces) of the granulated sugar and the Sevarome.
- In a medium pot with a cooking thermometer attached, mix together 530 grams (2¼ cups) water with the remaining 235 grams (1¼ cup) granulated sugar, the powdered glucose, liquid glucose, and trimoline inverted sugar. Cook the mixture over medium heat, whisking continuously as the temperature rises to 45°C/115°F to 50°C/120°F. Add the sugar-stabilizer mixture and continue to cook, whisking continuously, until the temperature reaches 85°C/185°F; do not allow the mixture to boil because it will lose water, which will change the structure of the solution. Immediately remove from the heat.
- Refrigerate, uncovered, until the mixture sets to a loose gel, about 3 hours.
- Transfer to an airtight container and keep refrigerated until ready to use.

Buckwheat is central to the culinary imagination of Brittany. Our love of buckwheat, like our love of butter, is an expression of a Breton identity that has never fully merged into the French national culture. Although the kingdom of Brittany was absorbed into France more than five hundred years ago, our ancestors didn't even start speaking French until the nineteenth century, and we've retained a fascination with buckwheat that dates back to the twelfth century, when the plant was introduced by travelers from the East and immediately thrived on our moors. Ground into flour and called *blé noir* ("black wheat"), buckwheat is actually much more nutritious than wheat; it is an excellent source of protein, naturally gluten-free, and endowed with all eight essential amino acids. Perhaps because Brittany has a long history of deprivation, many of our regional specialties call for *blé noir*, infusing a bit of health even into our cakes (*gâteau Breton*), potatoes (*kouign patatez*), and crepes (*galettes*).

I developed this recipe for buckwheat flatbread in 2013, when I was playing with the idea of opening a crêperie called Blé Noir. That project never materialized, but it intensified my interest in the history of buckwheat, especially the way this ingredient serves as an unacknowledged link between Brittany and Japan. (The Japanese word for buckwheat is soba, which is used interchangeably to mean hot and cold soba noodles.) I decided to add rice flour to my buckwheat flatbread to accentuate buckwheat's Asian origins. I've found that this buckwheat flatbread tastes great with many ingredients featured in sushi, from seafood to avocado to cucumber, but it is incredibly versatile. It can also stand in for blini (which are also made with buckwheat) in a caviar presentation, for bagels with lox and cream cheese, or for pita in a mezze platter. At Atelier Crenn, we serve it plain, on a slate, alongside our Squid with Lardo (page 133), and I love the way that the almost crunchy, smoky grilled bread pairs with the ham and truffle consommé. | *Makes 15 flatbreads*

Buckwheat Flatbread

INGREDIENTS

200 grams (1¼ cups) buckwheat flour

150 grams (1 cup plus 3¼ tablespoons) all-purpose flour plus more for dusting

40 grams (¼ cup) brown rice flour

2 grams (scant ½ teaspoon) sesame oil

2 grams (scant ½ teaspoon) fine sea salt

Maldon salt

>>>

- Heat a plancha or cast-iron skillet over high heat.
- Preheat the oven to 175°C/350°F.
- In the bowl of a stand mixer fitted with the dough hook attachment, combine the buckwheat flour, 180 grams (¾ cup) water, the all-purpose flour, brown rice flour, sesame oil, and fine sea salt. Mix on medium speed until a dough comes together.
- Transfer the dough to a work surface and knead gently four or five times.
- Use a kitchen scale to portion the dough into 40-gram (1.4-ounce) balls. Lightly flour each ball with all-purpose flour.
- Use your hands to flatten each ball and run it through a pasta roller at the thinnest setting.
- Season lightly with the Maldon salt and use a rolling pin to roll over each salted dough round one additional time to adhere the salt to the dough.

>>>

Buckwheat Flatbread, *continued*

EQUIPMENT

Plancha or cast-iron skillet

Stand mixer with dough hook
  attachment

Kitchen scale

Pasta roller

Rolling pin

Parchment paper

- Use a fork to puncture the dough in four or five spots. Stack the dough rounds with layers of parchment paper between each round to separate them.
- Working in batches, toast the flatbread on the plancha or cast-iron skillet, turning when it starts to bubble and rise irregularly, until the other side rises as well. Be careful not to burn the flatbreads.
- Transfer to a baking sheet and bake until crispy but not browned, 10 to 15 minutes.
- Allow to cool, uncovered, to room temperature, then store in an airtight container at room temperature for up to 1 week.

Although pumpernickel bread is not something I grew up eating, I have a peculiar fondness for this dark rye loaf, which feels earthy in a way that makes it perfect for grinding into the pumpernickel soil we make for A Walk in the Forest (page 79). And pumpernickel has a long, interesting history, beginning in fifteenth-century Germany as a soft loaf baked in a steamy oven for almost twenty-four hours, and transformed by nineteenth- and twentieth-century American Jewish delicatessens into a dark rye bread, flavored with molasses. Our pumpernickel has more in common with the deli version, which seems appropriate for me, another product of Europe that has evolved since arriving in America. | *Makes three 1,250-gram (2¾-pound) loaves*

Pumpernickel

INGREDIENTS

1,135 grams (8¼ cups) bread flour, plus
    more for dusting
1,135 grams (10 cups plus
    ¾ tablespoon) pumpernickel flour
225 grams (1 cup plus 1½ tablespoons)
    unsalted butter
28 grams (1 ounce) active dry yeast
28 grams (1 ounce) molasses
14 grams (½ ounce) vital wheat gluten

EQUIPMENT

Stand mixer with dough hook attachment
Bread lame (bread scoring blade) or
    very sharp knife
Wire rack

- Preheat the oven to 205°C/400°F.
- In the bowl of a stand mixer fitted with the dough hook attachment, combine 1,135 grams (4¾ cups plus 2¼ teaspoons) water with the bread flour, pumpernickel flour, butter, yeast, molasses, and vital wheat gluten and mix on low speed for 4 minutes. Raise the speed to high and mix for 7 minutes.
- Lightly flour a work surface with bread flour and scrape the dough onto it as a single ball. Cover the dough with a clean, dry towel and let rest at room temperature for 20 minutes.
- Portion the dough into 3 equal-size balls, cover with a clean, dry towel, and let rest at room temperature for 15 minutes.
- On a lightly floured work surface, gently pat one ball into a disc (keep the others covered as you work). Lift the edge closest to your body and gently roll away from yourself. Rotate the dough to orient the seam at the top and roll the dough in the other direction, this time leaving the seam at the bottom. Use your hands to gently pull the loaf along the work surface to shape into a soft hemisphere.
- Repeat the loaf-shaping process with the remaining 2 dough balls.
- Transfer the loaves to baking sheets. Use a bread lame or very sharp knife to score the top of each loaf with a symmetrical pattern, such as a tic-tac-toe board, meeting the surface at a 45-degree angle and penetrating ¼ inch to ½ inch deep.
- Bake the loaves for 35 minutes.
- Allow to cool on a wire rack to room temperature. Bread that will not be eaten immediately should be wrapped tightly in aluminum foil, placed in a resealable plastic freezer bag, and frozen.

Like pumpernickel, brioche dates back to the fifteenth century, but unlike pumpernickel, brioche was a huge part of my childhood, in one form or another. Brioche may be baked into a variety of shapes, from brioche à tête, which is shaped like a fluted muffin topped with a smaller ball of dough, to Juan's spiced brioche, which is baked in a loaf pan (see page 265), to brioche feuilletée, which is laminated with layers of butter, like a croissant. In this recipe, the butter layering is optional, and therefore, the amount of time in the oven is variable. But as my friend and baking guide Mehdi Boudiab points out, home ovens are hardly ever calibrated correctly, so it is always important to watch for browning when making a recipe for the first time.

Whatever the form, the essence of brioche is its beautifully fluffy crumb, which makes it perfect for making dehydrated squid ink brioche in our Beef Carpaccio (page 177). We also serve slices of brioche and butter immediately before presenting our Lobster Bisque (page 145), so that guests have a chance to enjoy the brioche on its own terms before tasting it in relation to the soup. | *Makes 36 muffin-size brioche or 3 full-size loaves*

Brioche

INGREDIENTS

1 kilogram (8¾ cups plus
    1½ tablespoons) pastry flour, plus
    more for dusting
200 grams (7 ounces) unsalted butter,
    plus 300 grams (10.6 ounces) cold
    unsalted butter for layering, if desired
150 grams (⅔ cup) beaten eggs
    (from 3 to 4 eggs)
100 grams (½ cup) granulated sugar
30 grams (2½ tablespoons) active
    dry yeast
18 grams (1¼ tablespoons) fine sea salt,
    plus more for the egg wash
2 whole eggs
1 egg yolk
60 grams (¼ cup) whole milk

EQUIPMENT

Stand mixer with dough hook attachment
Rolling pin (*optional*)
Brioche molds or loaf pans (*optional*)
Silicone basting brush
Wire rack

One day before baking:

- **TO MAKE THE LIQUID LEVAIN:** In a large storage container, combine the pastry flour and 130 grams (½ cup plus 2½ teaspoons) water and mix well. Cover tightly and let sit in a warm place until approximately tripled in bulk, 16 to 27 hours.

The day of baking:

- Set 200 grams (7 ounces) of the butter aside at room temperature to soften.
- In the bowl of a stand mixer fitted with the dough hook attachment, combine the liquid levain with 200 grams (¾ cup plus 1½ tablespoons) water, the eggs, sugar, yeast, and fine sea salt. Mix on low speed for 5 minutes. Raise the mixer speed to medium and mix for 4 minutes. Add the 200 grams (7 ounces) of softened butter and mix on medium speed for 5 minutes.
- Turn off the mixer and cover the bowl with a clean, dry towel. Let sit at 25°C/77°F for 30 minutes.
- **TO LAMINATE THE DOUGH TO MAKE BRIOCHE FEUILLE-TÉE, IF DESIRED:** On a lightly floured surface, use a rolling pin to shape the dough into a ½-inch-thick square. Stretch a large piece of plastic wrap on a flat work surface and place the remaining

>>>

Brioche, *continued*

300 grams (10.6 ounces) cold butter in the center. Cover the butter with a second layer of plastic wrap. Beat the butter with a rolling pin to flatten the butter. Use the rolling pin to roll the butter into a flat rectangle, as long as the dough on one side and half the size of the dough on the other. Unwrap the butter and place it on the dough in the center. Fold the ends of the dough over the butter so that they meet in a seam in the middle. Stretch the dough and fold again at the seam to make a double fold.

- Cover the dough (laminated or not) with plastic wrap and refrigerate for 45 minutes.
- Butter 36 brioche molds (for brioche feuilletée or brioche à tête) or 3 loaf pans.
- **TO SHAPE THE DOUGH FOR BRIOCHE FEUILLETÉE, IF DESIRED:** Use a rolling pin to flatten the dough into a rectangle ½ inch thick. Cut the rectangle into 2-inch-wide strips and roll the strips into spirals. Place the spirals in the buttered brioche molds with the coil showing at the top. Alternatively, shape the dough into brioche croissants or any shape appropriate to laminated dough.
- **TO SHAPE THE DOUGH FOR LOAVES:** Split the dough into 3 equal balls. Split each ball into 8 round balls and arrange them in the buttered loaf pans in 2 x 4-ball grids.
- **TO MAKE THE EGG WASH:** In a medium bowl, beat the whole eggs and egg yolk. Add the milk and a pinch of salt.
- Use a silicone basting brush to wash the tops of the dough with the egg wash.
- **TO PROOF:** Cover the brioche molds or loaf pans with a damp kitchen towel and let sit at 26°C/81°F until risen, 2 to 2½ hours.
- Preheat the oven to 180°C/355°F.
- Bake until golden brown, watching closely to prevent burning, for 20 to 25 minutes.
- Allow the brioche to cool in the molds or loaf pans for 5 minutes. Transfer to a wire rack and allow to cool to room temperature.

Literally "fermented dough," pâte fermentée is essentially a piece of old dough that has been allowed to acquire a bit of character from the ambient yeast in the air. As such, it is a beautiful reflection of a particular time and place. Many old-fashioned French bread recipes, including our Pain de Seigle and Pain au Son recipes (see pages 337 and 342) incorporate pâte fermentée. Traditionally, when every household made fresh bread every day, pâte fermentée was made by reserving a piece of dough from one loaf for use the next day, but here is a recipe for pâte fermentée for bakers on a less regular schedule. Note that unlike a liquid levain, which is used in our Brioche (page 333), pâte fermentée contains salt. | *Makes 480 grams (1 pound)*

Pâte Fermentée

INGREDIENTS

140 grams (1 cup plus 2 tablespoons) unbleached all-purpose flour

140 grams (1 cup plus 2 tablespoons) unbleached bread flour

0.2 grams (¾ teaspoon) fine sea salt

1.8 grams (⅔ teaspoon) active dry yeast

200 grams (¾ cup plus 1½ tablespoons) warm water (35°C/95°F to 38°C/100°F)

Neutral vegetable oil

EQUIPMENT

Stand mixer with paddle and dough hook attachments

Plastic wrap

NOTE: *This recipe makes enough pâte fermentée starter to make both the Pain de Seigle on page 337 and the Pain de Son on page 342.*

One day before baking:

- In the bowl of a stand mixer, mix together the all-purpose flour, bread flour, fine sea salt, and yeast. Attach the paddle attachment and add 175 grams (¾ cup) warm water. Mix on low speed until a ball forms, about 1 minute.
- Replace the paddle with the dough hook attachment and knead on medium speed until the dough is soft and pliable, about 4 minutes.
- Adjust the dough with up to 25 grams (1½ tablespoons) warm water or flour to keep it from becoming too dry or too sticky. As a test of the consistency, press your finger into the dough; you should be able to leave fingerprints on the dough, but not pull a large clump away with your finger.
- Lightly oil a large bowl. Transfer the dough to the bowl and coat in oil. Wrap the bowl with plastic wrap and let sit for 1 hour. Use your fingers to press the dough to release gas. Cover again with plastic wrap and refrigerate overnight.

Pain de seigle is a traditional French rye bread, popular in Brittany as an accompaniment to oysters and other fresh seafood. We shape it into a batard loaf, also known as a torpedo for its long, pointed shape. Because rye flour rises a bit less than wheat-based flours in the oven, we score the surface of the dough before proofing for pain de seigle, whereas most other breads are scored right before they go into the oven.

To create the perfect conditions for the yeast, we want to control the temperature of the dough. Many factors influence the temperature of the dough, including the starting temperature of the ingredients, the ambient temperature of the air, and the friction created during the kneading process. We really only have control over the temperature of the water, because different dough recipes will create different friction factors, so we want to add water at the correct temperature. We calculate the water temperature according to this formula, calculated in Celsius:

WATER TEMPERATURE = BASE TEMPERATURE – (ROOM TEMPERATURE + INGREDIENT TEMPERATURE)

For our pain de seigle, the base temperature is 50°C. | *Makes three 425-gram (scant 1-pound) loaves*

Pain de Seigle (Rye Bread)

INGREDIENTS

350 grams Pâte Fermentée (page 336)

500 grams (5½ cups) 100% rye flour
plus more for dusting

25 grams vital wheat gluten

15 grams (1 tablespoon) unsalted butter

15 grams (1¼ tablespoons) active
dry yeast

15 grams (1 tablespoon) fine sea salt

Olive oil

EQUIPMENT

Thermometer

Stand mixer with dough hook attachment

Clean kitchen towel

Bread lame (bread scoring blade) or
very sharp knife

Silicone basting brush

Wire rack

One to two days before baking:

• Make the Pâte Fermentée (page 336).

The next day:

• One hour before beginning, take the pâte fermentée and the butter out of the refrigerator to warm up.

• When you are ready to begin, calculate the temperature of the main ingredients: Take the temperature of the room, rye flour, and pâte fermentée in Celsius. If the rye flour has been stored in a pantry, it will be the temperature of the room. To get a weighted average of the ingredients, multiply the temperature of the pâte fermentée by 0.4 and the temperature of the rye flour by 0.6 and add them together. Add the temperature of the air. Subtract that number from 50, and that will give the correct temperature of the water in Celsius. It will probably be colder than you imagined, but the kneading action can raise the temperature as much as 2 degrees per minute, so you want to start with the dough at a cooler temperature.

>>>

Pain de Seigle (Rye Bread), *continued*

- In the bowl of a stand mixer fitted with the dough hook attachment, combine the rye flour, 355 grams (12.5 ounces) water, the pâte fermentée, vital wheat gluten, butter, yeast, and fine sea salt and mix on low speed for 5 minutes. Raise the mixer speed to medium and mix for 10 minutes.
- Leave the dough in the mixer bowl and cover with a clean, dry towel. Let rest for 30 minutes.
- Punch down the dough, which will have risen, and cover again with a dry towel. Let rest at room temperature for 30 minutes more.
- Divide the dough into 3 equal portions and gently roll into balls.
- **TO SHAPE THE DOUGH INTO A BATARD LOAF:** Lightly flour a work surface. Use your fingers to gently shape the dough into a rectangle oriented like a landscape relative to your body. Gently lift the edge closest to you and fold one-third of the rectangle toward the center. Use your fingers to gently press the edge into the center to seal the seam. Turn the dough 180 degrees and press one third of the dough toward the center. Use your fingers to pinch the seam together. Flip the dough over so that the seam is at the bottom of the loaf. Use your fingers to gently roll the ends into points. Transfer the loaves to baking sheets.
- **TO SCORE THE LOAVES:** Use a bread lame or very sharp knife to score each loaf with 2 parallel cuts, meeting the surface at a 45-degree angle and penetrating ¼ inch to ½ inch deep.
- **TO PROOF:** Cover the loaves with a damp kitchen towel and let sit at 25°C/77°F for 1 hour.
- Preheat the oven to 250°C/482°F.
- Use a silicone basting brush to wash the tops of the loaves with a generous layer of olive oil.
- Bake for 10 minutes, then crack the oven open, reduce the oven temperature to 205°C/400°F, and bake for 30 minutes more.
- Let the bread cool for 5 minutes on the baking sheets, then transfer to a wire rack and allow to cool to room temperature.
- Pain de seigle that will not be eaten immediately should be wrapped tightly in aluminum foil, placed in a resealable plastic freezer bag, and frozen.

Pain au son is a rustic French bread made with both bread flour and at least 25 percent bran. I love this recipe because it makes use of spelt, which is closely related to common wheat, but with a slightly different taste and a lower gluten content. When I was a girl, pain au son was one of my favorite breads to slather with butter, making it slightly less healthy than it might have been otherwise, but now I find that pain au son with cultured butter (page 299) pairs quite nicely with the vegetable dishes we serve at Atelier Crenn. | *Makes four 350-gram (¾-pound) loaves*

NOTE: *Please read about calculating base temperatures for baking in the headnote to our pain de seigle (page 337). For our Pain au Son, the base temperature is 56°C.*

Pain au Son (Spelt Bread)

INGREDIENTS

500 grams (1.1 pound) high-gluten flour

175 grams (6.15 ounces) spelt flour

130 grams (4.6 ounces) Pâte Fermentée (page 334)

22.5 grams (5 tablespoons plus 2 teaspoons) active dry yeast

15 grams (1 tablespoon) fine sea salt

15 grams (0.55 ounce) vital wheat gluten

7.55 grams (0.25 ounce) powdered milk

Olive oil

Spelt kernels (*optional*)

EQUIPMENT

Stand mixer with dough hook attachment

Silicone basting brush

Bread lame (bread scoring blade) or very sharp knife

Wire rack

Clean kitchen towel

One to two days before baking:

• Make the Pâte Fermentée (page 336).

The next day:

• One hour before beginning, take the pâte fermentée and the butter out of the refrigerator to warm up.

• When you are ready to begin, calculate the temperature of the main ingredients: Take the temperature of the room, high-gluten flour, spelt flour, and pâte fermentée in Celsius. If the flours have been stored in a pantry, they will be the temperature of the room. To get a weighted average of the ingredients, multiply the temperature of the pâte fermentée by 0.16 and the temperature of the high gluten and spelt flour by 0.84 and add them together. Add the temperature of the air. Subtract that number from 56, and that will give the correct temperature of the water in Celsius. It will probably be colder than you imagined, but the kneading action can raise the temperature as much as 2 degrees per minute, so you want to start with the dough at a cooler temperature.

• In the bowl of a stand mixer fitted with dough hook attachment, combine 500 grams (2 cups plus 1½ tablespoons) water with the high-gluten flour, spelt flour, pâte fermentée, active dry yeast, fine sea salt, vital wheat gluten, and powdered milk and mix on low speed for 10 minutes. Raise the mixer speed to medium and mix for 4 minutes.

- Let the dough rest in the mixer bowl, covered with a dry kitchen towel, for 20 minutes.

- Punch down the dough to deflate it, which will have risen, and cover again with a dry towel. Let rest at room temperature for 30 minutes.

- Divide the dough into 4 equal portions and roll into balls.

- On a lightly floured work surface, gently pat the ball into a disc (keep the remaining dough balls covered while you work). Lift the edge closest to your body and gently roll away from yourself. Rotate the dough to orient the seam at the top and roll the dough in the other direction, this time leaving the seam at the bottom. Use your hands to gently pull the loaf along the work surface to shape into a soft hemisphere.

- Repeat the loaf shaping process with the remaining 3 dough balls.

- **TO PROOF:** Cover the loaves with a damp kitchen towel and let sit at 25°C/77°F for 1 hour.

- Preheat the oven to 250°C/482°F.

- Use a silicone basting brush to wash the tops of the loaves with a generous layer of olive oil.

- Use a bread lame or very sharp knife to score the surface of the dough with a symmetrical pattern, such as a tic-tac-toe board.

- Bake for 10 minutes, then crack the oven open, reduce the oven temperature to 205°C/400°F, and bake for 30 minutes more. (In a professional setting, these loaves would be baked at 250°C/482°F with plenty of steam, but that would be dangerous in a home oven and we do not recommend it.)

- Let the bread cool for 5 minutes on the baking sheets, then transfer to a wire racks to cool until comfortable to touch.

- Pat the bread with a damp kitchen towel and dip in a layer of spelt kernels to coat, if desired.

- Pain au son that will not be eaten immediately should be wrapped tightly in aluminum foil, placed in a resealable plastic freezer bag, and frozen.

Conclusion

SUSTENANCE AND SUSTAINABILITY

IN THE COURSE of writing this book, I have had the pleasure of lingering over many childhood memories related to food, and to reflect on the ways that the history of food comes to influence our present enjoyment of it. I wonder, though: What kinds of memories will the children of today carry through their lives? Will food continue along an industrial course, toward so-called "meal replacements" and automated farming? Or can we recapture some of the meanings of food that have given me so much pleasure in my life and so much fodder for my art?

Fortunately, I feel that I am not alone in my concern for the long-term ramifications of food. Over the last few years, I've started to notice more activism and media coverage about the importance of connecting more deeply with the agricultural sources of our food. The Slow Food Movement and journalists like Michael Pollan and Mark Bittman are beginning an important conversation about what it means to be estranged from the larger network in which food is grown and distributed, and to imagine what we can do to change it. We are starting to recognize that mass-produced food is not only nutritionally inferior to local, organic, and heirloom foods, but there is also a spiritual inferiority in these sanitized "convenience" foods. When you factor in the ethical costs of the animal abuse and labor practices that often accompany low-cost food, it becomes quite clear that it is a bad bargain overall. Organizing our food culture around a principle of instant, cheap gratification is disastrous for our health, our environment, our economy, and our spirits.

I am hopeful, though, when I hear an emerging call to "put the culture back into agriculture." I interpret this slogan as drawing our awareness to the fact that food exists in a richer context that includes the farmers, the soil, the seeds, the prices, and the community that creates our food supply. And furthermore, it affirms that food is not merely fuel for our bodies, but also nourishes our hunger for culture, for meaning, for connection. As cooks, we must take a stand and become intimately acquainted with the origins of the foods we work with. We must align our choice of ingredients, from the land to the sea, with the natural cycles of the seasons. Perhaps most important, we have to think before cooking.

Thinking before cooking. That is my mantra, which I drill into my staff at Atelier Crenn. It covers everything from avoiding waste to dreaming up new techniques to learning about the soil and building relationships with farmers. Our sourcing choices have the power to influence what is being grown and how. Chefs can improve the entire food system through small choices—and so can home cooks. Everything from growing practices to ingredient selection to food preparation has both a cultural and environmental significance. As a new orientation to food is emerging in our culture, the agricultural side of the equation needs our attention, input, and care. Ultimately, this reimagining of our agricultural and socioeconomic landscape is profoundly empowering—even revolutionary—and those in the culinary community must engage in this field.

As a chef, I also see that we have a unique role to play as the artists of this (agri)culture. There has never been a great culture without art! As chefs, we must think before we cook so that we may use our platforms to educate and thereby usher a new food culture into existence. The culinary world is finally awakening to the fact that what is on a plate is not merely a commercial transaction between chef and guest, but an act of economic and environmental responsibility. We offer our guests a meal, surely, but more sustaining is the aesthetic experience we offer. If we are successful in our efforts, our guests have an opportunity to understand food in more profound ways. Our restaurants are ateliers where food, memory, and emotion mingle; where beauty is celebrated and consciousness is transformed.

"Harmony with nature is possible only if we abandon the idea of superiority over the natural world," said Bill Mollison, the father of permaculture, and restaurants offer a chance to reorient our relationship to nature. As chef-artists, we offer our guests pleasurable moments wherein they may experience themselves as sensuous beings, who are fluidly continuous with the entire natural world. I hope that my guests at Atelier Crenn experience a heightening of the senses in which they have come home to be nourished and inspired by nature.

To make sustainability sustainable, and not a mere "trend" in fine dining, we need to engage with food as one of our deepest connections to nature. Whether you are eating a peach from the farmers' market or dining in my restaurant, being part of a rich culture makes you feel so much more alive than absent-mindedly snacking on industrially produced calories. Our investment in sustainability is grounded in our own pleasure and our authentic nature as human beings. I invite everyone, and in particular chefs, to do everything possible to sustain the sustainable food movement.

INDEX

Note: Page references in italics indicate recipe photographs.

INDEX

INDEX

INDEX

INDEX

INDEX